*ORGANIZING
CRIME*

ORGANIZING CRIME

Alan A. Block
William J. Chambliss
University of Delaware

ELSEVIER
New York • Oxford

Elsevier North Holland, Inc.
52 Vanderbilt Avenue, New York, New York 10017

Sole distributors outside the USA and Canada:
Elsevier Science Publishers B.V.
P. O. Box 211, 1000 AE Amsterdam, The Netherlands

© 1981 by Elsevier North Holland, Inc.
Library of Congress Cataloging in Publication Data

Block, Alan A.
    Organizing crime.

    Bibliography: p.
    Includes index.
    1. Organized crime. 2. Crime and criminals. 3. Organized crime—
    United States. 4. Crime and criminals—United States. I. Chambliss,
    William J., joint author. II. Title.
HV6030.B55   364.1'06   80-25099
ISBN 0-444-99079-8

Copy Editor   Glen England
Desk Editor   Louise Calabro Schreiber
Design   Edmée Froment
Design Editor   Glen Burris
Openers/Mechanicals   José Garcia
Production Manager   Joanne Jay
Compositor   Typographic Services, Inc.
Printer   Haddon Craftsmen

Manufactured in the United State of America

To Marcia Block
and
Joseph H. Chambliss
Partners, friends, and fellow travelers

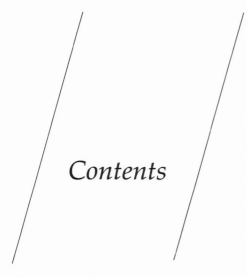

Contents

Acknowledgments

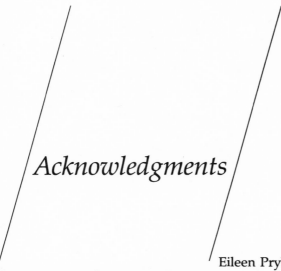

Acknowledgments

Eileen Prybolsky spent an inordinate amount of creative energy and patience on this project. To her, our students (especially Maureen J. Feeney), informants, and critics, we owe a special debt for the completion of this book. Paul Takagi was most helpful with comments on the chapter concerning the political economy of opium laws. Goran Elwin, Henrik Tham, and Lisa Stearns helped in the research and made invaluable suggestions.

Some of the material has appeared earlier, in slightly different form, in the following journals: *Crime and Social Justice, Criminology, The Public Historian.*

*ORGANIZING
CRIME*

Introduction: Perspective

1

The criminology of the 1950s was in some ways an enviable enterprise—it was one of those times when a discipline showed an almost complete consensus on the question to be asked and a great deal of agreement on the approach to be taken. The question was: Why do some people commit criminal acts while others do not? The question presupposed the approach: social psychology. True to the sociological tradition, efforts were made to show how differential association (a social psychological theory) implied "differential social organization"; and how reactions to "differential opportunities to achieve" (legitimately or illegitimately) were linked to the class structure of modern society. But basically the thrust and the emphasis of the theory was on how individuals came to behave anti-socially, criminally, or deviantly.

Criminology did not discover or create, though it may have contributed to, the fetish with juvenile delinquency that characterized the 1950s and early 1960s. Criminology expressed the same concern as Edward R. Murrow when he asked, "Who Killed Michael Farmer?"; as John Bartlow Martin when he investigated the senseless murder of a nurse in Ypsilanti, Michigan by a gang of young boys and wondered, "Why Did They Kill?" Warren Miller depicted Duke Custis as the Warlord of the Royal Crocodiles in "The Cool World," and Harrison Salsbury investigated gang life in New York for the *New York Times*.

In Britain, France, Germany, and the United States, delinquency was a national issue. Sociologists, criminologists, and psychologists dug into their bags of theory and their research strategies in an effort to shed what light they could on the issue.

All that changed in the 1960s and 1970s, but not as a result of "solving" the delinquency problem either politically or intellectually. Delinquency, delinquent gangs, and adolescent deviance remain as ubiquitous as ever and their causes are as much a mystery today as then. Writing in the early 1970s, Galliher and McCartney noted:

> . . . recent social changes have probably begun to dissuade many American scholars from a total acceptance of the activities of the American government; and therefore, we might expect a blossoming use of the internationalist and conflict perspectives . . . these alternative theoretical perspectives might lead sociologists to view juvenile delinquency as a subject matter created largely by government fiat . . . and lead to theoretical and methodological orientations where official definitions are taken as problematic.[1]

In the words of Thomas Kuhn, criminology underwent a "paradigm revolution." What for decades were accepted as the right question to ask and the appropriate methodology for investigation were challenged by a host of theoretical alternatives—some radical, some conservative—which led in part to the emergence of what was called "the new criminology."[2] The "crimes of the powerful,"[3]—from the crimes of nation states,[4] through the illegal and immoral acts of large corporations, to the misues of police and political office by local, state, and national powerholders—were increasingly examined.[5]

These issues were neither invented nor created by sociologists and criminologists. These, too, reflected the interests and concerns of journalists, politicians, and to some extent that omnipresent but difficult-to-pinpoint "public."

Sociologists and criminologists once again reached into their bags of tricks to find explanations and research methodologies that could be applied to the issues. Nothing very new was created, reflecting perhaps the wisdom of Alfred North Whitehead's observation that everything in Western social thought is only a footnote to Plato.

This time, what was resurrected from past criminologies and sociologies was more divisive than those favored in the 1950s; this was also a reflection of historical reality of the 1960s, which was itself more divisive. What emerged was a redirection of criminological inquiry along the boundary lines of any discipline: questions changed, perspectives and paradigms emerged that challenged extant ones and re-evaluated research strategies.

These changes were captured by Taylor, Walton, and Young in their 1973 publication of the (unfortunately titled) *New Criminology*. The critiques they generated against the delinquency-dominated criminology of the 1950s were not new, and their attempt to offer an alternative perspective was not particularly satisfactory. But for all of that, the book did speak to what was happening.

What Is the New Criminology?

The new criminology is mainly a restatement of threads and themes that have been part and parcel of criminology from time immemorial. It asks questions raised in the past, but which were largely ignored in the 1950s:

Why are some acts defined as criminal while others are not?

Why are some people who commit acts defined as criminal punished while others are not?

Are the incidence and distribution of criminal acts explicable in terms of political and economic forces?

Are law and crime best understood as a reflection of shared values or as a reflection of social conflict?

To what extent does political and economic power determine the workings of the law, its creation, and its implementation?

Thus the study of crime was broadened to reintroduce the questions raised by criminologists like Frank Tannenbaum, who said in 1938:

American criminal activity must be related to the total social complex. The United States has as much crime as it generates. The criminals are themselves part of the community in a deeper sense and are as much its products as are poets, philosophers, inventors, businessmen and scientists—reformers and saints. If we would change the amount of crime in the community, we must change the community.[6]

Hawkins and Waller, who said in 1936:

The prostitute, the pimp, the peddler of dope, the operator of gambling halls, the vendor of obscene pictures, the bootlegger, the abortionist—all are productive. All produce services or goods which people desire and for which they're willing to pay.[7]

Thorsten Sellin, who said in 1938:

Values which receive the protection of the criminal law are ultimately those which are treasured by dominant interest groups.[8]

Robert Merton, who said:

The distinctive function of the political machine for their criminal, vice and racket clientele is to enable them to operate in satisfying the economic

demands of a large market without due interference from the government. Just as big business may contribute funds to the political party
war-chest to ensure a minimum of governmental interference, so with
big rackets and big crime . . . . In both instances, many features of the
structural context are identical: (1) market demands for goods and services; (2) the operators' concern with maximizing gains from their enterprise; (3) the need for partial control of government which might otherwise interfere with these activities of businessmen; (4) the need for an
efficient, powerful and centralized agency to provide an effective liaison of
"business" with government.[9]

Merton also argued in the 1940s that organized crime and political
corruption were *not* economically distinguishable from legitimate business, and that failure to recognize this led sociologists to some "badly
scrambled" analyses.[10]

Edwin Sutherland called for studies and theories that took into
account the fact of white collar (corporate) criminality, professional
theft and the ubiquitous nature of crime across the class structure.[11]
Short and Nye expended great energy to show how omnipresent was
delinquency in *all* social classes,[12] and so forth.

The point of all this is simply to emphasize that much of what is
currently touted as "the new criminology" is reflective of a criminological perspective advocated and at least begun by an earlier generation
of students in the 1930s.[13] That this tradition was forgotten in the 1950s
is true enough, but that does not negate its earlier existence.

But there was and is more to the new criminology than a resurrection
of observations made in an earlier era. The critical criminology of the
1960s and 1970s goes beyond the empirical observations and the suggested themes of the critics of the 1930s to seek a link between criminological theory and broader social theory. In particular, the most important innovation and direction of the criminological enterprise of the
1970s is to take seriously the possibility that criminological inquiry can
be linked to Marxist theory. In this effort there are some side steps and
false starts, but these are only the first efforts at developing a truly
original perspective on crime.

Probably the most important false start of a Marxist criminology is
the attempt by some to build a criminological theory around the idea
that "in every era the ruling ideas are the ideas of the ruling class."
Taking this rhetoric literally has led some to argue that crime should be
fully understood as a result of the ruling classes' attempt to maintain
and perpetuate their own interest and ideology. Thus Richard Quinney invokes the idea that crime and law reflects extant ideology, but
integrates into this hypothesis the notion that extant ideology is largely
a reflection of dominant class interests:

As long as a capitalist ruling class exists, the prevailing ideology will be capitalistic. And as long as that ruling class uses the law to maintain its order, the legal ideology will be capitalistic as well.[14]

This interpretation of the Marxist theory of crime and law is in fact very un-Marxian, ignoring as it does the role of class struggle and the dialectical nature of social, political, and economic relations. In this sense, Quinney's theory is more akin to the pluralistic view articulated by social theorists such as Lawrence Friedman, who maintains that "What makes law, then, in not public opinion in the abstract, but public opinion in the sense of *exerted social force.*[15] Friedman goes on to recognize that there are differentials of power that make it more likely that some groups (and social classes) will be successful in "exerting social force to create law" than will other groups. The "explanation" proffered, then, is one of competing interest groups with different power bases as the moving forces behind the creation of laws.

These two views, of which the works of Quinney and Friedman are representative, are quite logically derivative from the earlier, less subtle characterizations of "ruling class" and "normative" theories of law. Several criticisms are nonetheless appropriate to the paradigms suggested by them. For one thing, neither is amenable to empirical test. As Friedman recognizes, if the test of whether one "interest group" has more power than another is that one is successful in its efforts to effect legislation while the other is not, then the theory is a mere tautology that tells us that those groups whose interests are represented in the law are the groups who succeeded in having their interests represented in the law. However, the view that the law represents the ideology of capitalism so long as there is a capitalist ruling class begs the question of how this comes about. Is there an automatic response of all law, or is there a process involved? Furthermore, this theory is also subject to the dangers of tautology. If we discover the passage of laws that are opposed by the "capitalist class," then does this contradict the theory? Perhaps it should, but if we invoke the idea that "in the long run these laws turn out either to be unenforced, or to represent in fact the interests of the capitalist class," then we have once again suggested a paradigm that becomes true by (a) definition, and (b) the invocation of auxiliary hypothesis. The fact is that the ruling-class theory of crime and law is patently false when it is unilaterally applied to law creation and law enforcement. Laws emerge and are enforced that are, at least on the surface, neither in the interests of nor a reflection of the ideology of the ruling class.

An equally untenable position is the social psychological explanation of the cause of criminal behavior proposed by Taylor, Walton, and

Young: that criminal acts are best understood as political statements of opposition to oppression and exploitation. Although such a view may have considerable merit as a rallying point for radical ideology, it has little merit as a criminological theory. To begin with, one must ask: Does this explanation posit a conscious recognition on the part of those who commit criminal acts? If so, it is a little out of touch with the consciousness (false or otherwise) of most people who commit crime. It is precisely because it is so rare that Eldridge Cleaver's claim that he raped white women as a way of attacking white man's property is such a powerful statement.[16] Most criminals tell us rather that they share the view held by their captors: that their acts are antisocial, immoral, and wrong. Others—professional thieves[17]—tell us that although their acts are labeled criminal, they are simply doing business like other businessmen. Although this may represent a reflection of the logic of capitalism, it can hardly be said that these offenders are striking back at capitalism—at least not consciously. If the theory is posited as an "unconscious motivation" for the criminal acts, then it is no more defensible than the Freudian interpretation of criminal acts as motivated by oedipal complexes and neurotic needs. Furthermore, the view that criminal acts can be understood as a reaction against oppression and exploitation fails to recognize one of the starting points for a radical analysis of crime, namely, that the "crimes of the powerful," the crimes of corporations and corporate executives, the crimes of nation-states and political leaders, are ubiquitous. Just as it makes little sense to see the crimes of the Nixons, Johnsons, and Callaghans, or of Lockheed, Gulf, and Rolls Royce, as explicable in terms of "delinquent subcultures," "differential association," or "labeling," so it makes little sense to see them as acts motivated by a desire to strike back at their oppressors and exploiters.

Thus the early efforts of "new criminologists" to provide an alternative theory of crime fell somewhat short of the mark. Through it all, however, a theme began to emerge that only now in the late 1970s is taking sufficient hold to give some hope that a truly "new" criminology will emerge. This theme is the serious attempt to apply dialectical theory to the study of crime. Not the naive, vulgar Marxism of ruling-class theory or the simplistic Marxist social psychology of the frustration–aggression hypothesis, rather it is a criminology that denies the deterministic nature of social theory, but does not fall prey to the equally erroneous assumption of voluntarism.[18] In essence, the theory argues that people in all social classes are responding to the contradictions of their historical conditions and in context are responding rationally to them. Rational responses may be criminal or noncriminal. Whatever the moral or cognitive component of the acts, they are best understood as people creating their own social world out of the inherited contradictions in the political economy of their existence.

Laws are seen as resulting from the contradictions that inhere in the political economy of (in our society) capitalism. The "ruling class" is central in the law-creation process, but it is not alone in the world: The ruling class and its political allies must take into account the extent to which the lower classes are demanding changes. Thus Marx's analysis of the law governing the length of the working day stands as a prototype of legal innovation, describing how it is the struggle of the ruling class against the conscious struggle of the working class over the length of the working day that lies behind the changing laws.[19]

The starting point, then, for that facet of the "new criminology" that holds considerable promise as a general theory of crime is *not* society, but the political economy. The new criminology follows the observation that our focus must be on whole political and economic systems rather than nation-states or societies. The analysis focuses on class relations (as opposed to social class as a category), as these are created and sustained by particular political economies. And finally, the methodology of determinism as practiced by social science is replaced with the methodology of dialetic-historical materialism.

Contradictions and Resolutions

Every historical era has its own persistent dilemmas and conflicts. The most important dilemmas and conflicts extant in a particular time and place are those that derive from the economic and political structures of the period. A contradiction is established in a particular historical period when the working out of the logic of the social structure and the ideology must necessarily destroy some fundamental aspect of existing social relations. This admittedly abstract depiction of what is meant by contradiction can best be comprehended by juxtaposing contradictions with other aspects of reality. Under capitalism, as Marx observed, there is a basic contradiction between capital and labor. This contradiction inheres in capitalism because if the workers and the capitalists both persistently and consistently pursue their own interests as defined by the logic of capitalism, then the ongoing relationship between workers and capitalists must eventually be destroyed. This basic contradiction of capitalism produces a wide range of dilemmas and conflicts. The attempt by workers to organize and demand higher wages, better working conditions, tenure of employment, etc., is a result of the basic contradiction. The attempt by owners to resist these demands creates conflicts. The dilemma for capital, labor, the state, and government is how to resolve the conflicts. Note, however, that it is usually the conflicts that precipitate the dilemma for the state, and it is conflicts that the state and the government attempt to resolve—not the basic contradictions. Note also that this process is a dynamic one: That is, the contradictions create conflicts and dilemmas that people try to resolve. In the resolution of particular conflicts and dilemmas, assuming that the basic contradictions are not resolved, we inevitably have the seeds for further conflicts. Often, resolutions of particular conflicts and dilemmas not only create further conflicts but spotlight as well other contradictions that may have been dormant.

Schematically, we can depict this model in the following way:

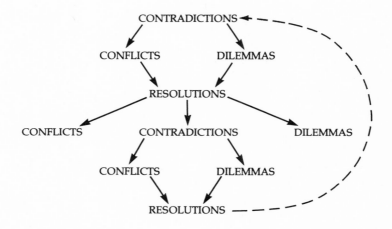

We purposely chose as our example of a basic contradiction in capitalist societies the relationship between capitalists and workers. This focal point lends itself to yet another insight to be gained from this perspective, namely, that the way people relate to the work that is done in the society—whether they own the means of producing the societies' goods or whether they work for others—is a feature of social structure that often generates profound contradictions. It is useful, then, to speak of historical periods and political economies according to the mode of production that characterizes them. A fundamental distinction in this regard is between societies where the means of production are owned privately and societies where the means of production are not. Obviously, there are many possible variations on these two ideal types: societies where the means of production are owned by the state (e.g. the Soviet Union) as contrasted with societies where the means of production are controlled by collectives of workers (e.g. Yugoslavia), or where the means of production are owned by collective units of workers, farmers, peasants, and other strata (e.g., China). Each of these different modes of production will manifest its own contradictions and therefore lead to quite different social relations and to different forms of crime and criminal law.

Capitalist societies, where the means of production are in private hands and where there inevitably develops a division between the class that rules (the owners of the means of production) and the class that is ruled (those who work for the ruling class), create substantial amounts of crime, often of the most violent sort, as a result of the contradictions that are inherent in the structure of social relations that emanate from the capitalist system.

The capitalist economy depends upon creating in the mass of the workers a desire for the consumption of products produced by the system. These products need not contribute to the well-being of the people, nor do they need to represent commodities of any intrinsic value; nonetheless, for the system to expand and be viable, it is essential that the bulk of the population be oriented toward consuming what is produced. In order to produce, however, the commodities that are the basis for the accumulation of capital and the maintenance of the ruling class, it is also necessary to get people to work at tedious, alienating, and unrewarding tasks. One way to achieve this, of course, is to make the accumulation of commodities dependent upon work. Moreover, as the system depends as it does on the desire to possess and consume commodities far beyond what is necessary for survival, there must be an added incentive to perform the dull, meaningless tasks that are required to keep the productive processes expanding. This may be accomplished by keeping a proportion of the labor force impoverished, or nearly so. If those who are employed become obstreperous and refuse to perform the tasks required by the productive system, then there is a reserve labor force waiting to take their jobs. Thus, always hanging over the heads of the workers is the possibility of becoming impoverished should they refuse to do their jobs.

Thus, at the outset, the structure of capitalism creates both the desire to consume and—for a large mass of people—an inability to earn the money necessary to purchase the items they have been taught to want.

Another fundamental contradiction of capitalism derives from the fact that the division of a society into a ruling class that owns the means of production and a subservient class that works for wages leads to conflict between the two classes. As those conflicts are manifested in rebellions and riots among the proletariat, the state, acting in the interests of the owners of the means of production, will pass laws designed to control those acts of the proletariat that threaten the interests of the bourgeoisie through the application of state-sanctioned force. In this way, then, some acts come to be defined as criminal.

It follows that as capitalism develops and conflicts between social classes continue (or become more frequent or more violent as a result, for example, of economic crises-inflation and recession), more and more acts will be defined as criminal and the amount of crime will increase.

From this perspective, criminal law and criminal behavior are best understood *not* in terms of customs, norms, or value-conflict and interest-group activity, but as directly linked to efforts by the state to create laws as a resolution to dilemmas created by conflicts that develop out of basic contradictions in the political economy.

In the chapters that follow, we will repeatedly turn to this general model of contradictions–conflicts–dilemmas and resolutions to make sense of and explain *how* various types of "organized crime" emerge, take their peculiar shape, and persist in capitalist societies. We will invoke middle-level theories about bureaucracy, social organization, and politics that supplement and buttress our paradigm. And we will range broadly over the territory of organized crime to accomplish our task. It might be useful here, however, to briefly discuss what is meant by the term "organized crime."

Defining Organized Crime

In a review of the United States Federal effort against organized crime, the General Accounting Office notes several times that there is no acceptable definition of organized crime.[20] It is stated that there is vast confusion among Federal agency personnel participating in America's so-called "war on organized crime." And their confusion is well founded." (The GAO Report is extensively discussed in Chapter 9.) In their critique of the Federal effort, the GAO suggests time and again that the root of the contemporary struggle against organized crime is hopelessly twisted because of the problem of meaning.[21]

The problems of Federal prosecutors with the meaning of organized crime have been mirrored within the American academic community where the search for acceptable definitions is just as difficult and is often unproductive. However, during the 1960s there emerged (or perhaps re-emerged) the notion that organized crime was an alien conspiracy brought to the United States by Sicilian immigrants. Promoted by mainstream social scientists, the view of organized crime's development was that of an inexorable march toward centralization and bureaucratization.[22] Organized crime, according to this interpretation, mirrored the well-known process of modernization that was itself discussed in a rather one-dimensional and simple-minded manner. Without stopping to criticize traditional modernization theory, it is enough to note that in the study of organized crime, its characterization as both an alien conspiracy and a continually rationalizing phenomenon was so compelling that almost surreptitiously the very term "organized crime" was carelessly transformed into meaning *the* monolithic organization of criminals. The identification tended to be complete: Organized criminals are members of the monolith; organized crime is whatever the members do.[23] In support of this view, interestingly enough, writers of criminology textbooks most often cited journalistic accounts or government documents. There were virtually no primary data generated by social scientists that supported the theory that there was a Mafia-type organization at the root of organized crime in America.[24]

With the emergence of a "new criminology" and a healthy skepticism about conventional views of crime, there emerged a group of researchers who questioned the prevailing view of organized crime.[25] Unfortunately, the connection between the term organized crime and the alleged alien conspiracy is so ingrained in our thinking that employment of the term often implies acceptance of this conspiracy. Indeed, to write about organized crime is to saddle oneself with at least the outline of the ineluctable drive toward consolidation and confederation. This is why historian Mark Haller abandoned the term organized crime altogether in favor of the term "illegal enterprises."[26]

Haller's suggested alternative conceptualization has some merit, in that it would avoid the tendency to conjure up images of a centralized, monolithic organization preying on innocent victims. However, the concept "illegal enterprise" does not differentiate very well among a wide variety of criminal activities. The "enterprise" of a gang of teenagers who siphon gasoline or illegally grow and sell marijuana fuses with the network of businesspeople, politicians, law enforcers, and racketeers who manage and profit from the sale of heroin or from gambling.

It is our view that the concept should be retained, but the definition should be altered to eliminate the difficulties of earlier usage. Thus we suggest that organized crime is a term that refers to those illegal activities connected with the management and coordination of racketeering (organized extortion) and the vices—particularly illegal drugs, illegal gambling, usury, and prostitution. This definition does not suggest *who* is involved, thereby leaving that question open for research. Nor does it include such a wide range of criminal activities (e.g., professional theft, organized burglary rings, or for that matter, the presistent criminality of a motorcycle gang) as to render it meaningless. By focusing on criminality that is organized to profit from vice and racketeering, we limit our scope and gain some ability to deal systematically with a set of social phenomena that share much in common and that are simultaneously differentiated from other criminal activities.

Summary and Conclusion

Criminology is a reflection of the times. The decade of the 1950s in capitalist nations was dominated by a view of the world that saw "society" as a real and living entity. "Deviance" was a manifestation of personal maladjustment. Delinquency was thus the focus of criminological attention, and theories of "how people got that way" made sense in the cosmology of the times. The 1960s forced a challenge to that view. In the attempt to construct a criminology built on a different foundation, criminologists resurrected ideas and observations of several generations earlier. In the end, however, it is necessary to forge a criminology from quite a different set of materials if it is to be more than a restatement of the theses of Merton, Sellin, Tannenbaum, and Sutherland. It is necessary to link criminology to Marxist theory in its most fundamental way. This will involve the development of a dialectical analysis with which to seek to understand how contradictions that are inherent in the political economy are linked to the incidence and distribution of criminality at particular historical periods. It is this point of view that is currently occupying the attention of the new criminology.

Thus it is that criminological inquiry is presently witnessing what Thomas Kuhn calls a "paradigm revolution." Beginning in the 1960s a "new criminology," variously labeled radical, critical, conflict, and Marxist, began taking shape. This book seeks to apply the perspective of the new criminology to the study of organized crime.

We have suggested here a theoretical model that will be used to explain how some kinds of crime come to be organized, survive, and take their particular form in capitalist countries. The nub of the argument is that every political and economic system contains within it certain fundamental contradictions: Criminal law and criminality can be explained by attempts of people in different social classes and positions in a society to accommodate to the conflicts and dilemmas created by these contradictions.

The second point made is concerned with definition of the concept "organized crime." As it is often used, this term is both confusing and misleading. The purpose of a definition is to provide limits within which to focus inquiry. Ideally, a definition isolates a relatively homogeneous set of phenomena that have certain characteristics from a wide variety of closely ralated but significantly different events. A good definition is neither so narrow as to be trivial nor so broad as to encompass more than is theoretically and empirically manageable. It is in this light that we suggest that organized crime be defined as (or perhaps better, limited to) those illegal activities involving the management and coordination of racketeering and vice.

One important, final point implicit in the foregoing is that our framework demands taking seriously the notion of *Organizing Crime,* the title for this book. Organizing crime—the processes that result in organized crimes—is going on constantly and ceaselessly. Organizing crime is one of the challenges offered by civil societies—and these civil societies are in motion, historical. To miss this is to miss the fundamental ground of dialectical analysis and to retreat into ahistoricism, one of the preconditions for sterile theorizing.

Going About Our Work

In the parts and chapters that follow, we intend to accomplish certain tasks. First, our approach is topical: The material is arranged under four topics, moving from narcotics to business and bureaucracy, to European issues, and finally to law. Under these topics we concentrate on two sorts of analysis: micro and macro. In each part we develop both theory and empirical research through case studies and more broadly ranging essays. We have chosen the topics because they are largely under-researched and because they quickly reveal the symbiotic relationships we hold important. We have written two sorts of chapter in order to make clear the manner in which theory and empirical research are mutually dependent in forming an overall perspective on vice and criminal rackets—that is, on organized crime.

NOTES

1. J.F. Galliher and J.L. McCartney, The Influence of Funding Agencies on Juvenile Delinquency Research. *Social Problems* 21:88 (1973).

2. T.S. Kuhn, *The Structure of Scientific Revolution*. (Chicago: University of Chicago Press, 1962).

3. F. Pearce, *Crimes of the Powerful*. (London: Pluto Press, 1976).

4. H. Schwendinger and J. Schwendinger, Defenders of Order or Guardians of Human Rights. *Issues in Criminology* 5 (1970).

5. W.J. Chambliss, Vice, Corruption, Bureaucracy and Power, *Wisconsin Law Review* (1971) No. 4. A. Platt, *The Politics of Riot Commissions*. (New York: MacMillan, 1971). R. Quinney, *The Social Reality of Crime*. (Boston: Little, Brown, 1970). A. Turk, *Criminality and Legal Order*. (Chicago: Rand McNally, 1969).

6. F. Tannenbaum, *Crime and the Community*. (Boston: Ginn & Co., 1978), p 25.

7. E.R. Hawkins and W.W. Waller, Critical Notes on the Cost of Crime. *Journal of Criminal Law and Criminology* 26 (1936).

8. T. Sellin, *Culture Conflict and Crime*. (New York: Social Science Research Council, 1938).

9. R.K. Merton, *Social Theory and Social Structure* p 134. (New York: Free Press, 1968).

10. Ibid. p 136.

11. E.H. Sutherland, *White Collar Crime*. (New York: Dryden Press, 1949).

12. J.F. Short and F.I. Nye, Scaling Delinquent Behavior. *American Sociological Review* 22: 326–331 (1957).

13. W. Bonger, *Criminality and Economic Conditions*. (Boston: Little, Brown, 1916). G. Rusche and O. Kirchheimer, *Punishment and Social Structure*. (New York: Columbia University Press, 1939).

14. R. Quinney, Critique of Legal Order, *Crime Control in Capitalist Society*. (Boston: Little, Brown, 1974), p 138.

15. L. Friedman, *Law and Society: An Introduction*. (Englewood Cliffs, New Jersey: Prentice-Hall, 1977), p 99.

16. E. Cleaver, *Soul on Ice*. (New York: McGraw-Hill, 1968).

17. E.H. Sutherland, *The Professional Thief*. (Chicago: University of Chicago Press, 1937). W.J. Chambliss, *Boxman*. (New York: Harper & Row, 1972).

18. R. Applebaum, Marxist Method, Structural Constraints and Social Praxis. *The American Sociologist* 13:73–81, 1978.

19. Karl Marx, *Capital* Vol. 1, p 231–302. (New York: International Publishers, 1972).

20. U.S. General Accounting Office (GAO), *War on Organized Crime Faltering*. (Washington, DC: U.S. Government Printing Office, 1977).

21. Ibid, p 8.

22. M.R. Haskell and L. Yablonsky, *Crime and Delinquency*. (Chicago: Rand McNally, 1970).

23. D.R. Cressey, The Structure and Functions of Criminal Syndicates, in *Task Force Report: Organized Crime*. President's Commission on Law Enforcement and Administration of Justice (Washington, DC: U.S. Government Printing Office, 1967).

24. J.F. Galliher and J.A. Cain, Citation Support for the Mafia Myth in Criminology Textbooks. *The American Sociologist* 9 (May, 1974).

25. W.J. Chamblis, *On The Take: From Petty Crooks to Presidents*. (Bloomington: Indiana University Press, 1978). J.L. Albini, *The American Mafia: Genesis of a Legend*.

(Appleton-Century-Crofts: New York. 1971). D.C. Smith, Jr., Mafia: The Prototypical Alien Conspiracy. *The Annals* 423 (1976). M.H. Haller, Organized Crime in Urban Society: Chicago in the Twentieth Century. *Journal of Social Hiistory*, (1971–1972) 5. A.A. Block, History and the Study of Organized Crime. *Urban Life* (1978) 6.

26. M.H. Haller, The Rise of Criminal Syndicates, paper read at Columbia University Seminar on the City (1975).

ORGANIZING
ILLICIT
ENTERPRISES

I

The Political Economy of Opium and Heroin

2

Traditional criminology asked three questions about drug use and its effects:

1. Why do some people use illegal drugs and others do not?
2. What effect does an individual's use of drugs have on that person's involvement in other types of crime?
3. How can people addicted to illegal drugs be rehabilitated?

Marxist criminology requires that we seek a broader view. It asks how opium and its derivatives (principally morphine and heroin) became products capable of generating profits in the capitalist economy. It asks how the profits from opium were legitimized and sustained. It asks what effects the widespread use of opium have on the social relations of a particular historical period. And it asks how opium use and opium markets relate to contradictions, conflicts, and conflict resolutions of a particular historical period. It is to these questions that we turn our attention.

The Magic Plant

The opium poppy is a plant that grows abundantly in warm climates at very high altitudes. It is also a plant that requires a very high investment in labor for its slow maturation. Such an unusual ecology is not found everywhere: It is found only in that chain of mountains that extends from Turkey through Iran, India, China, and Southeast Asia.

This stretch of mountains also contains a very large number of people who live at a low standard and who provide an abundant source of cheap agricultural labor.[1] Thus, for centuries this strip of land has had a corner on the world's supply of opium comparable to that held by the Middle East on the world's supply of oil.

Someone discovered that the juice that oozes from the opium poppy can be taken internally with some highly desirable effects, the most important of which was, in the early days, relief of pain. In areas of the world where medicine was (and is) not readily available and many debilitating diseases (such as tuberculosis, leprosy, and the more common diarrhea and toothaches) abound, an easily grown product that can relieve the pain of these diseases is most welcome.

So far as we know, Turkish traders were the first people to introduce opium to the rest of the world. In their search for exchangeable commodities, the Turks carried opium into India, China, and Southeast Asia. This took place in the eighth and ninth centuries. All indications are, however, that the trade in opium was small and relatively inconsequential. A full-fledged market in opium was not introduced into South Asia until the emergence of capitalism and its attendant search for labor, profits, and markets.

The European Way

As capitalism emerged from the ashes of feudalism in Europe, the newly formed economic necessities pushed both nations and capitalists to scour the world for new markets and products. Italy, Spain, and Portugal were at the forefront of this exploration and search for profits.

In the 1500s, the Portuguese arrived in Asia with crews searching for goods to take back to Europe and with items from Europe that could be sold. At the time, the economies of the Asian nations were self-contained. There was some trade and a minimal amount of migration among the Chinese who emigrated to neighboring lands, but commerce was limited between the countries.

Europe had little to offer Asia. While Asia had spices, tea, silk, and pottery that could turn a handsome profit on the European market, Europe had only silver or gold that interested the Asians. Using silver and gold to purchase commodities such as silk and tea soon became unpopular with European governments; it was apparent that the value of silver and gold was rising while the commodities they purchased were consumed.

When the Portuguese began setting up small enclaves on Asian shores, they also moved to control the sea traffic through plunder and piracy. In the course of plundering Asian vessels, sailors on the militarily more powerful Portuguese ships discovered that there was a small but already established trade in opium. At the time, opium was used primarily for medical purposes. Asian ships from Singapore and Bangkok carried opium to Indonesia, China, and other Asian ports where they traded it for other commodities. The trade was small and local enough that opium use was rare and relatively inconsequential.

The Portuguese traders, however, were quick to realize that for at least a small part of their trade they could use opium instead of gold and silver. First they crushed the Asian traders and ran their vessels out of the seas. Then they began purchasing opium from Turkish and Indian traders, trading the opium in turn for spices, tea, and silk that they could in turn sell profitably in Europe.

For the next three hundred years, European powers fought over the acquistion of Asian colonies. Colonial powers expanded into the interiors of the Asian nations, colonizing them to varying degrees. Increasingly, the European colonizers turned to the opium trade as a source of income to pay for the military excursions and as a way of obtaining purchasing power for the spices, tea, silk, and pottery they sought.[2]

Opium was a resolution of some important dilemmas for the expanding trade of European capitalist countries. The creation of capital through trade was an important and valued source of income for capitalists and nations alike. But so too was the accumulation of gold and silver reserves: Both precious metals had become the principal measure of a nation's wealth and, not inconsequentially, necessary for supporting the armies and navies essential to competition with other European capitalist nations. To increase capital through the exchange of commodities with Asia by bartering away the gold and silver reserves was to win a little and lose a lot. To the good fortune of European capitalists (and the bad fortune of the Asians) opium was discovered as a resolution to this dilemma.

Thus opium dens, controlled and managed by the European colonial governments or their local handmaidens, began appearing in the major cities of Asia.[3] India gradually replaced Turkey as the main opium-growing area. India's opium was produced mainly by the British East India Company, a private company that had been given almost total political and economic control over the Indian colony by the British government. The British East India Company, through its representatives in Asia and local colonial governments, encouraged and expanded opium addiction throughout Asia, especially among the enormous Chinese population. In the early years, the Chinese government, fraught with its own internal political problems and struggling to throw off the yoke of feudalism, paid scant attention to the growing spate of opium smoking. By the middle of the 19th century, China came to realize that it was trading away its precious metals especially silver, as well as its silks and tea, for opium.[4] As Europe had tried to do earlier, China sought to stem the outflow of silver. China did this by curtailing the importation of opium. The Manchu rulers announced a stringent antiopium policy with the explicit intention of stopping British and American traders. At the time, Whampoa was the major port through which opium flowed.[5] In 1839, the Manchu rulers appointed one Commissioner Lin to the task of stopping the opium importation. Although the basic issue was the outflow of silver, Commissioner Lin approached the problem moralistically and argued that it was a ". . . class of evil foreigner that makes opium and brings it for sale, tempting fools to destroy themselves."

Commissioner Lin demanded the right to inspect all incoming vessels and to confiscate any opium found. The American traders complied with this demand; the British traders refused. Meanwhile, one of the principal companies working under a franchise from the British East India Company began a lobbying campaign in the English Parliament to support its right to trade opium in China.[7]

The debate in Parliament was short-lived. Prime Minister Palmerston authorized the British fleet to seize Whampoa, Canton, and other major ports along the Chinese coast. Thus began the infamous Opium War between China and Great Britain, which lasted from 1839 to 1842. In the end the superior naval power of Britain brought the Manchu Dynasty a humiliating defeat. The terms of settlement after the war indicate the extent to which the British had subjugated the Chinese government:

1. Great Britain was given possession of Hong Kong.
2. British traders were given completely open access to five Chinese Ports, including Canton.
3. The Chinese agreed to pay $21 million in reparation for opium that had been seized and destroyed by Commissioner Lin prior to the war.
4. British traders would henceforth be subject *only* to British, not Chinese, laws when conflicts occurred.
5. Smuggling was outlawed, but opium was not specifically mentioned in the agreements. The responsibility for enforcing laws against smuggling was placed in the hands of the smugglers (the British), not the persons smuggled against (the Chinese).

Several years after the end of the War, a British consul in Shanghai seized three opium ships flying the British flag. He was subsequently removed from his post and transferred to India.[8]

After the 1839–1842 war, opium remained illegal by Chinese law, although in effect the British East India Company and its affiliates had a free hand to import and distribute opium in at least five Chinese ports besides Hong Kong:

> Opium smuggling entered new heights. The fastest ships available, mainly British, but also American and Indian, transported opium from Calcutta to the Chinese ports. These cargoes were moved to opium store-ships lying outside each treaty port. Opium was sold over the side of the ship to Chinese smugglers or sent on small lorchas (coastal ships) to agreed upon locations on the mainland.[9]

For the next 14 years the opium trade flourished. However, in 1856, the Chinese Commissioner of Canton seized a British-registered (but Chinese-owned) lorcha, the *Arrow*. There followed a second war between China and Great Britain that ended much the same as the first, except this time Britain was able to demand and get from the defeated Chinese the legalization of opium smoking and trading. The Chinese, however, did reserve the right to impose a tax on all opium imported: It was a decision which, paradoxically, would be a major factor in the decline of opium trading by the end of the 19th century.

The immediate consequence of China's legalization of opium was to vastly increase the potential and actual market. Now British traders could bring to bear all their skills and imagination to spread the opium habit to the interior of China. The market was truly overwhelming and couched in the nicest of terms when the head of one of the major opium trading companies noted that opium was a "comfort to the hard working Chinese."[10]

There was, however, a contradiction contained in this resolution: Legalization planted the seed that would eventually destroy the British opium monopoly and its profits. For with legalization came (a) taxes, and (b) the legal right of Chinese farmers to grow their own opium. Competition would shortly ruin the hard-won right to import opium from India into China.

Thus is the process of contradiction, conflict, dilemma, and resolution as illustrated by this early history of opium in Asia. The fundamental contradiction between developing a trade with Asian countries and having little to trade with them was resolved in favor of trading opium. Asian countries, however, were ill-disposed to permit this trade to flourish as it drained them of important economic resources (gold and silver as well as spices, etc.). It also took a toll in human suffering that many Asian leaders found intolerable. Attempts to stop the trade led inevitably to conflict between Asian and European countries. The superior military technology of Europe at this time spelled defeat for the Asian governments. Resolving the conflict through treaties that legalized opium trade was an immediate solution. The legalization of opium, however, utlimately led to competition from local growers, and this, combined with the tax imposed on imported opium, ultimately led to the demise of the opium trade by Europe. Interestingly, it was only at the point where local competition destroyed the profits from opium that European governments passed legislation making opium trading illegal.

Local competition, however, did not emerge immediately. Thus from 1856 until the end of the century, British capitalism in China flourished in part on the profits and labor advantages from the opium traffic. By the end of the 19th century, it was often said that China had become a nation of opium smokers.

The growing and expanding industrial revolution in Europe increased Europe's demand for markets and raw materials. Southeast Asia became a major pawn in the political economy of Europe's capitalist development. Burma was occupied and became British Burma; Malaysia became a British colony; Thailand fell under Britain's "sphere of influence." Laos, Vietnam, and Cambodia were brought together politically under French rule and were named "French Indochina." The Netherlands colonized Indonesia; Britain had possession of Hong Kong. China was formally independent, but in effect had a status similar to that of other British "protectorates."

You Can Lead a Horse to Water But You Can't Make It Drink

The creation of an adequate labor force reflected basic contradictions inherent in the imposition of capitalist economies onto feudalism. Still thoroughly in the grip of feudalism, the inhabitants of Southeast Asia were little inclined to move to the plantations of foreigners to grow rubber, sugar, cotton jute, and hemp. And the labor forces in Singapore, Hong Kong, Saigon, or Bangkok were disinclined to work on the docks at hard labor. Yet the demand for cheap labor was great. A famine in South China, the Tai Ping Rebellion, and the drain of silver from the opium traffic combined to provide a convenient solution. The population that had moved out of other provinces first concentrated in the Kwantung Provinces in the south of China and then soon began to emigrate to other cities of South Asia.

As the population of China's southern provinces reached a point of saturation, people began emigrating by the thousands. Some went as far away as the United States where they provided hordes of cheap labor for the railroads. Most, however, went to the nearby cities of Southeast Asia where they were employed as laborers on the docks. By 1910, there were over 100,000 Chinese in Saigon, 200,000 in Bangkok, and smaller numbers in every other major city in the area.

Not all of the Chinese migration was voluntary. Chinese "coolies" were an important source of profit for traders. There is also evidence that Chinese brought to the United States and other parts of America were kidnapped and sold into indentured service. In Cuba, for example, many of the Chinese laborers who were interviewed about the circumstances surrounding their leaving China insisted that they did not leave voluntarily, but were kidnapped.[12] The same is true of Chinese who were brought to the United States.

The Chinese brought with them the opium-smoking habits that had been so meticulously encouraged by British merchants and traders. The colonial governments were quick to recognize the value of encouraging the Chinese laborers to smoke opium. Profits were substantial, and an opium-addicted labor force was magnanimously compliant. In every major city of Southeast Asia, from Rangoon to Saigon, colonial and local governments developed opium dens. The opium trade was carefully, albeit corruptly, organized and controlled by an unholy alliance of colonial officials, local governments, and a new class of entrepreneurs who were given government franchises to import and sell opium. Opium sales provided 40%–50% of the income of colonial governments.[13] Opium profits helped finance railways, canals, roads, and government buildings—as well as the comfortable living conditions of colonial administrators.

From time to time local governments resisted the expanding opium trade. King Rama II of Thailand decreed a ban on opium trading in 1811, and in 1839 the death penalty was instituted for traffickers.[14] Unfortunately for King Rama II, British merchant ships that carried opium to the ports were beyond his control. When a British captain was arrested, the British government rumbled its warships, and the local government quickly released the opium smuggler. In 1852, King Mongkut of Thailand succumbed to British pressure, created an opium monopoly under Thai government control, and leased the monopoly to a wealthy Chinese merchant.[15] The king also established franchises in gambling, lotteries, and prostitution. The mainstay of the government revenues became opium. Opium was simultaneously the main thread on which the working class hung and the one by which it was enticed into providing labor for the European trade with these nations. It was opium, not religion, that was the opiate of the masses in Southeast Asia. By the 1940s there were in Indochina (Cambodia, Laos, and Vietnam) over 2500 opium dens which provided 45% of all tax revenues and an unmeasurable percentage of the unacknowledged salaries of both local and colonial government officials.[16]

Agri-Opium Business

The Chinese immigrants in Southeast Asia and the United States were not, of course, the sole or perhaps even the major market for opium. Opium smoking quickly spread to indigent American and Asian populations. The spread was encouraged by the same political and economic forces that had provided the impetus for its growth in China earlier.

British traders were joined in the late 1700s by American ships and merchants. However, the Hays Treaty of 1794 prohibited American merchants from dealing in commodities under British control. The profits from opium were, however, too appealing to be turned down, and American merchants began to introduce into China opium that was grown in Turkey—returning us, in some symbolically diabolical way, to the first opium route of the eighth century.

The American trade was less than that of its British competitors, but it was nonetheless large, profitable, and important for the development of American capitalism. In the years 1816, 1817, and 1818 there was an annual volume of 672,900 pounds of opium handled by U.S. merchants.[17] This volume of opium, according to the historians Latourette and Dulles, formed the capital which was basic to the growth of industrialization in New England.[18] The profits from opium trading were invested in the textile mills in Massachusetts and other New England states following the introduction of the power loom in 1814. Thus the following situation: Opium helped create a labor force for capitalist expansion in Asia and America, and the profits from the opium provided the capital for the development of the factory system in New England.[19]

From the period 1830–1860 (the period of the two opium wars) American clipper ships, sometimes referred to as Opium Clippers, competed successfully with the British in the opium market. But when the British introduced the steamship, American merchants lost their competitive advantage, and the British once again dominated the trade.

This change was combined with the fact that the "Treaty of 1856" had set the stage for the emergence of competition in the growth and distribution of opium, which was to emerge from the Chinese themselves. Chinese farmers discovered that the high mountains of South China were amenable to opium growing. As the profits from opium were higher than those from other crops there was a rather rapid transformation of the agricultural products—first in many mountainous regions of China and later in other parts of Southeast Asia. By the late 19th century, "British and American mercantile firms, seeking more profit from other goods, slowly withdrew from opium trade."[20] The British continued active trading until World War I, but the total trade in opium, once the mainstay of American and British mercantile operations in Asia, gradually declined after 1900.

The production of opium spread to the high mountain plateaus of neighboring countries. The border states of Laos, Burma, and Thailand quickly shifted from traditional crops to opium as the profits from opium (as well as the pleasures of local consumption) became increasingly apparent. Britain's loss of revenues was a boon for the impoverished hill tribes of Southeast Asia. World War I all but stopped the competition from British and American traders carrying Indian and Turkish opium, thus bringing down the curtain on the Asian opium drama begun some four hundred years earlier when the first Portuguese ships of war pirated opium from the small trading vessels that were at that time supplying a tiny market.

Between 1914 and 1940 the opium monopolies in Indochina (controlled first by the French, then by the Japanese colonial government) sought new, closer and more dependable sources of opium and found them among the Meo tribes of Laos. Indochina's opium production leaped from 7.5 tons in 1940 to 60.6 tons by 1944.[21] Similar leaps and changes occurred somewhat later in the other countries—Thailand and Burma—that now comprise the Golden Triangle. When the Chinese Liberation Army emerged victorious in 1949, the supply of opium from China disappeared. This further stimulated opium growing in the Golden Triangle.

As was the case in the early years of colonizing Southeast Asia, opium smoking and trafficking were encouraged and stimulated by both local and colonial governments. Addiction provided profits for the governments and kept at least the addicted segment of the labor force dependent on their employers. With the emergence of subterranean warfare conducted by colonial government intelligence units, the opium trade came to supply a new link in the armament of the colonial nations. France especially used the opium trade as a source of revenue to finance its clandestine intelligence operations in Vietnam, Cambodia, and Laos. The wedge provided by the opium trade was two pronged: First, there was money earned that paid for government administrative costs, and second, the opium trade was a carrot to be given to those hill tribes and local leaders who would support the French struggle against the indigenous communists.

When the United States took over the management of Indochina from France, it also inherited the link between military control and opium in these countries. It was necessary, and indeed highly expedient, to adopt the French policy of encouraging friendly tribesmen to grow and traffic in narcotics (opium) in return for fighting the communists. Thus, America's Central Intelligence Agency became a major trafficker in the international narcotics industry.[22]

Until very recently, the governments of Thailand, Laos, and South Vietnam were as dependent on the opium trade as they were at the end of the 19th century. The profits are immense. The former head of Thailand's police department is alleged to have put over 600 million dollars into European banks before he was forced to resign.[23] The three Kitchihoun family members who ruled Thailand's military dictatorship from 1964 to 1973 amassed over 200 million dollars worth of property in Thailand and an unknown fortune stashed secretly in foreign banks.[24] Much of this fortune derived from their share of profits from the opium trade. The South Vietnamese governments from Diem to Thieu profited immensely as well. In Laos, General Ouane openly admits that without the huge traffic in opium between his country and Saigon—which traffic he controlled—Laos could not have survived economically.[25] No wonder then that the U.S. provided the planes and the military equipment that enabled General Ouane to ship Laotian hill-tribe opium to Saigon, where it was processed into heroin and either sold to American soldiers in Vietnam or shipped back to the U.S.—sometimes in the coffins of American soldiers.[26]

Opium traffic still plays an important part in capitalism's political economy as a mechanism for reducing conflicts and dilemmas stemming from basic contradictions. In Southeast Asia, the Shan tribesmen with their own independent armies, the KMT (Chinese Nationalist Army), and the Laotian Armed Forces were, until the Cambodian revolution, three principal sources of transporting and marketing opium from the hill-tribe growers in the Golden Triangle to the middlemen who oversee its passage to the laboratories in Bangkok and Hong Kong. These three groups—the Shan, the KMT, and the Laotian Armed Forces—were supported by arms and technical assistance from the United States because they were believed to be serving U.S. interests by providing a wedge against the communist liberation armies in Burma, Laos, Cambodia, and Thailand.

Another parallel between conditions today and the historical roots of opium smoking in Asia is its function as both an expression of and a suppressor of social conflicts. In Vietnam, the widespread use of heroin by the American Army may have reduced the overt expression of rebellion so often commented on as a characteristic of the people fighting in a war without public sanction. Heroin in the ghettos of America's large cities may also serve the same purpose it did among the Chinese laborers of the late 19th century: It immobilizes a segment of discontented laborers who might otherwise more openly fight against the oppression and despair of their position at the bottom of the scale in a class society.

Opium and Heroin in the United States

The use of opium and heroin in the United States must be understood in the same general terms that have been applied to understanding its Asian background. The first major influx of opium smokers came when the Chinese emigrated to the west coast of America as "coolies" working in the gold and silver mines and building the railroads that would connect the eastern manufacturing centers with the western frontier.

Conditions of work for the Chinese immigrants were abominable. The workers were brought without families, were forced to labor long hours under the worst physical conditions imaginable and with little relief. Opium smoking was a way of lulling the psychological pain of the arduous conditions. It was also an extremely effective way of reducing the pain of physical illness for which medical care was practically nonexistent.

From the point of view of the employers, the laborers' opium smoking was a blessing. The employers, by controlling the importation and distribution of opium, made a profit from selling it to the workers. Furthermore, the threat of withdrawing the supply of opium kept many potential labor complaints from becoming serious threats to the employer.

It was in this social situation that opium smoking began a slow but steady growth throughout the American working class, especially in the west, where the work was often unbelievably demanding, and where there were few families in the mines and cities. In the late 1800s, when opium was legally imported and sold, the annual importation into the United States exceeded 500,000 pounds.[27] The market was supplied by normal business channels. Opium was still coming into San Francisco and some had begun to find its way east to Chicago and New York. Opium dens were found as far south as New Orleans and as far north as Montreal during the early 20th century.

Opium usage spread to the middle and upper classes as well. A study of patent medicines sold in Boston in 1888 showed that 14% of these medicines contained opiates, and in 1900 it is reported that 3.3 million doses of opium were sold each month in Vermont.[28]

By the 1880s, mining and railroad building began to decline in the west. Thus the need for cheap labor, such as had been supplied by Chinese immigrants, declined as well. The United States government became concerned over the growing number of immigrants entering the country who were rapidly becoming a burden rather than an economic asset. An envoy thus was dispatched from Washington to China with the mission of gaining Chinese cooperation in reducing emmigration to the United States. China was willing, it turned out, providing the United States would in turn take steps to reduce the opium being brought into China by American ships. The United States agreed: The opium business was substantial for a small group of shipowners, but the market inside China was rapidly declining, and the lion's share of the market was controlled by the British. The United States then passed the first antiopium legislation in the world: a statute at large passed in 1886 making it illegal to trade in opium.[29]

Thus, by the beginning of the 20th century the opium trade and traffic had shifted substantially. Southeast Asia was still a major market, as was China. The supply of opium, however, had begun to shift from India and Turkey to sources closer to home: mainly South China and the Golden Triangle. Turkey and India were still producing opium, which was shipped to Europe and the United States. Opium dens were run and organized by the governments of China and Southeast Asia, and the profits from these enterprises served to support not only local governments, but colonial governments as well. The United States had become a market of some importance for opium from Turkey, India, and Southeast Asia. Probably the major routes were for opium grown in India and Turkey to be manufactured into morphine in Europe and shipped to the United States and throughout Europe. Opium in its raw form was coming into the United States from Southeast Asia.

As the Asian opium trade became less profitable for Europeans, antiopium legislation began to appear in most western countries. A series of International Opium Conferences (Shanghai in 1909; The Hague in 1911–1914; Geneva in 1924) were the consequence of the changing economic realities that helped spread antiopium sentiment and subsequent legislation.

In 1898 a German pharmaceutical company, Bayer, began distributing a patented product called heroin, which, the manufacturer claimed, was a nonaddictive drug with the same medical value as opium but without the undesirable side effects.

In 1914 the U.S. Government passed the Harrison Act, which made it illegal to trade in opium or its derivatives (heroin included) without registering the with U.S. Government and paying a small tax. As a result of bureaucratic maneuvering (particularly the careful selection of cases for appeal) the Federal Bureau of Narcotics succeeded in getting a series of court decisions (especially in the U.S. Supreme Court Decision *Behrman vs. the United States*) that made it illegal for doctors to prescribe morphine, opium, or heroin to anyone who was an addict.[30]

World War I interrupted the European traffic in opium. The war provided an increased incentive to grow the poppy in China and Southeast Asia as trade routes with India and Turkey were now totally severed; it also interfered somewhat with the trade in opium into the United States. Nonetheless, enough opium and heroin were imported throughout the war to supply a stable addict population. World War I also inadvertently increased connections with Turkish and Middle Eastern opium sources.

It is not clear from the records how the opium and heroin business was organized after World War I. It seems likely that from 1918 to 1940 the opium–heroin business was highly competitive—run by local merchants who made special arrangements with merchant seamen and mercantilists. There is evidence that in the 1920s the New York trade was concentrated around some (but not all) of the same people (such as Arnold Rothstein and Frank Erickson) who were major organizers of the business in illegal whiskey.[31] In San Francisco, an underworld figure known as "Black Tony" was a central organizer of the opium–heroin trade.

> We all worked for the Narcotics Syndicate in San Francisco which at that time was run by Black Tony. It was a pretty big operation even then. The Syndicate used to get its morphine from Germany and its opium from China. The morphine came in through New York and was handled by the local narcotic wholesalers. Then it was shipped to the West Coast.[32]

Through connections with the Hearst newspaper chain, "Black Tony" used delivery boys and street corner paper sellers to distribute opium and heroin to his customers. Interestingly, this same pattern, involving Hearst newspapers, appeared in Chicago about this time.[33]

By 1938, the heroin business in the United States was one of the nation's larger industries. Senator John Coffee estimated that the sale of heroin at this time exceeded one billion dollars annually.[34] We know less than we should about the organization of this industry and the extent to which it was monopolized. (In the next chapter we will show how the cocaine trade was handled.) There is some evidence, however, that by the close of the 1930s, Vito Genovese had managed to gain control over some of the heroin business through working agreements with people in Italy and France.[35] Genovese may have worked closely with Frank Erickson, a Scandinavian who had inherited the illegal business empire of Arnold Rothstein after Rothstein was murdered in 1928.

World War II interrupted a great many things, including the smooth flow of morphine and heroin from Europe to the United States and of opium from Asia. According to Alfred McCoy, the addict population in the United States declined to such an extent that, following World War II, the "heroin problem" had become quite manageable.[36]

The affluence of the 1950s created unprecedented demand by the consuming American public for everything from refrigerators to ballpoint pens. The life and work conditions for many Americans created an unprecedented demand for narcotics as well. The iron law of capitalism is that where there is a demand there will be a supplier if the profit is high enough. Suppliers emerged throughout the United States, especially in the largest cities where life conditions and political forces combined to make the demand and distribution of heroin manageable.

Prohibition had produced a large number of businessmen with the knowledge and the capital capable of organizing international cartels for the production, shipments, and distribution of illegal goods. Meyer Lansky, Vito Genovese, and Joe Adonis had established a network of business and political contacts throughout Europe, Latin America, and the Caribbean that made the importation of illegal commodities highly profitable.

These businessmen and their associates also had very large profits from gambling and from real estate investments made during the 1930s and 1940s.[38] Capital was, of course, essential. Lansky is reported to have taken 20 million dollars to France in the 1950s to gain a monopoly on the heroin produced in Marseilles—heroin that was manufactured from opium base that came mainly from Turkey via the Middle East. The success of Lansky's mission was such that Turkey and Marseilles thereafter became the major suppliers of America's illegal opiates:

Although it is difficult to probe the inner workings of such a clandestine business . . . there is reason to believe that Meyer Lansky's 1949–1950 European tour was instrumental in promoting Marseilles' heroin industry. After leaving Switzerland (where he had set up Swiss bank accounts to take care of money transfers) Lansky traveled through France, where he met with highranking Corsican syndicate leaders on the Riviera and in Paris. After lengthy discussions, Lansky and the Corsicans are reported to have arrived at some sort of agreement concerning the international heroin traffic . . . . In future years, U.S. narcotics experts were to estimate that the majority of America's heroin supply was being manufactured in Marseilles.[39]

Our knowledge about the inner workings of the heroin industry is sketchy. We can safely conclude, however, that the profits from opium and heroin were growing at a rate that would have made even the growth rates of General Motors and International Business Machines seem modest. The average heroin addict in the United States in the early 1970s was spending $30,000 a year on heroin.[40] Although this is a very high figure, it is noteworthy that it is an average based upon the fact that not all heroin addicts are "street people." Many addicts are wealthy professional and business people who no doubt pay considerably higher prices for their "shit" than do the people in the ghettos and the slums.

Accepting, for the sake of argument, this average expenditure per addict enables us to also estimate the gross volume of business from heroin. If, as most experts agree, there are at least one million addicts in the United States, then this means that the annual gross sale of heroin in the United States today exceeds $30 billion.[41] Some sense of the importance of this industry to the national economy is gleaned from the fact that this would make the heroin industry comparable in gross volume of business to the largest corporations in the United States: In 1970, General Motors, Exxon, IBM, ITT, and a half-dozen other of the largest multinational corporations in the world had a gross volume of business *less than* $30 billion a year.[42] Indeed, there were only about 20 countries in the world with a gross national product in excess of the gross volume of business of the heroin industry in the United States.

The heroin industry is a highly competitive one. Although Meyer Lansky or Vito Genovese or Joe Adonis might gain a competitive advantage this does not mean they can do this without a struggle. Nor does it mean that their monopoly position is unassailable. There is evidence that the heroin industry is currently undergoing a substantial upheaval brought about by the emergence in the late 1960s of competitive forces with substantial political influence. To understand this, the latest chapter in the political economy of heroin, we must digress slightly.

The development of the state in the modern world is such that virtually every aspect of economic life is influenced by decisions of the states. Laws, regulations, government contracts, licenses—what the lawyer Charles Reich has called "The New Property"[43]—are the life substance of most industries in the capitalist world. Illegal businesses, including the business of heroin are no exceptions. State and government cooperation, especially the cooperation of those agencies responsible for regulating a particular industry, is an essential ingredient for protecting that industry's profits and maintaining its monopolistic advantages. State cooperation, in turn, depends upon being able to influence those political leaders who most directly affect the industry.

Throughout the period of 1930–1960 the major corporate executives who owned and managed the heroin industry in the United States were well represented by key people in state and federal government. The heroin industry had grown up during the heyday of the Democratic Party—quite predictably, their ties and allegiance to the Democrats were stronger than their connection with Republican politicians.

But the hegemony of the Democratic Party was undermined in the 1960s. Even old, established labor union ties, such as that between the Teamsters and the Democrats, began to show signs of wearing thin as Jimmy Hoffa was put in prison at the insistence of a Democratically controlled attorney general's office,[44] after the Teamsters shifted their allegiance from the Democrats to the Republicans.[45]

The emergence of Richard Nixon as a political force of substance posed a greater threat to the established monopoly in the heroin industry than any experienced since the 1930s. The Nixon administration adopted policies that were clearly inimical to the interest of the established monopoly. First, and perhaps most importantly, heretofore unheard of pressure was brought on Turkey to curtail its production of opium. At the threat of dissolving the massive allocation of foreign aid, the Nixon administration forced Turkey to enforce its long-existing laws restricting the growth of opium. Secondly, the Bureau of Dangerous Drugs (formerly the Federal Bureau of Narcotics) was expanded and given substantial encouragement to curtail the heroin traffic from Latin American and France—an importation route established and largely controlled by Meyer Lansky and his associates.[46]

The antiheroin war begun by President Nixon and his associates might have reduced the amount of heroin coming into the United

States except for one small thing: At the same time that effective programs to reduce the heroin from Turkey and Marseilles were being implemented, the supply of heroin from Southeast Asia was increasing dramatically. From 1968 to 1972 the amount of heroin coming from Turkey declined almost 50%. The amount of heroin consumed in the United States supplied by Southeast Asian sources increased 20%–30%.[47] Whereas in the mid-1960s it was estimated that over 95% of America's heroin was from Turkey by 1971 it was estimated that less than 50% was coming from Turkey.[48]

In 1968, Santo Trafficante, Jr. took a trip to Southeast Asia, visiting Bangkok, Thailand, Singapore, and Saigon.[49] This trip was to establish agreements between Southeast Asia producers and distributors for the importation of heroin into the United States. Trafficante is a Florida-based financier and organizer of illegal businesses whose connections with organized crime were inherited from his father. For almost 20 years he shared an uneasy alliance with Meyer Lansky. The roots of their competition are deep, beginning in the late 1950s when, at a crucial meeting in Florida, Trafficante agreed, under the threat of losing his life, to arrange for the murder of his close personal friend, Anastasia, allowing Lansky and his associates an opportunity to murder their chief competitor.[50]

Following Anastasia's murder, Lansky and Trafficante cooperated in investments in Cuba, the Bahamas, Florida and in the heroin trade. Trafficante also had close financial and business ties with Lansky competitors—among them, Bebe Rebozo.[51]

A number of events suggest that the 1968 trip of Trafficante was connected to an attempt to reduce Lansky's control of the heroin business. The major organizer of the opium and heroin traffic in Southeast Asia was a Chinese businessperson from Laos who organized the *Chiu Chow* Syndicate.[52] Huu was, among other things, the Laotian manager of the Pepsi Cola Company. The president of Pepsi Cola has been one of Richard Nixon's longest and most important friends and financial supporters.[53] In return, Pepsi Cola has received substantial help from Nixon, such as monopoly franchises in foreign countries, including a franchise on the Soviet Union market.[54]

Following Nixon's election as president, a campaign to expose and eliminate organized crime syndicates throughout the United States was widely publicized. In fact, the campaign was only directed at selected syndicates in cities where their support was inimical to Nixon and his Republican associates.[55] One city where this was the case was Seattle, Washington, where a Nixon-appointed United States attorney successfully spearheaded a campaign that exposed a criminal syndicate involving over 50 of the city's police officers and political leaders.[56] It was subsequent to this "clean up" of Seattle's "Mafia" that Seattle became a major import center for heroin coming into the United States: The heroin came from Southeast Asia, from the Chiu Chow connection, and in direct competition with Meyer Lansky's European connection. It is no wonder, then, that Meyer Lansky gave more than $250,000 in campaign contributions for Hubert Humphrey's presidential campaign in 1968 in an attempt to stop Nixon, nor that Lansky went to the state of Washington and offered to finance the gubernatorial campaign of the Democratic candidate in an effort to unseat the Republican governor who was an ally of Richard Nixon. Both Humphrey and the Democratic gubernatorial candidate lost and the Southeast Asia–Seattle heroin route opened up.

> Seattle was the only American City where the *Chiu-Chow* syndicates had been able to dominate the narcotics supply. After the abolition of Turkish cultivation in 1971 deprived the dominant Montreal Corsican syndicates of their sources, Vancouver's Chinese dealers increased their imports from Hong Kong and were soon supplying Canada's 9000 to 16,000 addicts with 80% of their heroin needs. Vancouver's Chinese began distributing to neighboring Seattle, and Southeast Asian heroin jumped from 12% of the city's identifiable seizures in 1972 to 40% in 1973.[57]

Narcotics Bureau's arrests and seizures of heroin from Europe were increasing at a dramatic rate. In 1968, the Federal Bureau of Narcotics was transferred from the Treasury Department (where it had been established at its inception) to the Justice Department. Dr. John Ingersoll was appointed head of the new bureau, which was renamed the Bureau of Narcotics and Dangerous Drugs.

In 1968 and 1969, the total seizures of illegal heroin coming into the United States were under 200 pounds. However, the reorganization resulted in the most effective attack on the international heroin traffickers ever put together by the U.S. Government. By the end of 1970, the government had seized more than three times as much heroin as in the preceding years (over 600 pounds).[58] And in 1971, the amount of heroin seized was over 1600 pounds.[59] In 1972 the combination of Customs and Bureau of Dangerous Drugs efforts resulted in the seizure of 2700 *pounds* of heroin—almost 15 times as much heroin as had been seized only four years before.

By 1972, the Nixon administration had serously disrupted the established monopoly. Furthermore, the emerging control over the Southeast Asian supply was becoming firmly established. At this point, the Attorney General and the President proposed yet another reorganization of the narcotics enforcement process. The reorganization culminated in the formation of the Drug Enforcement Administration. The seizure of heroin immediately plummeted to 900 pounds in 1973, and in 1974 it fell to less than 600 pounds. Dr. John Ingersoll resigned his post as head of the bureau and accused the Nixon administration of interfering with the agency.[60]

Watergate and a series of scandals undermined Richard Nixon's political power and he resigned the presidency. With his resignation went the shift from European to Southeast Asian heroin. Seattle's importation of heroin began to decline almost immediately. Dr. Robert L. Dupont, Gerald Ford's Presidential Adviser on Drug Abuse Prevention, wondered in testimony before Congress: "Why hasn't Southeast Asian heroin come more to the United States than it has?"[61] Other officials wondered why Seattle, poised as it is to become the major heroin port of the United States lost some of its momentum following Nixon's resignation.

The answer is that with the resignation of Nixon, the old established network of Lansky and his associates was able to reassert itself. Trafficante will not have resigned quietly, and indeed there is evidence that in Corsica, Amsterdam, and Southeast Asia there is at this moment considerable overt conflict and fighting for control of the international traffic in heroin. Southeast Asian producers have rapidly increased the market for and their control over heroin distribution throughout Europe—as one Drug Enforcement Administration officer put it—"from Spain's *Costa del Sol* to Oslo."[62]

Within the United States, the competition is fierce. Turkey is producing opium again. Marseilles once again is enormously busy and the routes through Latin America and Mexico are open. Seizures of incoming heroin are down, and although competition is intense, the supply is steady.

Government criminal charges of conspiracy and tax evasion brought against Meyer Lansky in Nevada and Florida during the years of Republican Party domination of the White House have been dropped. With the election of Jimmy Carter, Walter Mondale, a Democrat, has been placed in charge of the "narcotics problem," and Santo Trafficante, Jr. was recently called before a Senate Committee investigating organized crime. Arrests for heroin importation have taken place in cities throughout Southeast Asia (as they did not take place during the Republican years), but few major "busts" have occurred in Turkey, the Middle East, or France since the Democrats returned to power.

At the moment, there is "chaos in the industry." Southeast Asia has become an unreliable source of opium. Laos, Cambodia, and Vietnam are no longer the distribution and processing centers they were while the American Army was fighting its infamous war. There is, nonetheless, still a large growing area in Burma, Laos, and Thailand that produces magnificent poppies. There is also a well-worn and heavily used route through Thailand and Burma to heroin factories in Hong Kong. And there are traffickers in the United States—among them Santo Trafficante, Jr.—who are connected to the production and shipping of heroin from Asia. These people are not easily giving up their control of their profits simply because "their man in the White House" has moved to New York. There is open warfare in Corsica as different elements vie for monopolistic control over the distribution and processing of heroin. There is warfare among competing groups of middlemen in Latin America and Europe. Amsterdam has emerged as a major transfer point for heroin from Europe to the U.S. and Chinese merchants involved in the trade are killing each other. In the United States the battle for control is taking the form of marshalling political assistance from friendly government politicians as well as eliminating competition wherever and whenever possible. The end is not in sight, but the tendency to monopoly is strong. No one, least of all the police and cooperating politicians, wants the war to continue. They, as well as the most powerful executives in the industry, are doing everything possible to bring order into the industry and reestablish a smooth working monopoly. Exactly who will control the business when the present crisis ends is at the moment problematic. What is not problematic, however, is the state of this industry: It will continue to thrive, to expand, to reap large profits, and to support large numbers of law enforcement people, politicians, and specialists in illegal business.

The heroin industry is a mainstay of the political economy of much of the capitalist world and it shall not be eliminated any more readily than will the automobile, banking, or construction industries.

Conclusion

For the user, drugs represent a source of relief from the pains of living—physical, as in tuberculosis and leprosy, or mental, as in anguish and ennui. For the seller, they represent a source of profit and the satisfaction of "doing business." For the politician, they solve some pressing problems: How to keep some of the unemployed masses happy. For the academic they represent an endless source of data for theorizing.

The starting point for this analysis is capitalism as an economic system. Not a particular capitalist nation-state—but capitalism itself. For capitalism has been the moving force behind the development of the market in drugs—legal and illegal. Inextricably linked to capitalism are various political forms: colonial government, electoral politics, and the emergence of the state that have also played critical roles.

As we have seen, certain contradictions inherent in the economic system of capitalism and in the electoral politics of democratic countries coalesce to create a situation within which profiteering from opium trade is a resolution to a variety of contradictions and conflicts inherent in the system. It should be stressed that the sale and distribution of opium or its derivatives—either historically or in the modern world—is not an inevitable resolution of the conflicts and contradictions. It is simply one of many. Once discovered as a resolution, however, it would take a gigantic effort to eliminate it. People make decisions within a set of constraints inherited from their past. It is not impossible that a knowledgeable government would take adequate measures to eliminate the illegal heroin and opium traffic in the western nations. It is, however, unlikely that this will happen given the degree to which the profits from this illegal business help resolve contradictions of control over foreign populations (as recently, in Vietnam) and over indigenous labor forces that are otherwise a potential source of conflict. It is also unlikely, given the degree to which contradictions inherent in the financing of political campaigns and the relative concentration of wealth in capitalist countries creates a situation in which profits from illegal businesses are a ready solution to the dilemma posed by the heavy demands of financing political campaigns under electoral democratic political organizations.

NOTES

1. Paul Takagi writes: ". . . an important reason why opium is found in the areas you specified is because of the supply of a cheap labor force. Opium was cultivated in the United States during the 19th century. The morphine content did reach the desired level, around 14%, but the cost of labor made the experiment prohibitive. I once calculated the average yield per acre and it comes to around 8 pounds. The description of how it is harvested and the amount of time available to do the harvesting gave me the impression that it takes a huge amount of labor." For opium growing in the U.S., see *Consular Reports*, (1887) No. 86, 24:357, see also The Production of Opium in Alabama, *Hunt's Merchants Magazine* (1856), p. 249; and Stephen Holder, Opium Industry in America, *Scientific American* (1898), p 147.
2. T.T.B. Koh, Drug Use in Singapore, *International Journal of Criminology and Penology* (February 1, 1974) 2: 51–52. J.M. Scott, *The White Poppy: A History of Opium*. (London: Heineman 1969). H.G. Alexander, *Narcotics In India and South Asia*. (London: Unwin Brothers, 1930). Basil Lubbock, *The Opium Clippers*. (Glasgow: Brown, Son, and Ferguson, 1933).
3. T.T.B. Koh, op. cit., p 52.

4. D. Owen, *British Opium Policy in China and India* (New Haven: Yale University Press, 1934). See also J.K. Fairbanks, *Trade and Diplomacy on the China Coast.* (Cambridge: Harvard University Press, 1953).

5. P. Takagi writes: "I have the impression that Whampoa was the international settlement and the 'thieves' den of China at this time."

6. A. Haley, *The Opium War Through Chinese Eyes*, p 29. (London: Allen and Unwin, 1959).

7. B. Johnson, No Opium Policy Which Is Morally Wrong Can Be Politically Right, unpublished manuscript (1975). See also Clarkson Stelle, *Americans and the China Opium Trade in the 19th Century*, unpublished Ph.D. dissertation (Department of History, University of Chicago, 1938).

8. Wen-Tsao Wu, *The Chinese Question in British Opinion and Action.* (New York: Academy Press, 1928).

9. B. Johnson, op. cit.

10. Owen, op. cit., p 243.

11. V. Purcell, *The Chinese in Southeast Asia.* (London: University Press, 1951), p 58, 215.

12. Report of the Commission Sent to Cuba to Ascertain the Condition of Chinese Coolies in Cuba, in *The Cuba Commission.* (Shanghai: The Imperial Customs Press, 1876). We are indebted to Paul Takagi for pointing this out. He also writes: "Professor Ling Chi Wang at UC Berkeley says that there are Chinese documents showing that many Chinese who came to the United States were also shanghaied. Robert Schwendinger of San Francisco who is interested in maritime history mentioned to us that he has data from the logs of ship captains indicating the shanghaiing of Chinese workers."

13. A.W. McCoy, *The Politics of Heroin in Southeast Asia*, p 63. (New York: Harper & Row, 1973). C.U. Wen, Opium in the Straits Settlements 1867–1910, *Journal of Southeast Asian History* (1961) p 52–75.

14. G.W. Skinner, *Chinese Society in Thailand: An Analytical History*, p 118–119. (Ithaca: Cornell University Press, 1957).

15. Ibid., 119.

16. McCoy, op. cit., p 76.

17. F.R. Dulles, *The Old China Trade.* (New York: Library Editions, 1930); K.S. Latourette, *The History of Early Relations Between The United States and China 1784–1844.* (New Haven: Yale University Press, 1971).

18. Ibid.

19. Paul Takagi pointed this out to us.

20. B. Johnson, op. cit., p 18. See also Owen op. cit., p 260.

21. McCoy, op. cit., p 65–68.

22. Ibid.

23. *The Bangkok Post* (October 20, 1973).

24. *The Bangkok Post* (November 3, 1973).

25. *The Bangkok Post* (November 20, 1973).

26. McCoy, op. cit.

27. The Committee of Concerned Asian Scholars, *The Opium Trail: Heroin and Imperialism.* (Boston: New England Free Press, 1972).

28. We are grateful to James Inciardi for pointing this out.

29. Professor Paul Takagi, School of Criminology, University of California Berkeley, brought this statute to our attention in a letter.

30. A.R. Lindesmith, *The Addict and the Law*. (Bloomington: Indiana University Press, 1969).

31. M.A. Gosch and Richard Hammer, *The Last Testament of Lucky Luciano*. (Boston: Little, Brown, 1974).

32. W. Chambliss, *Boxman* p 5–6. (New York: Harper & Row, 1972).

33. Gosch and Hammer, op. cit.

34. *U.S. Congressional Reports* (1938).

35. Gosch and Hammer, op. cit.

36. McCoy, op. cit., p 30–57.

37. H. Messick, *Lansky*, (New York: G.P. Putnam's Sons, 1971).

38. U.S. Senate, Committee on Government Operations, Organized Crime and Illicit Traffic in Narcotics, 88th Congress, (Washington, DC: U.S. Government Printing Office, 1964).

39. McCoy, op. cit., p 28–29. See also A. Moscow, *The Merchants of Heroin*. (New York: Dial Press, 1968).

40. G.F. Brown, Jr., and L.R. Silverman, *The Retail Price of Heroin: Estimation and Applications*. (Washington, DC: Drug Abuse Council Inc., 1973). For estimates of prices paid by street addicts see W.E. McAuliffe and R.A. Gordon, A Test of Lindesmith's Theory of Addiction: The Frequency of Euphoria Among Long-Term Addicts, *American Journal of Sociology* (January, 1974) 79 (No. 4).

41. R.L. DuPont and M.H. Greene, The Dynamics of a Heroin Addiction Epidemic, *Science* (August 24, 1973).

42. Council of Economic Researches, *Guide to Corporations: A Social Perspective*. (Chicago: Swallow Press, 1974). *Fortune* magazine also publishes an annual review of the profits of America's 500 largest corporations.

43. C. Reich, The New Property, *Yale Law Journal* (1964) 63: 765–782.

44. W. Sheridan, *The Fall and Rise of Jimmy Hoffa*. (New York: Saturday Review Press, 1972).

45. *The New York Times* (December 9, 1972).

46. E. Clark and N. Horrock, *Contrabandista*. (New York: Praeger, 1973).

47. U.S. House of Representatives, Committee on International Relations, Proposal to Control Opium From the Golden Triangle and Terminate the Shan Opium Trade, 94th Congress: p 91. (Washington, DC: Government Printing Office, 1975).

48. McCoy, op. cit., p 29, 52–67.

49. Ibid., p 57.

50. See Messick, op. cit., p 209–215. See also F.J. Cook, *Mafia*. (Greenwich, Connecticut: Fawcett, 1973). See Gosch and Hammer, op. cit.

51. K. Sale, The World Behind Watergate, *The New York Review of Books* (May 3, 1973) 7.

52. A.W. McCoy, Report From the Golden Triangle, unpublished paper (1976).

53. L. Lurie, *The Running of Richard Nixon*. (New York: Coward, McCarr and Geoghegan, 1972). E. Mazo and S. Hess, *Nixon*. (New York: Harper & Row, 1968).

54. K. Sale, op. cit., p 1.

55. See W.J. Chambliss, *On the Take: From Petty Crooks to Presidents*. (Bloomington: Indiana University Press, 1978).

56. Ibid.

57. McCoy, Report from the Golden Triangle, op. cit.

58. F. Browning, An American Gestapo, *Playboy* (February, 1976), p 164.

59. Ibid., p 164.
60. Ibid., p 164.
61. U.S. House of Representatives, op. cit., p 101.
62. McCoy, *The Politics of Heroin*, op. cit., p 14.

Organizing the Cocaine Trade

3

An article in *Time* magazine claims that Americans today spend upwards of $20 billion a year on cocaine.[1] Cocaine is the "jet set high" and, even discounting the very large estimate made by *Time*, is doubtless a very large industry in the United States. But how did this happen? What are the historical roots of this industry? In this chapter, we focus upon the early days of the cocaine industry in New York City (1910–1918). Among the major reasons for selecting this particular historical period is that it was the time during which the state showed concern over narcotics, resulting in legislation such as the Harrison Act (1914). Also during this period, a supposedly scientific literature grew up detailing the destruction of thousands of lives through addiction.

An important part of the emerging viewpoint was the idea that drug use meant complete and total abandonment of will and purpose. Drug use signalled, moreover, a previously weak and disorganized character formation in the user. Addiction only proved what had been obvious on the surface—that vast numbers of the urban poor were "character deficient." Unable to successfully compete, willfully unpredictable, at best casually disciplined, drug addiction was the capstone of failed lives.[2] Within this litany of degradation, the only consistent picture of the drug distributor to emerge was fiendishly drawn. The distributor was the dope pusher, poisoner of countless young lives, destroyer of the weak.

Racial, sexual, class, and ethnic stereotypes abound in this literature and are carried over in innumberable studies. With remarkable ease, Progressive-Era formulations provide the intellectual bases for many of the contemporary conspiracy theorists who see the drug problem as simply a problem of evil pushers and weak users. The "dynamics" of the drug trade during the Progressive Period (1900–1917) itself have to be seriously examined outside the confines of Progressive morality.

Besides the important historiographical reasons for this case study, there are other substantial problems to be examined. Primarily these concern the manner in which a particular population at a particular time structured an illicit enterprise. We need this intensive analysis of a fixed point to provide the ground for discussion of both structure (in the sense of organization) and the social world of professional crime. It is of inestimable importance to demonstrate the relationships that were discussed earlier. And, it is equally important to understand the ways in which people go about organizing their illicit work.

The scene for our analysis is New York City in the years immediately prior to America's entry into World War I. The data employed come from the reports of an American–Jewish self-defense organization called the New York Kehillah. How and why the Kehillah became involved in investigating crime is thus our first concern.

Structural Forces

Capitalist nations that developed rapidly during and after the industrial revolution often faced labor-supply problems. Some, like the United States, needed large numbers of immigrants to supply the demand for cheap labor that came hand-in-hand with industrialization. As Colavito's research demonstrates so clearly, immigration laws reflected quite blatantly the desire of capitalists to have available a large and cheap labor supply.[3] Such a labor force, however, was not always as compliant as the capitalists or the host government would have liked. Some brought with them a socialist ideology and a labor militancy born in the throes of the European industrial revolution.[4] And all of them brought a healthy desire to improve their economic situation and accumulate some of the wealth that presumably lay like gold bricks on the streets of New York and Chicago. The reality of their lives was, however, not always consistent with their dreams.[5] Thus the contradiction between attracting a large supply of cheap labor by painting glorious pictures of the wealth to be had in America and the desire on the part of the capitalists and the government to provide the industrial sector of the economy with cheap and compliant labor often led to conflicts—some labor–management and some criminal. The immigrants resolved this contradiction in many ways, including labor militancy (see Chapter 4) and the creation of illegal businesses that, while risky (and therefore somewhat less appealing to those classes of people who could make money in safer ways), were nonetheless highly profitable. In those cases where connections with people in foreign countries were advantageous, the immigrants also had a business advantage over local competitors. At least on the level of distributing and retailing illegal products, immigration that solved the problem of labor supply also created the millieu in which illegal enterprises became organized for foreigners.

In the late summer of 1908, the immigrant Jewish population of New York was singled out by Police Commissioner Theodore Bingham as a center of criminality in New York's boroughs. Bingham's statement, which appeared in the *North American Review* said that about 50% of the criminal classes in New York City were Jews.[6] This charge of overwhelming Jewish criminality was reinforced a year later with the appearance of three articles in *McClure's Magazine,* calling attention to Jewish involvement in organized criminality.

The conspicuous concern with crime during this period marked a new and long season of reform for New York City. Fed by muckraking articles, government reports, published investigations, and the findings of a special grand jury, the public became privy to the details of a vast complex of prostitution and gambling.[7] Then, in 1912, when the recurrent absorption with lawlessness and immorality appeared to have run its course, the murder of the notorious gambler, Herman Rosenthal,[8] revitalized public concern with Jewish criminality, especially its manifestations in organized illicit businesses.

Jews from Europe had a long history of persecution at the hands of host countries who wanted them for their labor, but attempted to keep them from enjoying full benefit of membership in the society.[9] The contradiction here is obvious: Cheap labor of immigrant groups is necessary for capitalist society as long as the immigrant groups are not permitted to rise too rapidly in the class structure of the society, thereby threatening the position of established classes. With a long history of discrimination and anti-Semitism as a consequence of this contradiction, the Jewish community in Europe had institutionalized some resolutions to the attendant conflicts. One resolution was the formation of a Kehillah—an organization designed to oversee the moral and labor concerns of the Jewish community. The attacks by the police and muckraking journalists created a crisis in the Jewish community of considerable proportion, and the Kehillah responded.

In the summer of 1912, the Kehillah established an anticrime unit named the Bureau of Social Morals which was staffed by a number of private investigators whose province was primarily the six police precincts of New York's Lower East Side. The Bureau's task was to drive crime out of the Lower East Side by gathering as much hard evidence as it could through private investigations and by working cooperatively with Mayor William J. Gaynor and the police. Judah L. Magnes and the Bureau's counsel, Harry W. Newburger, brought to the Mayor lists of criminal establishments they wanted closed; the Mayor was to make sure that the police raided the offending places. To back up the police, the Bureau had an attorney attend those criminal court cases that involved the Lower East Side and Jewish organized criminals.[10]

The effectiveness of the Bureau of Social Morals was sharply reduced after its first year of operation when Mayor Gaynor, whose support was absolutely crucial, died in September, 1913. Without Gaynor, the Bureau's political influence was severely curtailed. Quiet for a number of years, the Bureau came back to life for only a short period of time in 1917, when Magnes tried to revitalize it by garnering money from a number of wealthy Jewish philanthropists. Receiving some financial aid, the Bureau concentrated one last time on uncovering crime among New York's Jewish population.[11]

Until 1917, the Bureau's reports had been rather discursive, documenting a wide range of criminal activities and influences. But in the spring of 1917, during the last phase of Bureau activity, it centered on what was considered to be the most pressing criminal problem in the Jewish neighborhoods—narcotics. There is no mistaking the seriousness of the Bureau's perception of the problem as shown by its statement that prefaced the reports. Jewish drug dealers, it remarked, "were creeping into the homes on the East Side, Bronx, Harlem, and Brooklyn with their poisonous drugs and if this thing is not curbed . . . tens of thousands of our men and women will be hopelessly addicted to the use of cocaine and opium." It was added that "the mind and body of Jewry" were being "attacked and poisoned" by fellow Jews, which for the Bureau was the cruelest irony of all.[12]

Interestingly, the knowledge of Jewish involvement in the illegal drug trade did not bring on anything that resembled the earlier nativist articles and accusations. The issue of Jewish criminality that had been fed by the revelations of Jewish gamblers, prostitutes, pimps, and madams had obviously expired by 1917. In fact, Jewish crime was so dead an issue by the second half of the decade that there is hardly a reference to be found in either contemporary or historical literature (except, of course, for the Bureau's primary material) concerning crime which discusses Jewish criminals and the drug trade during the 1910s.[13]

The following discussion is based upon the information contained in the Bureau's reports on narcotics. There was no final comprehensive report on the menace of drugs, and there was no particular organizational scheme evident in the material. The investigators' purpose was to document Jewish involvement in narcotics and then to turn the evidence over to the appropriate municipal agencies, which did nothing. The reports are day-by-day accounts of the information uncovered by the investigators with little attempt to coordinate one day's findings with the next. But within the mass of material there are data concerning age, ethnicity, criminal occupations, kinship, arrest records, geographical locations of criminal hangouts, functions in the narcotics trade, and membership in particular mobs when it applied for 263 identified drug dealers. There are some things to be noted about the data, however. The information is not consistent for all members of the sample; for some, all that was reported was name and age; for others, name and arrest records; for still others, nickname and location of hangout. The material has been arranged to answer three interrelated questions: first the personal background of the dealers; second, the structure of the illicit narcotics trade; and third, the structure and stability of the mobs involved in the trade. Mobs, hereafter called combinations, are defined as collectives having at least three apparently equal partners. One final point concerns the drugs themselves: With very few exceptions, all the dealers were in the cocaine business—probably one of the "unintended consequences" of the Harrison Act and its fixation on heroin, as well as a consequence of the severe disruptions of settled patterns of international trade caused by World War I.

Personal Background

Given the Bureau's purpose and concern, ethnicity is the first aspect of personal background to be examined. Ethnicity has been determined by either the Bureau investigators' explicit statements or by our judgment based on the reported names. Because of the uncertainty in such a method, ethnic identity has been conservatively estimated with 122 of the 263 criminals so identified. There are 83 Jews, 23 Italians, eight Irish, five blacks and three Greeks. Even at this stage, two important points seem fairly clear: Jews were disproportionately over-represented in the cocaine trade; and it was not an exclusively Jewish business. The latter point is more apparent when consideration is given to the Bureau's desire to ferret out Jewish criminals—probably to the exclusion of some others. The three smallest groups are only of passing interest because of their very limited involvement in that segment of the underworld investigated by the Bureau. The Greeks were members of a small retail operation located in a Greek restaurant on Sixth Avenue in Manhattan. Unlike the Greeks, the five blacks were independent dealers. Griff Richardson sold narcotics out of a pool parlor on West 135th Street in Harlem. The four remaining black dealers were Dick Green, Blackie, Bob Kemp (considered a large dealer whose operation was located in a restaurant on Lexington Avenue in Harlem) and Dick Brown who worked the Lower West Side of Manhattan. Concerning the Irish dealers, the Bureau's investigators provided no information beyond names. The Italians, as will be discussed later, played a variety of roles in this predominantly Jewish underworld.

Two other categories of personal background are sex and drug use. There were four women dealers among the 263 criminals. None of them worked alone.[14] Three of them were members of two combinations, held together by marriage and kinship. Concerning drug use, the Bureau stated that 57 of the dealers were users. However, users were relatively more prevalent in simple partnerships (two individuals) than in combinations. Out of the 38 people constituting the 19 partnerships found in the sample, 26% were users, while only 9.5% of combination members were similarly inclined. Not much should be made of this, though, as it was a rare partnership in which both members were reported as users. The bulk of the users—about two-thirds—came from the ranks of independent and small dealers.

Another important area in the personal backgrounds of the dealers concerns their involvement in other illicit activities. Apart from narcotics, 20 different criminal enterprises were conducted apparently simultaneously with drug dealing. The 20 collaterial activities fall into five fairly distinct types of enterprises: stealing, gambling, vice, criminal management (which included fencing of stolen goods, political fixing, and managing or owning of criminal establishments), and extortion. The number of drug dealers who were found participating in the five major collateral criminal occupations is: stealing, 50; gambling, seven; vice, 32; management, 32; and extortion, 21.

The collateral occupations are exceptionally significant. They indicate the complex interplay of criminal activities, revealing, for example, the relationships between drug dealers who were pimps and the groups of retailers who primarily sold to prostitutes. The range of collateral activities also establishes that drug dealers were more likely to be criminal generalists rather than specialists, and that drug dealing was typically part of an expanding criminal repertoire. These last points are, of course, important factors in the social structure and stability of combinations.

Some confirmation of the spread of criminal activities is found in the Bureau reports that mentioned arrest records. About 100 of the dealers were found to have been arrested for offenses ranging over 12 different crimes, including murder, stealing, burglary, armed robbery, pimping, gambling, strikebreaking, prostitution, and narcotics violations. By far the most common arrests were for drugs with various forms of stealing a distant second. About one-fifth of the dealers arrested had been arrested at least once before.

Drug dealing during this period was clearly the kind of enterprise that demanded some sort of criminal maturity. It was not the sort of activity readily engaged in by juvenile delinquents or exceptionally youthful criminals, according to the reports. Age was one of the areas in the personal background of the criminals more extensively recorded. The ages of 86% of the dealers were given and they ranged from 18 to 45 years, with the average age being 28. Although the largest clustering falls in the years 25 through 29, with 99 of the dealers in this group, it is striking that 84 others were over 30. Only 44 of the dealers were younger than 25 and almost half of this group were 24 years old.

The drug—more properly cocaine—industry uncovered by the Bureau of Social Morals in the summer of 1917 was staffed by a population that was heavily Jewish, although not exclusively so, and overwhelmingly male. At least one-fifth were habitual drug users and more than one-third had been arrested at least once. It follows that they were, in the main, knowledgeable about the operations of the city's criminal justice system—strangers neither to the criminal courts, the city's jails, nor the legion of bondsmen (and women) and lawyers who worked the system. Again, in the main, this population was criminally mature and involved in a multiplicity of illegal activities, which aided them in developing the contacts and capital resources to deal successfully in drugs.

The Structure of Cocaine

As this population was essentially concerned with the distribution of cocaine, it roughly divided itself into importers, wholesalers, and retailers—the structure of the industry as a whole. The division, however, was neither well defined nor equal, with the vast majority of dealers engaged solely in retailing. Disposed to seizing all sorts of criminal opportunities, the 234 dealers for whom there is information about their marketing habits actually comprised seven different and overlapping categories. There were two dealers who were exclusively importers, ten wholesalers, and 173 retailers. But there were also four individuals who were both importers and wholesalers, two importers and retailers, 27 wholesalers and retailers, and 16 who were engaged in all phases of marketing.

The two individuals who were exclusively importers were Uncle Joe DeGorizia, a well-known figure in the underworld of Paterson, New Jersey, and Dave Lewis, equally as famous in the underworld of both Manhattan and Brooklyn. As a member of the Kid Springer gang, Lewis usually could be seen in a restaurant on Pitkin Avenue in the Brooklyn neighborhood of Brownsville. There is, however, enough material on the 22 other part-time importers to roughly indicate points of cocaine entry. For instance, John the Sailor, who participated in all three distribution categories, worked ships that berthed in New Orleans where he presumably received cocaine. Other areas noted were Buffalo, New York, Philadelphia, various New Jersey ports, and Canada.

The material on wholesaling is more substantial. Most wholesaling was carried out by nonspecialists. Additionally, over two-thirds of this group were members of combinations. Outside of a few major independent wholesalers, it seems that this aspect of the trade was dominated by the combinations, although only one combination confined itself totally to the wholesale trade. Among the ten individuals who specialized in wholesaling, four formed a single combination that was headquartered in a saloon on West 45th Street in Manhattan. But the four marketing specialists were still criminal generalists: Three were pimps and the fourth was a bookmaker.

Probably the most important independent wholesaler was Al Lampre, known as "Cockeye Al of 14th Street." Lampre supplied at least ten dealers whose reach was citywide. Additionally, he franchised cocaine, selling it to Eddie Friedman, Hyman Nigger, and Jimmie McDonald, who retailed it and then returned part of their profit to Lampre. Friedman sold in downtown Brooklyn, Nigger on Avenue B in the Lower East Side, and McDonald along the Bowery including Harry Callahan's political club. Among the retailers who bought cocaine outright from Lampre were Sammy Klein, Joe Stagger, Sammy Cohen, and partners Farge and Dago Jimmy, and Charlie Palmer and Mike Goodman. One of Lampre's sources of supply was identified. He was Harry Witt who was located in a saloon in West New York, New Jersey. Next to Lampre, the most significant independent cocaine wholesaler was Ike (Pheno) Brown who could usually be found in Wolpin's restaurant on Broadway in the theatre and night club district. Brown's business was structured in the same manner as Lampre's, only on a somewhat smaller scale. Those dealers noted as Brown's customers dealt only in Bowery hotels and pool parlors. Although the investigators did not directly mention his supplier(s), they did suggest that Abe Kutner of Buffalo was probably one. Another wholesaler who adds to the geographical picture of the cocaine trade was Johnny Daly, who lived and worked in Schenectady, New York. Buying from Daly was a retailer, Tony Abato, who brought the narcotics back from upstate New York and sold it along the Broadway theatre district.

Two other areas outside of New York City were also mentioned as places where New York wholesalers worked: Boston and Philadelphia—the latter being much more important. The criminal connections between New York and Philadelphia, which have never been explored, were lucrative and well established. Besides the already noted importation of cocaine in Philadelphia, a number of the New York combinations also sold there. One example is the Britt Brothers' combination which worked both the Lower East Side and Philadelphia. Another New York group prominent in the Philadelphia underworld was formed by Abie Cohen, Desperate Little Yidel, Fatkie, and Little Jimmy.[15] New York's largest drug combination, Silver and Ream, was also represented in Philadelphia. Representing this combination in Philadelphia was Johnnie Burt, who had an extensive criminal background in New York and Chicago and who sold cocaine along Noble, Vine, and Race Streets in Philadelphia. Silver and Ream also had one of its partners located in Boston. There were at least six wholesalers representing several combinations working in Philadelphia—as well as two in Boston.

The predominant activity in the drug trade was, of course, retailing: 74% of the 234 dealers whose marketing habits are known were strictly in the retail trade. If the part-time retailers are added, retailing encompasses 93% of the sample. The characteristics of retailers were obviously those of the dealers in general. There are, nevertheless, some points to be made. There were at least nine different types of place in and on which retailers conducted business: parks, drug stores, hotels, restaurants, saloons, pool parlors, theatres, public buildings, and certain street corners throughout New York City. To determine geographical concentrations of cocaine retailers, a list was drawn of the 129 specific addresses found in the Bureau's reports. The two areas of greatest concentration were (roughly) the Lower East Side, with 44% of the addresses, and the Broadway district, with 15.5%. Other areas that showed clusters were Harlem, several sections in Brooklyn, and the area of Mott and Mulberry Streets in Manhattan, adjacent to the Lower East Side.

In addition to location, the investigators reported on four different types of retail consumers: prostitutes, actors and actresses, soldiers and sailors, and newspaper people. Those who dealt either solely or primarily with prostitutes were partners: Mike Butler and Bill Ronan, Smiling Frank and Pete Braga, Charlie Palmer and Mike Goodman, Hymie Sindler and Dago Alec, and Jim Malloy and Tony Cousine. Besides the partnerships, two combinations' retail trade was oriented toward prostitutes. One was the Klein combination; the other was formed by Max Frank, Sam Freidman, and Sam Goldstein. The material on Goldstein reveals something of the web of business relations between dealers and vice entrepeneurs. Goldstein had both business and personal relationships with a bondswoman, Winnie Meyer, who had once been a madam. It seems that she both solicited customers for Goldstein, who sold only to prostitutes, as well as protected him from prosecution by using her political influence with local magistrates.

Those whose prime market was actors and actresses were the LeRoy combination and two independent retailers, Johnny Fox and Franklin. Both Fox and Franklin worked in the same establishment, the New York Victoria Hotel on West 47th Street right off Broadway; there is no evidence that they worked together. Although the connection between show people and vice (including narcotics) was, if not widely known, at least deeply believed,[16] a similar exchange relationship involving the military was not. Nevertheless, soldiers and sailors furnished an extensive market for some of the dealers. All of the reported sales to the military took place in Brooklyn at the Brooklyn Navy Yard or at the 47th Regiment Armory. One of the dealers specializing in this area was Skelly, whose operation employed at least a dozen men as sellers. The other dealers were Max Gardner and Johnny Spanish, who were among the most notorious criminals in New York.[17] Gardner and Spanish were partners in this aspect of the cocaine trade, as well as fellow members in the Kid Springer gang. Another member of the gang was importer Dave Lewis, although there is no evidence that Lewis worked with either Spanish or Gardner in cocaine. To add to the organizational confusion, Gardner was also reportedly in a separate drug combination with his three brothers.

The last consumer group was newspaper people, who played several roles in the cocaine trade. In addition to being consumers, there were two unnamed "newsboys" who were retailers selling exclusively to streetwalkers. One peddled both newspapers and narcotics in front of (Pheno) Brown's headquarters, Wolpin's restaurant. Newsboys also functioned as spotters and contacts for a number of dealers. Several newsboys worked as sellers for Joe Rocks and, lastly, one of the dealers in the sample is Dutchy, a 26-year-old "newsboy" who worked for wholesaler Charlie Young.

The particular marketing specialties for some of the dealers may be explained by geographical proximity. For example, two of the dealers who sold to prostitutes lived in the same building at 311 East 14th Street. On that same block were four different female institutions, including the Little Mothers Aid Association, the Little Sisters of the Poor, and the Hebrew Technical School for Girls. Joe Rocks also lived on that block and it is notable that the Newsboys Club was on the corner of East 11th Street and Second Avenue—only a short distance away.

Cocaine was imported, wholesaled, franchised, and retailed: It moved from South America to New Orleans, Canada, Buffalo, Philadelphia, West New York, New Jersey, and so on. It traveled back and forth from Broadway and the Forties to the Lower East Side, Harlem, Brooklyn, back to Philadelphia, and to Boston. It slid up and down the Bowery, Second Avenue, and Third Avenue, across 14th Street where it circled Tammany Hall, then it slipped down toward Mott and Mulberry Streets—perhaps ending up at the Essex Market Court on First Street and Second Avenue (where it was sold, not used for evidence) or at the Odd Fellows Hall at 98 Forsythe Street.[18] It was sold many times over by a variety of dealers (who were also at times, consumers) to show people, the military, newsboys, prostitutes, Jews, Italians, blacks, and so on. It was traded in movies, theatres, restaurants, cafes, cabarets, pool parlors, saloons, parks, and on innumerable street corners. It was an important part of the coin of an underworld that was deeply embedded in the urban culture of New York: supporters as well as exploiters of the myriad establishments that made up the night life of the city. And finally, cocaine was something of a bonding agent bringing criminals together in a variety of ways.

Combinations

There were 22 combinations central to the cocaine trade; the largest probably had 17 members,[18] the smallest had only three—the minimum number of partners that defined a combination. Ten of the combinations had only this minimum size; five had four, and two others had five. The last four combinations had six, seven, eight, and nine members. The average size of a combination was about five members, although if the largest and most atypical one is discounted, the average dips to just over four members. The combinations were heavily Jewish: 85% of the ethnically identifiable members were Jewish. The only other identified group represented were Italians who made up the remaining 15%. The ten Italians were distributed in seven different combinations, always in partnership with Jews. There were three combinations in which Italians and Jews reached parity, and 13 others which were totally Jewish as far as can be determined. Both the predominant Jewish cast of the combinations and the evidence of some interethnic cooperation are notable.[20]

The marketing preferences of 85 combination members is known and they ranged as shown in Table 1.

TABLE 1. Marketing Preferences of Combination Members in Number and Percent Along with Comparable Percent of the Remainder of the Sample

	Wholesale	Retail	Import wholesale	Wholesale retail	Import wholesale retail
Number from combinations	4	42	2	22	15
Percent from combinations	4.7	49.4	2.4	25.9	17.6
Percent from remainder of sample	4.0	87.9	1.3	3.4	0.67

Combinations were obviously much more deeply involved in the wholesale and import aspects of the trade than the rest of the dealers. In fact, adding the part-time and full-time wholesalers together, about one-half the combination members did some wholesaling compared to 9.4% of the other dealers. In importing, the corresponding figures are 20% for combination members to about 5% for the rest. Retailing was still, however, the predominant activity even for combinations, with eight of them exclusively in the retail trade. Although importing and wholesaling were more likely to have been carried out by combinations (a probability of three to one), it is also clear that combination members were somewhat less likely to have been marketing specialists than the rest of the dealers. This means that the social structure of these organizations was not typically marked by any particular, enduring division of labor structured around set marketing tasks.

Not only were combinations usually small groups, engaged in changing marketing activities suggestive of informal organizations, but ten of them were at least partly forged out of kinship ties. Already mentioned are three—LeRoys, Kleins, and Gardners—who were nothing more than kin groups. In five of the remaining seven kin combinations, at least half of the members were related. For example, one was composed of the three Newman brothers along with Charlie

Straus and Joe the Wop; another featured two sets of brothers working with two unrelated dealers. One other example is the combination formed by Irving (Waxey Gordon) Wexler, his brother, known as Harry Irving, and two others.

Small, loosely structured, often kin-centered, combinations were also notable for their lack of both stability and solidarity. Members had a pronounced tendency to divide both their time and ties among other criminal groups. For instance in the Newman combinations, one of the brothers divided his loyalty by working for another mob—managing a crap game in Harlem. Obviously, collateral activities reduced the commitment to any particular combination. This same sort of division or splitting also took place within the cocaine trade as select individuals moved from one drug combination to another without forfeiting membership. This kind of situation was alluded to earlier in the discussion of the drug partnership of Max Gardner and Johnny Spanish, which coexisted with the Gardner brothers' combination as well as Max's involvement with the Kid Springer gang. Perhaps the best example of this movement is in the activities of Irving Wexler who participated in five different cocaine combinations at the same time. One was formed with his brother and two others to work Harlem; another operated in Philadelphia; a third was composed of Little Simon, Hershel Chalamudnick, and Wexler, and worked out of a tea room on Grand Street on the Lower East Side; the fourth was founded by Wexler, Hymie Fishel, and Mahlo and was headquartered in the Odd Fellows Hall at 98 Forsythe Street, also on the Lower East Side; the last was made up of Wexler, his oldest associate Jonesey the Wop, and six others working around 14th Street. Wexler's many pursuits were independent ventures in the sense that no other members of the five combinations, including his brother, crossed the same combination lines. Various members of them did, however, cross other lines and enjoyed parallel memberships both in drug combinations and collateral mobs. Several examples follow: Jew Murphy, one of Wexler's partners in Philadelphia was also a partner in another combination in New York; Hymie Fishel divided his time between a Wexler group and another combination headquartered in a saloon on Madison Street; Jack Pipes, the third man in Wexler's Philadelphia combination, was also in a separate group that worked Philadelphia; and Hershel Chalamudnick, an associate in the tea-room combination, was the fence for several burglary mobs operating around Coney Island, Brooklyn. Concentrating on just cross memberships in drug combinations and leaving out the examples of membership in collateral enterprises and organizations, there were 12 combinations affected. This means that over one-half of the drug combinations contained members who had working interests in other drug combinations.

Clearly, these groups had few of the attributes of "formal organizations."[21] This does not mean, however, that they functioned poorly. On the contrary, they were among the vehicles through which drugs were processed and fortunes made. In fact, their informal structures and probably short lifespans were exceptionally responsive to the necessities of the drug trade. First of all, entry into the trade was fairly simple, involving few costs beyond the initial capital investment, few contacts in the area of supply, and hardly any organization for distribution. But there was one catch: Everything was contingent on overseas suppliers who could not be controlled by the American entrepreneurs. It would have been foolish to stake one's criminal career around a particular combination, given the chances that there would be nothing to sell. Unable to control the delivery of the commodity, it made little sense to surround oneself with a formal marketing organization. The field was lucrative, but it demanded entrepreneurs who were flexible, who had numerous contacts, and who were able to raise capital at unexpected times and to pull together a small organization with little effort. Nothing adapted itself quite so well to these circumstances as ties of kinship, which could be invoked to form the nucleus of a more or less spontaneous combination. Combinations, because they did not compete for limited sources or for a limited market, were complementary. Combination structure, because it was dependent on the inefficiencies of supply, was exceptionally loose.

Discussion

At this point, one may legitimately ask what the preceding exercise has taught us; it is after all, a rather detailed analysis of a highly selective segment of New York's underworld. First, of course, it is a corrective of the common notion that organized crime has been and is some sort of monolith marching in lock-step toward ever-increasing centralization. Quite the contrary is true, at least in drugs, where decentralization was clearly the norm. The drug industry uncovered by the Bureau of Social Morals was fragmented, kaleidoscopic, and sprawling. It was organized and coordinated, not by any particular organization, but by criminal entrepreneurs who formed, reformed, split, and came together again as opportunity arose and when they were able. In 1917, after several decades of drug trafficking, there was little tendency toward either centralization or indeed bureaucratization. And despite what Pace and Styles imply,[22] decentralization has probably always been the norm in the narcotics trade. Consider the similarity between the trade in 1917 and the contemporary scene described recently by Patrick Murphy, the former Police Commissioner of New York. Murphy states:

> The illegal drug industry today can more accurately be compared structurally to the garment industry. Many sources of raw materials exist. Many organizations, large and small, buy and process the raw materials, import the product into this country, where it is sold to and processed and distributed at retail by a host of outlets, some large and small, chain and owner-operated. . . .Organization in the drug business is largely spontaneous, with anybody free to enter it at any level if he has the money, the supplier and the ability to escape arrest or robbery.[23]

Second, the analysis places the narcotics trade during the second decade of the 20th century within the broader context of a multiplicity of illegal enterprises engaged in for profit. It suggests that the entrepreneurs were in reality criminal-justice entrepreneurs acutely responsive to a broad panoply of activities that often bridged the gap between illegal enterprises and positions within New York's criminal justice bureaucracies. It also details the manner in which criminal careers were structured—not within a particular organization, but through an increasing web of small but efficient organizations. This chapter provides us with one fixed point illuminating some of the ways in which illegal work was really organized and coordinated. It also reveals a great deal about the people themselves involved in this aspect of New York's underworlds.

Moreover, we can more clearly see the value of viewing organized crime within an urban, historical context by noting the many examples of the mesh between drug dealing and such urban structures as saloons, pool parlors, restaurants, and theatres, as well as those aspects of New York's economy that recruited and supported prostitutes, actors and actresses, and newsboys. The interplay between the particular illegal enterprise and the organization of urban life reveals something of the structural contradictions manifest in organized crime—and, perforce, the necessity for concretizing our analysis.

Finally, we have seen in this chapter, as we did in the preceding discussion of opium, how the social relations of illegal business enterprises and networks reflect responses to basic contradictions of political economy. Drugs in all their variety of manifestations represent resolutions to conflicts created by a myriad of contradictions. The fact that the sale and distribution of drugs is legal or illegal affects rather importantly the composition of the social relations that develop to supply the commodity, create markets, and generate profits; but the character of the business does not define its existence nor its persist-ence. The contradiction between declaring the sale and distribution of some commodities and services as illegal within an economic and political culture that is based on the accumulation of capital through the sale of commodities changes the form of the particular social relations generated, but it does not eliminate, indeed in some cases it enhances, the structural forces pushing toward the creation and per-petuation of these illegal activities. Some social classes (immigrants, for example) may be more disposed to the pressures that lead to participation in these illegal activities than other classes or social groups, but the moving force behind the creation of crime networks remains firmly fixed in the political economy of the society.

NOTES

1. *Time* (January 28, 1979), p 23.

2. N.H. Clark, *Deliver Us from Evil: An Interpretation of American Prohibition.* (New York: W.W. Norton, 1976), p 217–226.

3. K. Calavita, "Sociological Analysis of U.S. Immigration Law, 1820–1924," unpub-lished Ph.D. dissertation (University of Delaware, 1979).

4. P.S. Foner, *History of the Labor Movement in the United States* Vol. IV *The Industrial Workers of the World, 1905–1917.* (New York: International Publishers, 1965). D. Bell, *Marxian Socialism in the United States.* (Princeton: Princeton University Press, 1967).

5. J.A. Riis, *How the Other Half Lives: Studies Among the Tenements of New York.* (New York: Hill and Wang, 1957). T. Kessner, *The Golden Door: Italian and Jewish Immigrant Mobility in New York City, 1880–1915.* (New York: Oxford University Press, 1977).

6. A.A. Goren, *New York Jews and the Quest for Community: The Kehillah Experiment, 1908–1922.* (New York: Columbia University Press, 1970).

7. T.A. Bingham, The Organized Criminals of New York, *McClure's Magazine* (Novem-ber, 1909). S.S. McClure, The Tammanyzing of a Civilization, *McClure's Magazine* (November, 1909). G.K. Turner, The Daughters of the Poor: A Plain Story of the Development of New York City as a Leading Center of the White Slave Trade of the World Under Tammany Hall, *McClure's Magazine* (November, 1909). O. Handlin, *Race and Nationality in American Life.* (Garden City, New York: Doubleday, 1957).

8. A. Logan, *Against the Evidence: The Becker–Rosenthal Affair.* (New York: Avon Books, 1974).

9. See S.M. Dubnow, *History of the Jews in Russia and Poland.* (Philadelphia: Jewish Publication Society, 1916). W. Laqueur, *A History of Zionism.* (New York: Holt, Rinehart, Winston, 1972), especially p 3–39.

10. The high point in the Kehillah's anticrime drive came in 1913. In February of that year, Mayor Gaynor appointed Newburger the Third Deputy Commissioner of Police and agreed that in addition to Newburger's regular duties," 'everything affecting the the First Inspection District would go through him.' " Accompanying Newburger as his secretary was Abraham Schoenfeld, the Kehillah's chief investiga-tor. Newburger "ordered and led raids" while Schoenfeld was in charge of "one of the two roving 'strong arm' " squads. Goren, op. cit., p 170–175.

11. A.A. Goren, op. cit., p 183–185.

12. Information on the Bureau of Social Morals was obtained from the Judah L. Magnes Archives, The Central Archives for the History of the Jewish People, Jerusalem, Israel. We first became acquainted with the material in the Magnes Archives through Goren's study noted above. In his note on sources, he states that the Magnes Archives in Jerusalem "contain an outstanding collection of sources for the study of Jewish life in New York and Jewish communal politics in America from 1908 to 1922. . . . The largest part of this material consists of the Kehillah's records which contain a wealth of sources on Jewish education, religious life, philanthropic organizations, industrial conditions, and crime." Using Goren's citation for the specific material on crime—MA (SP/125-SP/139)—I wrote to the Central Archives for the History of the Jewish People, Jerusalem, Isarael, and requested a microfilm copy of the almost 2000 "case histories of Jewish criminals prepared by the Kehillah's chief investigator and based on information supplied by his informers and agents." Ms. Hadassah Assouline of the Central Archives was kind enough to fulfill our request.

13. M. Rischin, *The Promised City: New York's Jews, 1870–1914.* (New York: Harper & Row, 1970). I. Howe, *World of Our Fathers: The Journey of the East European Jews to America and the Life They Found and Made.* (New York: Harcourt Brace Jovanovich, 1976). A.F. Landesman, *Brownsville: The Birth, Development and Passing of a Jewish Community in New York.* (New York: Bloch, 1971). I. Metzker (ed.), *A Bintel Brief: Sixty Years of Letters from the Lower East Side to the "Jewish Daily Forward."* (Garden City, New York: Doubleday, 1971). H. Roskolenko, *The Time That Was Then: The Lower East Side 1900–1914, an Intimate Chronicle.* (New York: Dial Press, 1971). J. Slonim, The Jewish Gangster, *Reflex* (July, 1928). D.R. Taft, Nationality and Crime, *American Sociological Review* (1936) 1. S.D. Hubbard, The New York City Narcotic Clinic and Differing Points of View on Narcotic Addiction, *Monthly Bulletin of the Department of Health, City of New York* (February, 1920). C.B. Pearson, A Study of Degeneracy as Seen Among Morphine Addicts, *International Record of Medicine.* (1919). Mayor LaGuardia's Committee on Marihuana, The Marihuana Problem in the City of New York, in D. Solomen (ed.), *The Marihuana Papers.* (New York: New American Library, 1966). H. Asbury, *The Gangs of New York: An Informal History of the Underworld.* (New York: Alfred A. Knopf, 1927).

14. For a discussion female criminality in the Lower East Side during the 1910s, see A.A. Block, Aw! Your Mother's in the Mafia: Women Criminals in Progressive New York, *Contemporary Crises* (1977) 1.

15. Most of the Philadelphia connections reported on by the Bureau seem to have originated with the activities of Benjamin "Dopey Bennie" Fein, one of the most important Jewish mobsters, whose career spanned a few years before 1917. A large number of the dealers who worked both in New York and Philadelphia had at one time been affiliated with Fein; Little Jimmy was his cousin. In a report filed by the Bureau's investigators in the summer of 1913, dealing with labor racketeering, it was noted that Fein also operated in Philadelphia as a labor thug. (SP/134, Story #700).

16. A.F. Harlow, *Old Bowery Days: The Chronicles of a Famous Street.* (New York: D. Appleton, 1931).

17. H. Asbury, op. cit., p 261–264.

18. The Odd Fellows Hall was, without doubt, the most popular meeting place and distribution center in the cocaine trade: Seven combinations were found to congregate there in 1917. The building continued to serve as a narcotics center through the 1920s, as a story in *The New York Times* (June 12, 1926, p 17) indicates. On the preceding day, federal narcotics agents had arrested six men at the Odd Fellows Hall and confiscated $25,000 worth of cocaine, morphine, and heroin. Unknown at the time, one of the men arrested was Irving Bitz, who was, along with his partner Salvatore Spitale, one of the area's leading narcotics dealers. For a disguised version of Bitz's career, see Halpern, Stanislaus, and Botein, *The Slum and Crime: A Statistical*

Study of the Distribution of Adult and Juvenile Delinquents in the Boroughs of Manhattan and Brooklyn, p 131–153. (New York City Housing Authority, 1934).

19. There is some confusion in the reports on the size of the largest combination known as the Silver and Ream Syndicate. In some reports it appears to have 17 full partners—in others no more than five.

20. In the more-or-less traditional histories of organized crime, interethnic cooperation and multiethnic syndicates are supposedly a feature of the restructuring of organized crime that took place in the early 1930s. Prior to this time, the underworld was supposedly notable for its ethnic divisions and, indeed, wars.

21. P.M. Blau and W.R. Scott, *Formal Organizations: A Comparative Approach.* (San Francisco: Chandler, 1962).

22. D.F. Pace and J.C. Styles, *Organized Crime: Concepts and Control.* (Englewood Cliffs, New Jersey: Prentice-Hall, 1975).

23. Murphy's statement is contained on p 187 of *The Heroin Trail* (New York: New American Library, 1973), compiled and written by the staff and editors of *Newsday.*

ORGANIZING CRIME: BUSINESS AND BUREAUCRACY

II

The Role of Business in Organizing Crime

4

In Chapter 1 we defined organized crime as those illegal activities that organize the rackets and vices. The principal activities covered are: (1) the manufacture and distribution of illegal drugs; (2) illegal gambling; (3) usury; (4) prostitution; and (5) organized extortion. Thus far we have focused upon the historical roots and contemporary parameters of the illegal drug industries that have grown up around opium, heroin and cocaine. We have tried to show how these industries have become an integral part of our modern political economy.

In this chapter we will analyze the role of business in the emergence and sustenance of labor-union racketeering. The traditional perspective in the sociological literature finds the roots of labor-union racketeering in the unions themselves. Looked at from the perspective of the new criminology and taking into account historical development, however, serious doubts are raised as to the validity of this interpretation.

The sociological literature makes frequent allusion to, but little systematic analysis of, corruption in labor unions. The one major exception is the classic study by Daniel Bell of the "Racket-Ridden Longshoremen."[1] Bell's analysis has, for the most part, been uncritically accepted in the sociological literature as the definitive statement on the subject. Although Bell's analysis is unquestionably insightful and imaginative, it is seriously flawed because of its uncritical acceptance of the functional paradigm as the lens through which racketeering in the Longshoremen's Union is viewed. From the perspective of functionalism, it is sufficient to seek an explanation for any phenomenon simply in terms of the "function" or "consequences" the phenomonon has for maintaining order and stability at a particular point in time. From this starting point, it then makes perfectly good sense to seek an explanation for the pervasiveness of racketeering in the Longshoremen's Union in terms of the contribution racketeering makes to smooth functioning, stability, and the predictability of the tasks to be accomplished: in this case, the loading and unloading of ships in New York Harbor. Accepting the legitimacy of this starting point, then, Bell's "explanation" for the pervasiveness of racketeering in the Longshoremen's Union, which stresses how racketeering solves the problem of getting ships loaded and unloaded rapidly in a harbor fraught with physical–geographical problems that are magnified by the unpredictable nature of shipping, is quite logical. The problem is that this interpretation is not only misleading, it is also quite untenable when viewed from a broader perspective. Rather than tracing the historical development of racketeering in the New York Longshoremen's Union, Bell seeks to "explain" the phenomenon solely in terms of the "functions" served by the existence of racketeering at the time of his study. As is characteristic of research employing the functional paradigm, Bell also fails to ask: functional for whom? He is therefore misled into believing that "what is good for shippers is good for everyone."

Looking at only one part of the harbor in New York and the activities of one union distorts even a generalization about racketeering in New York's Longshoremen's Union. For instance, by concentrating on Manhattan's West Side piers as the "hub of the port,"[2] Bell commits a serious mistake that is compounded when he goes on to discuss aspects of racketeering resulting from the peculiar physical layout of Manhattan's dock area. It was not Manhattan but Brooklyn that contained the "premier port" in America at the time.[3] Brooklyn's piers handled 54% of all the seaboard traffic of the entire port of New York,[4] which included all the docks on the New Jersey side of the Metropolitan region. Furthermore the Brooklyn waterfront was more completely dominated by racketeers and their collaborators in the shipping and stevedoring companies than Manhattan ever was.[5] Needless to add, the configuration of Manhattan's streets can tell us nothing about the structure and functions of racketeering on the Brooklyn waterfront, and therefore of New York waterfront racketeering—much less of labor racketeering in general.

It is our intention to trace the social relations that were responsible for the institutionalization of racketeering and other forms of criminality in some labor unions in the United States. To accomplish this, we will look in detail at the historical roots of corruption and racketeering among garment industry unions in New York and less intensely, but nevertheless suggestively, at the same phenomenon in the Teamsters and the United Mine Workers.

The Scope of Racketeering

Consider the following list of industries in New York City that were pervaded by "racketeers": bead, cinder, cloth shrinking, clothing, construction, flower shops, Fulton market, funeral, fur dressing, grape, hod carriers, ice, Kosher butchers, laundry, leather, live poultry, master barbers, milk, millinery, musical, night patrol, neckwear, newsstand, operating engineers, overall, paper box, paper hangers, shirt makers, taxicabs, waterfront workers, and window cleaners. All of these industries and trades, as well as others, were subject in one fashion or another to racketeering, which was well defined in the 1930s as organized extortion.[6]

The question for researchers, obviously, is how to account for such an extraordinary development in which so many of New York's and indeed America's key trades became the province of power syndicates. The general answer to such an inquiry lies in the often violently antagonistic relations between labor and capital, workers and bosses, in the modern era. The history of trade unionism in the United States reveals the violent methodologies adopted by employers to prevent, contain, and destroy unions.[7] Among the methodologies was the use of hired thugs to engage in strikebreaking. Very often, the services of strikebreakers were purchased from a burgeoning industry known as the private detective trade, dominated by such agencies as Pinkerton, Burns, and Farley. Agencies engaged in strikebreaking were not timorous in announcing their services. For example, the journal of the National Association of Manufacturers in 1906 carried an announcement of the Joy Detective Service of Cleveland, which stated: " 'WE BREAK STRIKES . . . . We guard property during strikes, employ non-union men to fill places of strikers.' "[8] Many of the individuals recruited by private detective agencies were local gangsters—some of whom because of their "ethnic and community identification" were doubly useful to employers. Noting a complaint from a New York trade union official, Jeffreys-Jones comments:" 'The private detectives employed by these agencies are recruited from East Side gangs, the same gangs that support the politicians . . . ,' with the result that politicians persuaded the police to side with employers.'"[9]

Within the general social situation in which employers resorted to local power syndicates masquerading as private detective agencies for strikebreaking and labor mediation, there was room for duplicity and the double-cross. Jeffreys-Jones reports on a meeting between David Silverman, an executive board member of the Neck Wear Makers' Union, and Max Schlansky, of the United Secret Service Agency in 1914.

> Schlansky entered into conversation with Silverman about the strike in progress against the business of Oppenheimer, Franc and Langsdorf. The guard business arising out of the dispute was being handled for the notorious Val O'Farrell Agency by its chief agent, Schultz. The engagement was yielding $300 weekly for Schultz, but was now coming to an end. Schlansky averred that Schultz did not know his business, for he had let slip by many opportunities to prolong the strike. Perceiving an opportunity to extract some money from the situation, Schlansky proposed to Silverman that the union leader hire some of his plug uglies to beat up Schultz' men. Schlansky pointed out that in this event, Oppenheimer and partners would probably fire Schultz, and engage Schlansky. Then, presumably for a future fee, Schlansky would ensure that the union won the strike.[10]

Having created an arena of violence by their intransigence, employers soon found that extortion could be a double-edged sword. Nevertheless, even with the machinations of some power syndicates who turned their violence against employers, it is clear that the one consistent victim throughout all this turmoil was the rank and file worker. Control of workers through violence and the threat of violence lined the pockets of employers first and foremost—and then professional criminals and corrupt union officials. The ends to which this private violence was employed—besides the immediate pecuniary ones—included strikebreaking, sweetheart contracts, price-fixing, monopoly, and oligopoly.

The Needle Trades

Among the most significant racketeers to work in the garment industry in the United States was Louis "Lepke" Buchalter who, along with his partner, Jacob "Gurrah" Shapiro, had virtual control of the clothing industry in Manhattan from the late 1920s through most of the following decade.[11] Their dominance in the field of criminal labor relations was not seriously challenged until the fall of 1936, when the federal government tried them on charges of extortion in New York's almost

Byzantine fur dressing industry, one of the garment trades. To understand the roles played by Buchalter and Shapiro, and in whose interests they acted, it is important to relate something of the history
of the garment industries and their corrresponding trade union
movements.

The clothing industry provided a place for the Jewish immigrant,
according to Moses Rischin, "where the initial shock of contact with a
bewildering world was tempered by a familiar milieu."[12] Although the
manufacture of men's clothing was already an important segment of
New York's economy, the arrival of the East European immigrant Jews
drastically changed the ready-made clothing industry's organizational
pattern. The contractor was revived who had been ousted in the 1870s
as factories had replaced outside manufacture. This time, however, the
contractor introduced a unique type of production known as section
work, which exploited new recruits through a minute and deplorable
division of labor. Because loft and factory rents were so high, the
contractor supplied the perfect solution to the destructively competitive economics of seasonal manufacture. Upon the contractor was
placed the burdens of manufacture production risks and the responsibility for supervising and recruiting a labor force. In return, contrac-
tors, attempting to lower production costs, developed the task system.
This system, Rischin notes, was described as "the most ingenious and
effective system of overexertion known to modern industry."[13]

The changes in the labor process went hand in hand with technical
improvements, innovations, and the influx of cheap immigrant labor,
which altogether were responsible for the exceptional growth of the
garment trades that began in the 1880s. Most of this growth was in the
area of men's clothing. The phenomenal expansion of women's ready-
made clothing had to wait until the turn of the century when "labor
costs fell, techniques of design improved, and women gradually
emancipated themselves from the home."[14] The fur industry, in turn,
emerged in conjunction with the women's clothing industry. Rischin
concludes that by 1910, around 75% of the workers as well as the
majority of manufacturers in the fur trades were immigrant Jews.[35]

Commenting on the overall importance of the garment trades, Rischin states that from 1880 to 1910, the social economy of New York was
reshaped by the clothing industry. He notes that in 1880, almost 10% of
Manhattan's factories were engaged in manufacturing clothing and
that they employed over 28% of the industrial labor force. By 1910, the
figures had changed to 47% of the factories manufacturing clothing
employing 46% of the industrial labor force. In a study of the demogra-
phy of the American Jew based on the 1900 census, Ben B. Seligman

finds that 36% of the 143,337 employed persons described as Russian—almost all of whom were Jewish, living in New York, Chicago, Philadelphia, Detroit, Boston, Pittsburgh, and St. Louis—were employed in the needle trades.[16] Remarking on the economic and occupational status of American Jews between the two world wars, Seligman states that "three-fourths of the New York City Jews engaged in manufacturing in 1937 were in the clothing and headwear industries, where they constituted more than one-half of the total number employed in these industries." It is also estimated for 1937 that "6% of the New York City Jews in industry were furriers, and they constituted about four-fifths of those in the fur industry."[17] Along with the spectacular and increasing Jewish domination of the needle trades went pitiful wages, extended hours, innumerable slack seasons, contracting and subcontracting, home work, and the lack of even rudimentary safeguards of health and decency that made the needle trades infamous as a "sweated" industry.

As a consequence of conditions like these, and a number of other factors, a dynamic trade union movement developed. The founding institution for the Jewish labor movement was the United Hebrew Trades, begun in 1888. The major purpose of this group was obviously the organization of Jewish workers into trade unions. In a large number of cases, the unions that were formed, either with the initiative or help of the UHT, were local or regional bodies that had next to be affiliated with an existing national organization. In the garment trades, however, there were no national organizations until 1891 when the United Garment Workers was started for the men's clothing industry. Will Herberg describes this group as "at bottom a coalition of men's tailors, largely radical-minded immigrant Jews and Italians, on the one hand, and conservative American overall and work clothes makers, on the other."[18]

Workers in the women's garment industry waited until 1900 for their national organization—the International Ladies Garment Workers Union. Although the ILGWU started well, the 1903 business depression halted its growth. Subsequently, the ILGWU suffered through a difficult period that ended in 1909 when an economic upswing provided the most important surge of trade unionism that Jewish labor experienced until 1933. In the next five years, (1909–1914) there developed what Herberg calls "a tremendous transformation in the power and status of the Jewish labor movement."[19] The major events during this period in the women's garment industry were the "uprising of the 20 thousand" and the "great revolt."

In the fall of 1909, a spontaneous rebellion of almost 20,000 shirt-

waist makers in New York, mostly women, was enormously successful. At the time of the strike, the entire membership of the ILGWU was
only 2000; at the end, the shirtwaist makers union itself had over
10,000 members.[20] Closely following the rebellion of shirtwaist makers
was the strike of the New York cloak makers known as the "great
revolt." Unlike the earlier action, this strike took place in an industry
that employed primarily men and in which there was a strong and
deep tradition of trade unionism. The strike was called for July 10,
1910, and about 60,000 workers responded. Like the earlier strike, this
one, too, was a victory with most of the workers' demands granted.
Following the example of the women's garment workers, the furriers
called a general strike that was successful and led to the formation, in
1913, of the International Fur Workers Union.

The trade union movement among the men's clothing workers during these years was hampered by a serious conflict between the leaders
of the United Garment Workers and the rank and file tailors. One of
the primary differences was found in the extreme reluctance of the
UGW leaders to become involved in labor struggles, especially strikes.
The militant tailors, however, had great faith in the power of the strike.
Increasingly, the tailors viewed their national leaders as indifferent to
their problems, primarily interested in containing their militancy. The
rift in the United Garment Workers widened in 1910 and again in 1912
when a general strike was called at the instigation of the New York
Brotherhood of Tailors. At first, the leaders of the UGW refused to
recognize the action. Later, "behind the backs of the workers and even
many of the strike leaders, the UGW officials . . . tried to bring the
strike to an end with an agreement that enraged the strikers because it
ignored the question of recognition and other essential demands."[21] In
1914, the conflict between the tailors, who represented a majority of
the unionists, and the conservative leadership resulted in the formation of the Amalgamated Clothing Workers of America, an independent union under the leadership of Sidney Hillman and Joseph
Schlossberg. The Amalgamated was almost immediately called a "dual
union" and therefore a betrayal of labor solidarity by the American
Federation of Labor. The other Jewish unions, however, ignored the
slander and viewed it as a bona fide union. The Amalgamated soon
established itself as both an integral and significant element of the
labor movement wherever men's clothing was manufactured.

So-called labor racketeering—which in its simplest form, is direct
extortion by the imposition of union sanctions—originally developed
in the needle trade unions out of the necessity to fight scabs and thugs
hired by employers. In this century prior to World War I, known

criminals such as Benjamin Fein and Irving Wexler fought employer goons and became semipermanent fixtures in a number of needle trade locals and in the United Hebrew trades.[22] From policing strikes it was a short step to helping to organize workers and dominating key locals. Continuing labor management and internal union struggles throughout the 1920s enabled others, such as Buchalter and Shapiro, to attain positions of influence.

Their first labor–management efforts were in the men's clothing industry. Buchalter helped organize truck owners and self-employed drivers into an employers trade association that was perhaps the most significant act in the development of what should be called business racketeering. To make the point clearer, one of the first actions of the association was to raise the cartage costs for men's clothing, which was followed by the sharing of the windfall profits by the members of the association.[23] At the same time, Buchalter became what John Hutchinson modestly calls "influential in the clothing drivers' local of the Amalgamated," thus completing what we will see is the classic equation of business racketeering. Finally, it was at this time that Buchalter and Shapiro bought into some clothing firms, thus moving into the arena of business crime.

Let us expand upon the methods by which racketeers became entrepreneurs. First, consider the details of Buchalter's and Shapiro's relationship with businessman Joseph Miller as reported by the FBI:

Miller has been in the coat front manufacturing business since 1907, and in 1933 the name of his firm was changed to the Pioneer Coat Front Company, Inc. In that year, Miller took Shapiro and Buchalter into his business as one-third partners, following their investment of $20,000 each. In 1934, Miller sold his New York plant to Samuel Weiner for $50,000 and moved to Philadelphia. At this time Weiner ascertained that Buchalter and Shapiro were stockholders in the New York Pioneer Company and they demanded to be placed on Weiner's payroll, stating even though Miller had moved to Philadelphia under an agreement not to open up in the coat front manufacturing business in New York City nor to sell to his old customers, nevertheless, he would not keep his agreement and Weiner would need the services of Buchalter and Shapiro for forcing Miller to keep his promise. At this time, Buchalter and Shapiro, without any capital investment whatsoever, were taken into the Perfection Coat Front Manufacturing Company, and received $300 each, weekly. They were not satisfied with the salaries paid them by Weiner and took additional money from the Perfection Company in the nature of loans; resulting in losses to the organization of $75,000 from April 12 to September 1, 1934. The company then could not obtain additional credit unless Joseph Miller returned to New York to take over management of the company. Buchalter and Shapiro, in an effort to force Miller to return to New York from Philadelphia, stopped him from selling coat fronts manufactured in Philadelphia to his New York customers.[24]

What seems clear from the FBI account, although not commented on by them, is that Buchalter, Shapiro, and Miller had entered into a scheme to defraud Weiner. Obviously, Miller had not lived up to his part of the original agreement and was busy selling to his former New York customers. It is also apparent that both Buchalter and Shapiro knew well in advance that Miller would fail to fulfill his contract and that would provide their rationale for bilking Weiner, which would cause Miller to be brought back into the business.

A further indication of the business machinations engaged in by Buchalter and Shapiro, along with Miller, concerns the formation in 1933 of Leo Greenberg & Company, Inc. This corporation was founded with Nathan Borish and Joseph Miller, who invested $10,000 and $5,000 each. Then, in 1934, Jacob Shapiro also invested in the company an amount sufficient to obtain one-half interest. The company's name was changed to Greenberg and Shapiro, and Jacob Shapiro brought his brother Carl in as manager of the company. The following year the company was reorganized into the Raleigh Manufacturers Company with Nathan Borish, Carl Shapiro, Jacob Shapiro, Louis Buchalter, and Louis Miller each having a 20% interest.

One final example of the methods by which Buchalter, Shapiro, and other "union organizers" joined the ranks of owners deals with the outcome of a work stoppage called by the Amalgamated to prevent garment work from being carted out of New York to nonunion firms located primarily in Pennsylvania. One of the garment trucking firms balked at the stoppage, claiming that it had been "double-crossed by the Amalgamated once before."[25] Buchalter countered that argument by assuring the boss of the company, Louis Cooper, that he had nothing to worry about—that he (Buchalter) was now the Amalgamated. Cooper responded that he would only agree to stop his trucks if Buchalter would become his partner. Buchalter agreed and the trucks stopped.[26]

In 1931, Buchalter attempted to take control of the cutters' union, Local 4 of the Amalgamated, and thereby precipitated what Matthew Josephson, in his laudatory biography of Sidney Hillman, terms the "terrible emergency."[27] The strategic importance of the cutters' union is described by Joel Seidman.

> The jobber-contractor system is particularly vulnerable to gangster influence. Under the system of inside production, with workers of all degrees of skills under the same roof, the superior economic power of the highly

skilled worker can be utilized to help unionize the entire plant; so long as the relatively small number of skilled workers refuse to work under nonunion conditions, the plant can scarely operate, whether or not it enjoys the protection of gangsters. Under the contracting system, however-er, the cutters, comprising a large percentage of the skilled workers, may work in the jobber's shop under union conditions. If the cut goods can then be shipped to nonunion contracting shops, anywhere within a radius of a hundred miles or even more, the enterprise can undersell its completely unionized competition. The function of the gangsters is then to protect the trucks that haul the cut goods to the contractor and bring the finished product back. Protection of trucking at or near the jobber's office is more important than safeguarding the contract shop against union organizers: the gangster may indeed perform both functions, though in many small towns, the police may stand ready to repel the union organizing drives, without extra cost to the garment manufacturer.

The two points of control are therefore the cutting room and trucking. When the union is functioning properly, it checks the volume of goods cut with the volume received by inside and authorized contract shops, and learns from the truckers where the balance is being taken. If some of the cutters can be persuaded to send false figures to the union office, however, receiving part of the net savings as their share of the loot, and if in addition, the metropolitan politicians or police are bought off so that the gangsters riding the trucks are not molested in the performance of their duties, then indeed the business that receives gangster protection will prosper and the union tailors and the legitimate employers will suffer.[28]

Seidman added that this was exactly the situation in the metropolitan New York men's clothing industry.

Buchalter gained control of the cutters, according to Assistant District Attorney Burton Turkus, by convincing some of their leaders that it would be advantageous if his mob replaced Terry Burns and Ab Slabow, who were then Local 4's enforcers. At the same time, Jacob Orlofsky, who had been a business agent for the union, became the manager of the cutters' local. In the battle between Hillman and Orlofsky, Turkus contends that Buchalter used Orlofsky as a pawn, trading him off for a deal with Hillman. This maneuver was followed by the designation of Bruno Belea, the general organizer of the Amalgamated, and of two Buchalter hoods, Paul Berger and Danny Fields, as the new intermediaries between Buchalter and the union. Later, another of Buchalter's men received $25,000 from Hillman himself for delivery to Buchalter. With his position with the Amalgamated supposedly secured, Buchalter next turned to management. He extorted anywhere from $5,000 to $50,000 from both truckers and individual manufacturers. One of Buchalter's most important operatives, Max

Rubin, stated that from 1934 to 1937 he took part in shakedowns of $400 to $700 per week—and he was only one of many collectors. Turkus also notes that it had been charged "that reputable garment trucking firms alone yielded Lepke a million dollars a year for ten years."[29] Not calculated, however, was the amount of money saved by employers engaged in price fixing, restraint of trade, and wage freezes.

By 1932, Buchalter became involved in the fur dressing trade. Buchalter was approached by members of the fur dressing industry who asked if he would help in overcoming resistance to an organization of manufacturers. The request, obviously criminal in intent, called for the formation of a syndicate under Buchalter's direction, which would work in concert with an earlier criminal conspiracy formed by employers. As we have already seen with the formation of an employers' associations among garment truckers, so-called labor racketeering "flourishes most effectively in conjunction with trade associations formed and maintained in demoralized industries."[30] These employer associations are, of course, a device to stablize competition and to raise commodity prices. In some cases, however, "the temptation to attract business by price-cutting may be so strong, that coercion becomes necessary to compel members to remain in the association or competitors to join it."[31] In these kinds of situations, racketeers, usually through intimidation of local union leadership or as partners with corrupt trade unionists, are able to threaten labor problems against those recalcitrant firms attracted by the advantages of price cutting.

The fur industry was both demoralized and exceedingly competitive, according to Hutchinson. Because fur manufacturing was a skilled trade, resistant to mechanization and performed largely by hand, access into the industry was simple. The majority of firms were small: About 25% had only one or two employees and more than one-half employed four workers or less. In addition, Hutchinson writes that the fur trade was highly susceptible to fashion changes, quite unstable in prices, an arena replete with business and economic failures and, finally, a kind of ethical wasteland. Also, the depression struck the fur industry harder than any of the other needle trades, with fur imports dropping by 1932 to one-quarter and exports to one-third of the 1929 base. These grave difficulties increased the employers' normally competitive, secretive, and suspicious behavior toward each other. They were notoriously uncooperative in facing common industry problems.[32]

Prodded by desperate competition, after three years of the Great Depression, in what was probably the most cutthroat part of the fur industry, the fur dressers invented two organizations they hoped would promote both stability and profit. The Protective Fur Dressers Corporation (Protective) was formed early in 1932 and comprised 17 of the largest rabbit skin dressing companies in the country; the Fur Dressers Factor Corporation (Factor), including 46 of the largest dressers of fur other than rabbit skins, was formed the same year. As outlined later by the Federal Bureau of Investigation, the purposes and functions of the two corporations were to eliminate from the industry all dressing firms that were not members, to persuade all dealers to work only with firms that belonged to the corporation, and to prevent them from dealing with nonmembers.[33] The associations were to set prices and to implement a quota system ensuring that the different members of the corporations received a fixed percentage of the entire business handled by the member firms. The associations also set up a system of credit that enforced frequent settlements and blacklisted dealers who did not pay on time.

Once the corporations were organized, all the dealers and manufacturers were notified that henceforth their business was to be given to a firm designated by the Association. They were also told that prices would be increased immediately and all accounts were to be settled every Friday in full. When the Protective was first organized, the individual members set the price for dressing the cheapest rabbit skins at five cents apiece; subsequently, prices were raised until the minimum was seven cents and the maximum ten cents. The FBI estimated that this association controlled about 80%–90% of the trade in 1932 and about 50% the following year. Those dealers and manufacturers who refused to cooperate with the Protective and continued doing business with independent fur dressers were subject to telephone warnings first, and then beatings and the destruction of their goods and plants by corrosive acids and stench bombs. In extreme cases, some firms were told to close down permanently or they would be blown up.[34]

Buchalter and Shapiro were brought into the fur industry through the efforts of Abraham Beckerman, previously a high official in the Amalgamated and subsequently general manager of the Fur Dressers Factor Corporation and the Associated Employers of Fur Workers, Inc. Beckerman's initial problems as general manager of the Factor were organizational and, accordingly, he solicited the help of Buchalter and Shapiro, both of whom he had known from the Amalgamated. Beckerman explained to Buchalter and Shapiro that there was a need for "organizational work," meaning violent coercion. Beckerman then said, according to the FBI, that before he became associated with the Factor, it had contracted with gangster Jerry Sullivan, a member of the Owney Madden gang, to handle the organizational problems.[35] Sullivan's work had been unsatisfactory, and Beckerman was requested to get the association out of the deal. He now had this done by contracting with Buchalter and Shapiro.

The work performed was the obvious: Informed by contact men within the industry which dealers, dressers, manufacturers, and union officials were not cooperating, they directed their men to intimidate and coerce these individuals into joining the Association. The FBI concluded that all together, more than 50 telephone threats were made, along with 12 assaults, ten bombings, three cases of acid throwing, two of arson, and one kidnapping.[36]

Buchalter and Shapiro had relatively short careers in the fur industry; they lasted from April of 1932 until the summer or fall of 1933. The decisive factor in the termination of their activities lay in the deteriorating relationship between the Protective and the Needle Trade Workers' Industrial Union, perhaps the most radical union in the garment industry.[37] It is not clear in Hutchinson's account why this turn of events was, in fact, decisive—unless it displayed Buchalter's inability to control labor in the industry and thus turned the employers against him. Perhaps as important was a Federal investigation that resulted in indictments of the two trade associations, Buchalter and Shapiro, and others in the fall of 1933. In any case, by the spring of 1933, something like open warfare existed between Buchalter and the Industrial Union. A telling incident that is descriptive of the fragmenting cooperation or unalterable opposition between the Protective and the union concerned Morris Langer, one of the union leaders. Langer, called by Philip Foner a "Martyr of Labor,"[38] and by Hutchinson, an organizer for the Protective,[39] was told by the racketeers to organize strikes against three companies that had refused membership in the association. Langer balked because the firms were unionized. Langer also began to talk against the Protective. Before a month had passed, on March 23, 1933, Langer was killed by a bomb placed under the hood of his car.

The event that finally ended Buchalter's and Shapiro's involvement in the fur industry came in the form of a miniwar on April 24, 1933. During the morning, thugs hired by Buchalter and Shapiro staged an armed attack on the headquarters of the Industrial Union while a meeting was in progress inside. Contrary to expectations—and even though armed with revolvers, lead pipes, and knives—the gangsters were beaten back by the union men inside the building. As word of the attack spread, more workers streamed into the building and severely beat a number of the hoodlums who had been unable to escape. When all was over, two men were dead and many injured; another man died months later from injuries sustained in the battle.[40]

Buchalter and Shapiro had been hired by fur dressers in an effort to achieve the benefits of monopoly by forcing competitors into trade associations that dictated prices and allocated resources and markets. Garment manufacturers, including fur dressers, found it exceptionally difficult to escape competition and maintain profits through expansion because the industry was typically "confronted with a continually changing product," which hampered the development of large firms and dominant plants. This meant that garment businesses usually could not "afford to accept the rigidities involved in specialization and growth."[41] Instead, manufacturers relied on subcontractors and others for operations and services that otherwise they might have considered providing from inside the firms. Also, the structure of the industry encouraged the entry of entrepreneurs with limited capital, further increasing the competitiveness. In many cases, highly competitive, small-size, local-product businesses such as the needle trades developed illegal associations staffed by gangsters. All this means that the logic of competitive capitalism in industries, such as the clothing trades, leads inexorably to the formation of organized crime. Consumed by the desire for profit which, it seemed, could only be achieved by the creation of illegal monopolies and the elimination or more likely neutralization of trade unions, businessmen were instrumental in establishing some of the most vicious criminal syndicates in urban America. Paradoxically, some employers were themselves the victims of terror campaigns waged by racketeers, which sometimes rivaled those aimed at both progressive trade unionists and much of the rank and file. More often than not, however, the instigators of violence against employers were themselves employers.

It should be clear that even though extortion was practiced against some employers in the form of initiation fees and membership dues that ended up in the pockets of trade association racketeers, it was still monetarily advantageous for firms to belong. A graphic example of the benefits to employers who joined can be seen by looking momentarily at the restaurant racket operated by Arthur "Dutch Schultz" Flegenheimer. Flegenheimer worked along with a trade association to extort initiation fees of $250 and membership dues of $260, annually, in addition to remunerative shakedowns of scores of restaurants in Manhattan. But because of Flegenheimer's dominance over restaurant locals, salaries were never raised, despite what appeared to be vigorous union activity. It was estimated, "on the basis of wage increases granted to the union in 1936 after the fall of the racket," that one employer saved about $136,000 from 1933 to 1936—even after paying $36,000 to the association. It is no wonder that it was strongly alleged that Flegenheimer "was brought in by the restaurant owners to stave off the activity of Locals 110 and 119."[42]

Finally, it must be added that the single most effective organization in combatting racketeers was the Needle Trade Workers' Union, surely the most radical trade union to confront organized crime in our sample. One might well want to argue, therefore, that the more progressive the union, the more militant the rank and file, the less likely it is to be penetrated and seduced by organized crime.

Dave Beck of the Teamsters

Toward the end of one of the hearings conducted by the McClellan Committee investigating corruption in the International Brotherhood of Teamsters, Senator Frank Church of Idaho delivered a most revealing opinion: "I submit . . . that these men are capitalists and exploiters in the same tradition as the robber barons of old."[43] At that moment, Church was commenting on the character of certain teamster leaders from Chicago, including Joseph Glimco, a notorious criminal, and John T. O'Brien, secretary of Teamster Local 710 and a vice-president of the International Teamsters. The Committee had just finished listening to some of the most tawdry accounts of blatant stealing and corruption in the history of organized labor. What Church sensed, and aptly noted, was the triumph of capitalism as unregenerate greed at the very core of one of America's largest trade unions. The ideology that sustained the leaders of the International Teamsters was "gutter" capitalism, as far removed from the traditional ethos of trade unionism as Bonapartism was from Marxism in the 19th century. What is unique about these modern robber barons, then, is the sordid but curious perversity of crooked capitalists running one of America's most significant national labor unions. In this case, it is organized labor as organized crime.

Dave Beck was one of the most infamous of labor leaders and the man generally given credit for the unprecedented growth of the International Brotherhood of Teamsters (a union that began by organizing truckers, but now includes a wide range of workers in many different types of industry). Beck's career as a teamster began in Seattle, Washington, in the 1920s. Beck was involved in relatively low-level union-organizing activities, and he served as Business Agent for Teamsters Local 566. In 1924, Beck was elected secretary of the local, and in 1925 the national organization hired him as a labor organizer.

The economic crash of 1929–1930 strengthened the unions' appeal to workers, and the election of Franklin Delano Roosevelt in 1932 provided them with unprecedented political clout. In 1933, the National Recovery Act was signed, and section 7a of that act provided that workers had the right ". . . to organize and bargain collectively through representation of their own choosing . . . ." The Seattle Teamsters chose Dave Beck to bargain for them.

Early attempts at union organization (in the late 1800s) in the United States met with an incredible amount of violence. Business and industry employed strikebreakers who did not hesitate to shoot or maim in order to break a strike. Fledgling unions in turn employed people who became virtually professional specialists in violence. Dave Beck was unusually effective in creating a coterie of union organizers who specialized in the selective enforcement of Beck's organizing activities.

Beck's more important innovations, however, were not along the lines of organized violence. They were in the area of union–management cooperation. Among other things, David Beck is generally given the dubious credit of having developed the "sweetheart contract," that is, a contract between the union and an owner that requires the owner to kick back to the union leaders a certain amount of money in exchange for a union contract that the owner finds favorable. More generally, Dave Beck's policies were from the beginning designed to create peace and harmony—he referred to it as "order "—in the businesses with which he dealt. Beck said publicly in the early 1930s, "Some of the finest people I know are employers." Some years later, a teamster worker remarked, "Dave used to say some of his best friends were bosses. Now I'll bet he tells the bosses some of his best friends drive trucks."[44]

In the early days of union organizing, as mentioned, the unions employed musclemen to counterattack strikebreakers employed by owners. These musclemen, however, in the case of the Seattle Teamsters were used for a variety of purposes, including the intimidation of workers who did not readily accept Beck's leadership and his contracts. "Professional bullyboys made it unhealthy to drive anything for pay if you didn't wear a Teamsters button. Trucks were sideswiped and overturned. Men who voted wrong at the Central Labor Council were beaten up. People heard the apocryphal Teamster slogan: 'Vote no and go to the hospital.' "[45]

These techniques of entering into secret pacts with owners and coercing workers to accept his leadership were largely effective in maintaining stability for those who negotiated with the Teamsters. Occasionally businessmen who refused to cooperate were attacked, and their businesses were sometimes destroyed. Al Rosser, a Teamster organizer under Beck, was sent to prison for burning down a box factory when the owner refused to allow the Teamsters to organize the workers.

Beck's most powerful weapon—and the one that eventually enabled him to become one of the nation's most influential labor leaders—was his willingness to cooperate with the owners. It was often said, as often by Beck as by business leaders, that Seattle had the most peaceful labor relations in the country. These relations were built upon the complicity of union leaders with business interests—complicity that not only meant wage agreements that were favorable to business, but that involved labor leaders in a set of economic links with the owners.

Dave Beck was not the only West Coast union leader to gain national prominence in the 1930s. Harry Bridges of the Longshoremen's union which was based in San Francisco, was also rapidly rising as a powerful labor leader. Bridges and Beck confronted each other in Seattle, where Beck's union was allied with the AFL and Bridges' union with the recently formed Congress of Industrial Organizations. In Seattle, Teamsters and Longshoremen literally waged war. Longshoremen and sailors armed themselves with grappling hooks and fists wrapped in steel tape; Teamsters relied on sawed-off baseball bats that fit under their coat sleeves. In the end, the Teamsters won this war because the local politicians, businessmen, and police supported them. Longshoremen were arrested while Teamsters were allowed to go free after confrontations. Bridges was described by business as "the worst red peril to hit America since the Russian Revolution." Beck put the matter squarely when he addressed Seattle's businessmen: "The town is going to be organized. Choose me or Bridges."[46]

They chose Beck—a wise (and realistic) choice from their point of view. Beck promised and delivered labor stability:

> Our aim has been to develop better understanding between industry and labor. This is our contribution toward good government and the community. We have inculcated the concept that there is a definite understanding between those employed and those who invest capital. We do our part to make the system work. We observe our contracts to the letter.[47]

It was no surprise that the business and political community of Seattle backed Beck in his struggle for power against Bridges. Harry Bridges had said in Seattle:

> We take the stand that we as workers have nothing in common with the employers. We are in a class struggle, and we subscribe to the belief that if the employer is not in business, his products will still be necessary and we still will be providing them when there is no employing class. We frankly believe that day is coming.[48]

Dave Beck, by contrast, was an anticommunist, believed that private property was sacred, and should not be blemished by "sit down strikes." As a member of the Board of Trustees of the University of Washington, Dave Beck recommended that faculty members who refused to testify about their alleged Communist Party affiliations before committees on the state and national level should be fired.

Beck bought stock in some of the companies and worked not only to assure labor stability, but price stability as well. When some of the breweries of the Northwest lowered prices to gain a competitive edge, Beck approached the owners and threatened union action if they did not fall into line with the prices set by the majority of other brewery owners, including himself.

By 1947, the Teamsters were the largest labor union in the United States and Dave Beck was the national union's executive vice-president. In 1952, Beck took over as president of the national union. He continued to do favors for local businessmen and to organize the Teamsters around racketeering practices that served business interests.

Beck was active in both stealing and corruption and he permitted or condoned it on the part of others in positions of leadership.[49] No better example of the type of activities that were rampant in the Teamsters during Beck's leadership can be found than in some of the highlights of the career of Johnny "Dio" Dioguardi. In the early 1950s, Dioguardi was the regional director of the UAW-AFL in addition to being the business manager of one of the New York locals. Dioguardi concentrated his attention on paper locals composed of the most abused segments of the working class population—blacks and Puerto Ricans. The vast majority of these locals were operated as money machines for Dioguardi and his associates.

> The typical contract was never seen by the employees, provided a wage rate below or just slightly above the federal minimum wage, offered no other benefits, and was unenforced. There were no union elections, no general meetings of the members, and employers usually attended the shop meetings that were held. There was no grievance process, and in many cases the union officials involved were unknown to the members.[50]

Investigating activities of Dioguardi, a Senate Committee's only analogy to the conditions uncovered in Dioguardi's locals was the condition of the serfs of the Middle Ages. These conditions were so blatantly rotten and so obviously criminal that Dioguardi was expelled from the UAW-AFL in 1954. But his career as a leader of organized labor was hardly over. The following year, Dioguardi and several of his associates received charters for four local Teamster unions. Concerning these new Teamster locals, the McClellan Committee noted:

The officers and directors of these locals read like a rogue's gallery of the New York labor movement. They include such convicted extortionists as Joseph Cohen, Nathan Carmel, Aaron Kleinman, Milton Levine, Dominic Santa Maria, Harry Davidoff, Sam Goldstein, and Max Chester. So phony were these locals that, in the mad dash which occurred in the Teamsters to get them chartered, officials were chosen who had never been members of the union, false addresses were given for the offices, and the stationery of five of the locals was jointly printed and kept under wraps in the office of one of the locals.[51]

As for Beck himself, probably the least criminal or corrupt activity he engaged in was the transfer of large amounts of Teamster funds (the Central States Pension Fund alone, by 1952, contained over $20 million) out of Indianapolis banks (where the union was headquartered) to Seattle banks. Among the rest of his deals consummated while President of the Teamsters were highly unethical if not illegal ones involving the Fruehauf Trailer Company, a toy manufacturing company, the Occidental Life Insurance Company, and the Seattle First National Bank.

Dave Beck's friendship and support of politicians was, however, eventually his undoing. He built his empire on cooperation with businessmen and with successful politicians. From 1932 to 1952, successful politics meant Democratic politics. With Eisenhower's election as president (and Richard Nixon's as vice president), Beck's empire was in trouble. Federal investigators uncovered enough evidence of Beck's misuse of union funds to send him to prison in 1956. He was replaced by Jimmy Hoffa, who was sent to prison a decade later.

Beck's rise and fall in the Teamster's Union shows the extent to which the "success" of union organizers in the United States in the 1930s, 1940s, and 1950s depended upon their being able to cooperate with business and politics sufficiently to receive their support. The workers were for the most part organized by coercion and violence. Business support was gained through offering labor stability and an alternative to radical labor representation (such as Harry Bridges), and politicians were bought through campaign contributions and votes. The racketeering that transpired was indeed rampant, the corruption ubiquitous—but it was racketeering and corruption that did not emerge from the "needs of the system" or from the seamy character of union leaders, but rather from the ability of business and politics to support that kind of union leadership and to squelch opposition. In the end, labor racketeering was in reality business racketeering that was "functional"—for business interests and business profits—but "dysfunctional" for workers and for labor unions as a force in American politics and economics.[52]

The Bosses and the United Mine Workers

So far we have dealt with two classic examples of business racketeering that have been erroneously labeled labor racketeering—a device to shift the onus of blame for aspects of organized crime onto the trade union movement and away from competitive and corporate capitalism. Our last example, however, is in large part such an obvious case of corporate gangsterism that only rarely and in special circumstances has the term "labor raceteteering" been applied. What follows is primarily an account of business racketeering in its most primitive form: the use of criminals (goons, thugs, enforcers) to prevent labor from organizing. The social environment in this case is so unsophisticated that we are confronted with pure criminal conspiracies that were engineered by corporate leaders who could easily marshal criminal armies to bully, if not murder, nascent trade unionists. This is a world apart from the political economy of mid-century New York or Seattle where so many contentious, squabbling urban entrepreneurs were anxiously willing to deal with local power brokers, like Buchalter, Dutch Schultz, or Beck, to ensure profits. Equally removed from this world are the machinations of pseudo-trade unionists, like Dioguardi, Jimmy Hoffa, and Joseph Glimco, whose romance with corporate capitalism was built on the back of the rank and file.

The coal mines of the Cumberland Plateau, located in the hills of Kentucky, West Virginia, and Tennessee, suffered along with the rest of the nation in the economic crisis of the 1920s and 1930s. The time was ripe for labor unions and the National Recovery Act of 1933 gave formal legal support for organizing. The U.S. Supreme Court, however, quickly declared the Act unconstitutional:

> The darkness of despair descended upon the region when the Supreme Court shattered the Recovery Program by declaring the Congressional Act unconstitutional. By the mandate of the court, the fair codes were dissolved and prices and wages plummeted to the old subterranean levels. In the gloom that followed the apparition of trade unionism was replaced by the appearance of the genuine article. Organizers for the United Mine Workers of America entered the field under the determined direction of a battlehardened warrior, John L. Lewis.[53]

Few of the miners had had any real experience with the union movement. Any movement toward collective bargaining was often viewed as an infringement on the right of the individual to work for such employer—and at such wage—as the workman might choose. In the union membership drives of the early 1920s, most miners spurned the entreaties of the "field workers."

But in the intervening years, their outlook changed radically. They were now willing to listen to anyone who offered a possible solution to their problems. No longer were the advocates of unionism disdained. To the contrary, when rumor spread the word that a representative of the union was in the vicinity, miners sought him out.

The organization of local unions was bafflingly difficult. The operators knew each man in their respective camps. Any act or word indicating pro-union leanings came promptly to the attention of the new bosses. The sheriffs and judges were little less than hirelings of the coal corporations, and the men who successively occupied the governor's office were wholeheartedly sympathetic with the operators' point of view. Sheriffs could be depended upon to arrest any union representative who "loitered" or "breached the peace," and the judges were certain to reform him with a jail sentence. Also, the governor could be relied on to send national guard units "to preserve the peace" in the coal towns. The majesty and power of the law were on the side of the operators.

Under statutes then in effect, "industrial peace officers" were employed by the coal companies. It was their duty to protect company property and preserve the peace. The larger coal companies and associations of the smaller ones hired small armies of such industrial policemen. The sheriffs appointed many of them as deputies so they could act as both private and public peace officers, as occasions might require. In addition, private sleuths were engaged from Pinkerton's Detective Agency and other similar firms. These latter sometimes masqueraded as miners, finding underground employment and ferreting out evidence of union activities among their fellow workmen.

"Bloody" Harlan County acquired its famous prefix during these years because the Harlan County Coal Operators Association, marshaled by the United States Coal and Coke Company, fought a violent, lengthy campaign to prevent their employees from taking the "obligation" required of United Mine Workers.

The blacklists came back and any man known to have joined the union or suspected of being sympathetic to its objectives was summarily dismissed and his name added to the ban. Some companies publicly posted their blacklists by payroll windows. Gangs of heavily armed "goons" were imported from Chicago and other crime-ridden cities to beat, murder, and intimidate organizers and miners. In automobiles and on motorcycles, they patrolled the camps and highways of the county. They wore the uniforms of the iniquitous industrial police and were as arrogant as Nazi storm troopers. Their testimony was accepted by the courts in preference to that of any number of coal miners. The tactics of these desperados violated both state and federal constitutions and have rarely been equalled.

The company-directed law officers were unbelievably numerous and were on constant outlook for union agents. If a stranger came into a coal camp, he was accosted and his business and identity demanded. If he could offer no explanation for his presence that suited the company, he was told in no uncertain terms to "get off company property and out of town."

Despite these tactics and the goons employed by owners, the realization that organization and collective action were essential to their future led increasing numbers of workers to join the United Mine Workers. Under the tough and experienced leadership of John L. Lewis, the workers struck back: "When his wife packed the miner's dinner bucket she frequently reserved space for his .38 caliber revolver. And the armed and sullen men began to strike back with violence as deadly as any the companies meted out."[54]

In the end, the mine owners were forced to sign contracts with the union. Then came the inevitable attempts to slander and discredit. The UMW was accused of being a communist front that took orders from Moscow. This chorus was taken up, not only by mine owners, but their lawyers, local law enforcement officers, the mass media, and even the governor of Kentucky. In the years to come, however, the complaints lessened. As was the case elsewhere, the owners came to realize that the UMW might be the lesser of alternative evils. When the Progressive Miners Union tried to organize a more militant brand of labor organization, they were crushed by a coalition of the UMW and the mine owners.

From the outset, John L. Lewis was a staunch advocate of technological innovation in the mining industry. The rhetoric was impressive: More machines would reduce the arduousness of the job and increase the safety in the mines. It would also increase profit for the owners and, though this was not mentioned, swell the ranks of the unemployed. As the courts began to see the benefits of technology and strong union leadership, they increasingly supported the UMW.

The advance of technology to increase profits was rapid and effective. The electric drill replaced the manual breast auger; the cutting machine displaced the pick. Conveyor belts carried the coal out of the mines and the ultimate in coal mining equipment, "the coal mole," drilled mercilessly into the mountains of black earth and transformed the industry. The increased profits were shared by the owners, union leaders, and, to a lesser extent, those miners who were not made redundant by mechanization: "Production capacity climbed while payrolls shriveled. The same industry which had required 700,000 men in 1910 was able to provide all of the same fuel required by a vastly larger nation in 1958 with fewer than 200,000 men."[55] The union did nothing for the 500,000 men and their families who were displaced.

Meanwhile, with the aid and support of the mine owners, the UMW institutionalized racketeering practices second only to the International Brotherhood of Teamsters. Sweetheart contracts, a blind eye to company policies, use of union funds for personal gain by union leadership, profit sharing with owners, and outright stock-ownership by union leaders assured a relatively peaceful and predictable (albeit somewhat higher paid) labor force.[56] To secure the position of the union, members who complained were fired, threatened, and, if necessary, shot.

Most interesting, the profit potential of a violently conservative labor union was recognized by others besides the collaborationists in charge of the union and the corporate capitalists whose attitude had shifted from opposition to contented acceptance. The professional classes, for instance, also enriched themselves at the expense of the rank and file and thus became supporters of the union. Doctors and morticians dipped into union funds by operating on anyone who came near the examining room of the doctor, and billing the union pension fund for exorbitant burial fees for those who died:

> Despite the bellowing of the American Medical Association that the UMW medical fund was a venture in 'socialized' medicine, many camp doctors promptly recognized the Welfare Fund as a gravy train. They climbed aboard with alacrity and plundered it with great skill. The empty rooms in their little hospitals were filled with beds and new cubicles were opened. Chronic ailments for which the patient had already taken bags of pills and gallons of tonics now required bed rest and hospitalization. Surgery was undertaken for trivial complaints. Bushels of tonsils, adenoids and appendices were removed. The "head nurse" at one of these establishments described the situation in her hospital in inelegant terms: "It's all a woman's sex life is worth to even walk through this place. It's got so the doctors spay every woman who comes in the door.[57]"

Mine owners, union leaders, medical doctors, morticians, politicians, law enforcers—all were made richer by unionization. Miners' complaints of misuse of union funds were, if heeded at all, easily and quixotically dismissed as the inevitable result of labor racketeering. What, after all, could one expect from a bunch of lower class types whose success in union organizing was a function of their ability to corner the use of violence? No one asked why those tactics had been necessary. No one asked why the companies chose to sign contracts with some unions rather than others. No one questioned the process by which these racketeering practices evolved. After all, the mines kept operating, the coal kept spewing out, and profits remained high. When profits were finally exhausted, the owners sold out, the union withdrew, and the medical clinics and mortuaries closed.

Contradictions and Conflicts

If people were as manipulable as animals, many of the contradictions that create turmoil and strife in capitalist nations would disappear. People who work for wages have the unfriendly habit (from the perspective of the capitalist) of joining together to demand higher wages and better working conditions. The owners of the factories and shops where these people work are thus forced to either do battle with the workers or accommodate their demands. In the early history of capitalist development, owners clearly chose the whip rather than the carrot as a means of resolving the conflicts caused by the contradiction between needing labor and not wishing to interfere with maxium profits by sharing the profits with the workers. In time, labor unions formed. In this chapter we have oulined how the owners and managers accommodated the formation of labor unions by encouraging and cooperating with those labor union organizers who promised to minimize labor strife by the institutionalization of racketeering in the unions. The owners, of course, paid a price for the cooperation: They, too, were often the victims of, and sometimes the partners in, the racketeering that developed. That price, however, was apparently preferred to the potential of more militant, radical unionization that would have demanded a greater share of the profits for the workers.

Wherever one delves into the development of rackets or corruption in labor unions the same theme is repeated: Business and industry are frightened by unionization, in the face of militant and demanding union leadership; compliant unions or union leaders (often with a background in strikebreaking) are sought out and encouraged; contracts are drawn up that sometimes raise wages and improve conditions while simultaneously establishing a network of collaboration between union leadership and owners. Labor stability is thereby assured, profits increased, and the threat of unionization turned into a mild annoyance. There are, of course, a host of even more vicious scenes in which the working class is simply brutalized as a prelude to the drive for monopolization.

Clearly, "labor racketeering" is a most inappropriate and misleading term for describing what takes place in the corruption of unions and in the arena of "labor–management relations." Business co-optation of the labor movement through corruption and violence to protect the short-term interests of business and union leaders is a more apt description. But the tenacity of the term "labor racketeering" signals a deep-seated prejudice against organized labor. It also points out how deeply ingrained are the myths of private enterprise as the engine of public good. Labor unions are per se suspect; criminal capitalists are simply the bad bananas of an otherwise efficient, if not benevolent, bunch. Consequently, social scientists and popular writers alike focus on the "racketeers" and the "rackets" rather then the symbiosis between business and corrupt labor practices.[58]

From the perspective of functional theory in sociology, racketeering is understood as emerging from "the system." This functional perspective is more interesting for the things it fails to see than for those it reveals. It certainly highlights the extent to which economic realities shape the development of labor union activities. But, because of its premature closure of the analysis, it is unable to analyze the phenomenon adequately, thus failing to see both sides of this functional argument: Although the development of racket-ridden unions may be "functional" for business and labor racketeers, it is "dysfunctional" for the workers and for the development of organized labor. The creation of racket-ridden unions makes possible the manipulation of union leadership by owners at the expense of an independent labor union that would represent the interests of the workers. Quite a different picture of union racketeering emerges if we look more systematically at the historical roots of union racketeering, which suggest that the development of corruption and racketeering comes about through a coalition between the least desirable elements in the trade union movement and the owners of business and industry. More importantly, the impetus for criminal conspiracies comes from employers. The conspiracies dominated by the needs of both large and small capitalists in a variety of industries provide the groundwork for the more publicized kind of corruption—the domination of both locals and certain national unions by the likes of Jimmy Hoffa, Frank Fitzsimmons, Dave Beck and Tony Boyle, who enrich themselves and their associates in the business world by looting union treasuries and by stealing from the rank and file through institutionalized loan sharking and other criminal activities. This mutuality of interest between employers and union leaders also serves the "function" of eliminating radical and militant trade union efforts.

In his discussion of political machines and criminal rackets, Robert K. Merton clearly recognized the "function" of racketeering for business:

Business corporations, among which the public utilities . . . are simply the most conspicuous in this regard, seek special political dispensations which will enable them to stabilize their situation and to near their objective of maximizing profits."[59]

The preceding analysis of the emergence and development of racketeering in labor unions makes essentially the same point: Racket-ridden labor unions are in the interest of business and a few so-called labor leaders. The struggle between social classes for control of the profits from production led to a situation in the early 1900s where business was faced with a serious challenge to its control of labor. The inherrent contradiction between labor and capital created organizational efforts on the part of labor unions sufficient to threaten the owners with the very real possibility that they would lose control of the labor force. Among other serious threats perceived by capital was the introduction of communist and socialist ideology into the labor movement. The dilemma thus created for business was whether to join into an unholy alliance with some union leaders or to risk the possibility of losing the entire game in the form of a labor force that would demand not just higher wages, but control of the means of production. The dilemma was resolved in favor of supporting and joining those in the labor movement who employed illegal and violent means to circumvent the demands of workers.

NOTES

1. See D. Bell, Racket-Ridden Longshoremen: The Web of Economics and Politics, in *The End of Ideology*. (New York: Free Press, 1962).

2. Ibid., p 161.

3. District Attorney of Kings County and the December 1949 Grand Jury, *Presentment* (Feburary 1, 1955).

4. Ibid., p 199.

5. A.A. Block, *East Side–West Side: Organizing Crime in New York, 1930–1950*. (Cardiff, Wales: University of Cardiff Press, 1980).

6. *The New York Times*, (September 1, 1931), p 14. This is the full text of an investigation conducted by Samuel Seabury into the District Attorney's office in Manhattan.

7. S. Lens, *The Labor Wars: From the Molly Maguires to the Sitdowns*. (Garden City, New York: Doubleday, 1973). M. Dubofsky, *We Shall Be All: A History of the Industrial Workers of the World*. (Chicago: Quadrangle, 1969). S. Yellen, *American Labor Struggles*. (New York: Harcourt, Brace, and Co., 1936). R.O. Boyer and H.M. Morais, *A History of the American Labour Movement*. (New York, 1955). L. Huberman, *The Labor Spy Racket*. (New York: Modern Age Books, 1937). P.S. Foner, *The Industrial Workers of the World, 1905–1917*. (New York: International Publishers, 1965). G.R. Jeffreys-Jones, Plug-Uglies in the Progressive Era, in *Perspectives in American History*. D. Fleming and B. Bailyn (eds.) Cambridge, Massachusetts: Charles Warren Center, 1974). I. Bernstein, *The Lean Years: A History of the American Worker, 1920–1933* Baltimore: Penguin Books, 1966).

8. G. R. Jeffreys-Jones, op. cit., p 524.

9. Ibid., p 525.

10. Ibid., p 534.

11. See A. A. Block, op. cit.

12. M. Rischin, *The Promised City: New York's Jews, 1870–1914*, p 61. (New York: Harper & Row, 1970).

13. Ibid., p 64–66.

14. Ibid., p 62–66.

15. Ibid.

16. B.B. Seligman, The American Jew: Some Demographic Features, in *American Jewish Yearbook* (1950) 51:56.

17. Ibid., p 57.

18. W. Herberg, The Jewish Labor Movement in the United States in *American Jewish Yearbook* (1952) 53:9–10.

19. Ibid., p 16.

20. Ibid., p 17–18.

21. Ibid., p 23–24.

22. Information on Fein, Wexler, and other professional criminals involved with the United Hebrew Trades can be found, as noted earlier, in the Judah L. Magnes Archives, the Central Archives for the History of the Jewish People, Jerusalem, Israel. Specifically check reports Number 1, 700, 719, and 871.

23. J. Hutchinson, *The Imperfect Union: A History of Corruption in American Trade Unions*. (New York: E.P. Dutton, 1970).

24. U.S. Department of Justice, FBI, "The Fur Dress Case" I.C. #60–1501. (Washington, DC, November 7, 1939).

25. Court of Appeals—Brooklyn, New York. The People of the State of New York against Louis Buchalter, Emmanuel Weiss, Louis Capone. May–June 1942; 7944, Vols. 1–5, pp 1333–1347.

26. Ibid.

27. M. Josephson, *Sidney Hillman: Statesman of American Labor*, pp 336–339. (Garden City, New York: Doubleday, 1952).

28. J.L. Seidman, *The Needle Trades*, pp. 190–191. (New York: Farrar and Rinehart, 1942).

29. B.B. Turkus and S. Feder, *Murder, Inc.: The Story of the Syndicate*, p 338. (New York: Farrar, Straus, and Young, 1951).

30. Legal Implications of Labor Racketeering. *Columbia Law Review* (Summer, 1939).

31. Ibid.

32. See J. Hutchinson, op. cit.

33. FBI, op. cit., p. 9.

34. Ibid., p 10.

35. Ibid., p 11.

36. Ibid., p 12.

37. J. Hutchinson, op. cit., p 81.

38. P.S. Foner, op. cit., p 338–401.

39. J. Hutchinson, op. cit., p 83.

40. FBI, op. cit., p 15–16.

41. E.M. Hoover and R. Vernon, *Anatomy of a Metropolis: The Changing Distribution of People and Jobs Within the New York Metropolitan Region*. (New York: Doubleday, 1962).

42. *Columbia Law Review*, op. cit., p 998–999.

43. J. Hutchinson, op. cit., p 252.

44. M. Morgan, *Skid Road*. (New York: Ballentine Books, 1951).

45. Ibid.

46. Ibid., p 250.

47. Ibid.

48. M. Morgan, op. cit., p 248.

49. W.J. Chambliss, *On the Take: From Petty Crooks to Presidents*. (Bloomington: Indiana University Press, 1978).

50. John Hutchinson, op. cit., p. 234.

51. Ibid., p 234–235.

52. It is tempting to speculate, for example, that the failure of America to develop a Labor Party similar to those that emerged in Sweden, Norway, and Denmark during the 1920s and 1930s was the result of the difference in the effective co-optation of unions in the United States as compared to other countries.

53. H.M. Caudill, *Night Comes to the Cumberlands*. (Boston: Little, Brown, and Co. 1962), p 123.

54. Ibid., p 187.

55. Ibid., p 27.

56. North American Congress on Latin America, Channeling Labor's Early Struggles, in *Latin American and Empire Report* (May–June, 1977) XI (5).

57. H.M. Caudill, op. cit., p 44.

58. A recent *Washington Post* article (Tuesday, March 21, 1978, p C1) suggests that the symbiosis may take many forms. For example, the practice of "lumping" in the trucking industry. "Lumpers" are nonunion gangs who load large trucks for warehouses and who charge the truck drivers for this service. "Receivers of perishable goods, such as larger supermarket warehouses, allow the 'lumpers' to avoid hiring additional laborers."

59. See R.K. Merton, *Social Theory and Social Structure*. (New York: Free Press, 1969).

Corruption, Bureaucracy, and Power

5

In the Middle Ages, when Anglo-American criminal law was being formed, there was no pretense of applying the law uniformly across class lines. When prostitution, gambling, public intoxication, drug use, and the like were made criminal, it was not intended, nor was it the practice, to apply these laws indiscriminately to all social classes. The upper classes were free to gamble, engage prostitutes, or take drugs without fear of interference from the state.

In time the emerging commercial, mercantile, and industry-owning classes sought to use the state as a means of equalizing their position *vis-a-vis* the heretofore-dominant landed aristocracy. The law was one of the means through which this struggle was resolved. By insisting on the right to a trial by jury, by establishing an adversary system of justice, and by creating a set of social relations built around contractual obligations, the emerging class of businessmen and manufacturers was able to bring the landed aristocracy to heel; at least the two ruling classes were made more or less equal in the law. The lower classes were of course excluded from this equality. The necessity of paying an attorney for protection in the courts assured that neither the aristocracy nor the *nouveau riche* would have to share state power with the working classes.[1]

Thus a solution was forged; but so, too, were the seeds of conflict planted by that solution. Relying on the moral principle of equality before the law and depicting the state as a value-neutral organ for settling disputes gave rise to endless criticism from those who observed that "some are more equal than others."

This process repeats itself over and over in the history of law: A solution is forged that attempts to resolve conflicts arising out of basic contradictions in the structure of social relations and creates social relations that generate other conflicts reflecting underlying contradictions—thereby generating further attempts to resolve the contradictions.

The first laws prohibiting gambling, bribery, official corruption, vice, prostitution, drug use, and usury were each in their turn an attempt to resolve problems stemming from contradictions. Some were intended to help control the "teeming masses of urban dwellers who walk the streets seeking money by any means fair or foul." Others, such as anti-opium laws, came as a consequence of international competition as it developed into a worldwide, all-encompassing economic system.

Laws against usury are illustrative: They helped stabilize the banking industry by reducing competition. The laws enacted established legal limits to the amount of interest that could be charged. This solved the problem of competition among moneylenders, helped stabilize financing for both industry and banking, made life more predictable and thus more conducive to the formation of monopolies in the banking industry. At the same time, usury laws made it possible for people to operate illegally; if the banks could not charge excessively high rates of interest, then they would not make loans to people who were considered poor risks. But, risky people have as much need for money as those with good credit. Not being able to get credit in a bank does not reduce one's desire to borrow, but it may increase one's willingness to pay higher than legally allowable interest. Enter the usurer: The usurer can charge excessively high interest and therefore make a profit even from customers who are a greater risk than banks will accept as borrowers. Consequently, a structurally induced illegal business is created as soon as the solution to competition and "chaos" in the banking industry is solved by establishing legal limits to interest—all, of course, done with the best of intentions.

However, those who engage in usury confront a number of administrative problems not faced by banks. Most important is the fact that usurers, because they are engaged in illegal acts, cannot turn to the state and ask that the law be invoked to force debtors to pay back what they have borrowed. Usurers, in order to protect their investments and guarantee their profits, must establish their own law-enforcement arm. They must employ a staff of people who are capable of "persuading" those who have borrowed, but have failed to pay back their debts that it is better to pay the debts than to have them hanging over their heads. Usurers use many of the same techniques that the law employs in the service of banks: They confiscate property or threaten to expose the person to public shame. If none of these is effective, they resort to corporal or at times even capital punishment. The latter is of course used only as a means of demonstrating to other would-be renegers that it is unwise not to pay one's debts. The same principle, need it be said, underlies the justification for capital punishment when it is imposed by the state on people who presumably have committed acts that are "beyond the tolerance limits of the community." The acts vary; the problem that gives rise to them is identical—namely, that some people are not living up to the standards that others with more power believe they should. To keep the heresy from spreading, a life is taken.

It is ironic that those who are least likely to be able to afford the high interest of usurers are those most likely to need to turn to them for loans; the poor as well as the rich are protected from being charged more than the legal limit on interest by banks and licensed financiers.

It is an ironic manifestation of political economic contradictions that the laws that prevent many illegal activities from being rampant in the "better neighborhoods" have the effect of concentrating them in precisely those parts of the city where the people are most likely to be already disillusioned by "The System," that is, in the slums. Thus a further contradiction: Laws that were not initially intended to be enforced against the rich push illegal businesses into areas where the poor and working classes live, thereby revealing the hypocrisy of law in everyday life.

A recent study of Seattle, Washington,[2] illustrates the workings of vice and corruption in modern American cities. A conspicuous number of Seattle residents share with their contemporaries elsewhere a smug complacency and a firm belief in the intrinsic worth of the area and the city in which they live. Their particular smugness may be exaggerated due to relative freedom from the urban blight that is often the fate of larger cities and to the fact that Seattle's natural surroundings attract tourists, thereby giving the citizenry proof of their faith that Seattle is, indeed, a Chosen Land.

However, a less visible but large minority of the population do not believe they live in the Promised Land. These are the inhabitants of the slums and ghettos that make up the center of the city. Camouflaging the discontent of the center are urban renewal programs that ring the slums with brick buildings and skyscrapers. But satisfaction is illusory; it requires only a slight effort to get past this brick and mortar and into the not-so-enthusiastic city center—a marked contrast to the bubbling civic center less than a mile away. Despite the ease of access, few of those living in the suburbs and working in the area surrounding the slums take the time to go "where the action is." Those who do go for specific reasons: to bet on a football game, to find a prostitute, to see a dirty movie, or to obtain a personal loan that would be unavailable from conventional financial institutions.

Bureaucratic Corruption and Illegal Business: A Study in Symbiosis

Laws prohibiting gambling, prostitution, pornography, drug use, and high interest rates on personal loans are laws about which there is a conspicuous lack of consensus. Even persons who agree that such behavior is improper and should be controlled by law disagree on the proper legal response. Should persons found guilty of committing such acts be imprisoned or counselled? Reflecting this dissension, large groups of people, some with considerable political power, insist on their right to enjoy the pleasures of vice without interference from the law.

In Seattle, those involved in providing gambling and other vices point out that their services are profitable because of the demand for them by members of the respectable community. Prostitutes work in apartments on the fringes of the lower-class area of the city, rather than in the heart of the slums, precisely because they must maintain an appearance of ecological respectability: Their clients must not feel contaminated by poverty. Although professional pride may stimulate exaggeration on the part of the prostitutes, their verbal reports are always to the effect that all of their clients are very important people. Our observations of the traffic in several apartment houses where prostitutes work generally verified the women's claims. Of some 50 persons seen going to prostitutes' rooms in apartment houses, only one was dressed in anything less casual than a business suit.

Observations of panorama—pornographic films shown in the back rooms of restaurants and game rooms—also confirmed the impression that the principal users of vice are middle and upper class clientele. During several weeks of observations, over 70% of the consumers of these pornographic vignettes were well dressed, single-minded visitors to the slums, who came for about 15 minutes of viewing and left inconspicuously. The remaining 30% were poorly dressed, older men who lived in the area.

Information on gambling and bookmaking in the permanently established or floating games is less readily available. Bookmakers report that the bulk of their "real business" comes from doctors, lawyers, and dentists in the city:

It's the big boys—your professionals—who do the betting down here. Of course, they don't come down themselves; they either send someone or they call up. Most of them call up, 'cause I know them or they know Mr. —— [one of the key figures in the gambling operation].

Q. How 'bout the guys who walk off the street and bet?

A. Yeh; well, they're important. They do place bets and they set around here and wait for the results. But that's mostly small stuff. I'd be out of business if I had to depend on them guys.

The poker and various card games held throughout the city are of two types: (1) the small, daily game that caters almost exclusively to local residents of the area or to working-class men who drop in for a hand or two while they are driving their delivery route or on their lunch hour; (2) and the action game that takes place 24 hours a day and is located in more obscure places such as a suite in a downtown hotel. Like the prostitutes, these games are located on the edges of the lower-class areas. The action games are the playground of well-dressed men who were by manner, finances, and dress, clearly well-to-do businesspeople.

Of course, there are the games, movies, and gambling nights at private clubs—country clubs, Elks, Lions, and Masons clubs—where gambling is the mainstay. Gambling nights at the different clubs vary in frequency. The largest and most exclusive country club in Seattle has a "funtime" once a month at which one can find every conceivable variety of gambling, plus a limited, but fairly sophisticated, selection of pornography. Although admission is presumably limited to members of the club, it is relatively easy to gain entrance simply by joining with a temporary membership—paying a two-dollar fee at the door. Other clubs, such as the local fraternal organizations, have pinball machines present at all times; some also provide slot machines. Many of these clubs have ongoing poker and other gambling card games that are run by people who work for the crime network. In all of these cases, the vices cater exclusively to middle- and upper-class clients.

Not all the business and professional men in Seattle partake of the vices: some of the leading citizens sincerely oppose the presence of vice in their city. Even larger numbers of the middle and working classes are adamant in their opposition to vice of all kinds. On occasion, they make their views forcefully known to the politicians and law enforcement officers, thus requiring these public officials to express their own opposition and appear to be snuffing out vice by enforcing the law.

The law enforcement system is thus placed squarely in the middle of two essentially conflicting demands: their jobs obligate them to enforce the law, albeit with discretion; at the same time, considerable disagreement rages over whether or not some acts should be subject to legal sanction. This conflict is heightened by the fact that some influential persons in the community insist that all laws should be rigorously enforced while others demand that some laws should not be enforced—at least not against themselves.

Faced with such a dilemma and the obvious contradictions, the law enforcers do what any well-managed bureaucracy would do under similar circumstances: follow the line of least resistance. Using the discretion inherent in their positions, they resolve the problem by establishing procedures that minimize organizational strains and that provide the greatest promise of rewards for the organization and the individuals involved. Typically, this means that law enforcers adopt a tolerance policy toward the vices, selectively enforcing these laws only when it is to their advantage to do so. As the persons who are most opposed to vice rarely venture into the less prosperous sections of the city, the enforcers can control visibility and minimize complaints by merely regulating the ecological location of vice. Limiting the visibility of such activity as sexual deviance, gambling, and prostitution appeases those who demand the enforcement of applicable laws. At the same time, since controlling visibility does not eliminate access for persons sufficiently interested to ferret out the tolerated vice areas, those demanding such services are also satisfied.

This policy is also advantageous because it renders the legal system capable of exercising considerable control over potential sources of real trouble. For example, as gambling and prostitution are profitable, competition among persons desiring to provide these services is likely. Understandably, this competition is prone to become violent. If the legal system cannot control those operating these vices, competing groups may resort to war to obtain dominance over the rackets. If, however, the legal system cooperates with one group, there will be a sufficient concentration of power to avoid these uprisings. Similarly, prostitution can be kept clean if the law enforcers cooperate with the prostitutes; the law can thus minimize the chance, for instance, that a prostitute will steal money from a customer. In this and many other ways, the law enforcement system maximizes its visible effectiveness by creating and supporting a shadow government that manages the vices.

Initially this may require bringing in people from other cities to help set up the necessary organizational structure. It may mean recruiting and training local talent or simply co-opting, coercing, or purchasing the knowledge and skills of entrepreneurs who are at the moment engaged in vice operations. When made, this move often involves considerable strain, as some of those brought in may be uncooperative. Whatever the particulars, the ultimate result is the same: A syndicate emerges—composed of politicians, law enforcers, and citizens—capable of supplying and controlling the vices in the city. The most efficient network is invariably one that contains representatives of all the leading centers of power. People in business must be involved because of their political influence and their ability to control the mass media. This prerequisite is illustrated by the case of a fledgling magazine that published an article intimating that several leading politicians were corrupt. Immediately, major advertisers canceled their advertisements in the magazine. One large chain store refused to sell that issue of the magazine in any of its stores. When one of the leading network members was accused of accepting bribes, a number of the community's most prominent business leaders sponsored a large advertisement declaring their unfailing support for and confidence in the integrity of this "outstanding public servant."

The network must also have the cooperation of business in procuring the loans that enable them, individually and collectively, to purchase legitimate businesses, as well as to expand the vice enterprises. A member of the banking community is therefore a considerable asset. In Seattle, the vice-president of one of the local banks (who was an investigator for a federal law enforcement agency before he entered banking) is a willing, knowledgeable participant in business relations with network members. He not only serves on the board of directors of a loan agency controlled by the network, but also advises network members how to keep their earnings secret. Further, he sometimes serves as a go-between, passing investment tips from the network on to other business members in the community. In this way the network serves the economic interests of business indirectly, as well as directly.

The political influence of the network is more directly obtained. Huge, tax-free profits make it possible for the network to generously support political candidates of its choice. Often the network assists both candidates in an election, thus assuring itself of influence regardless of who wins. Although there is usually a favorite, ultracooperative candidate who receives the greater portion of the contributions, everyone is likely to receive something.

The Bureaucracy

Contrary to the prevailing myth that universal rules govern bureaucracies, the fact is that in day-to-day operations rules can—and must—be selectively applied. As a consequence, some degree of corruption is not merely a possibility, but rather it is a virtual certainty that is built into the very structure of bureaucratic organizations.

The starting point for understanding this structural invitation to corruption is the observation that application of all the rules and procedures comprising the foundation of an organization inevitably admits to a high degree of discretion. Rules can only specify what should be done when the actions being considered fall clearly into unambiguously specifiable categories, about which there can be no reasonable grounds of disagreement or conflicting interpretation. But such categories are a virtual impossibility, given the inherently ambiguous nature of language. Instead, most events fall within the penumbra of the bureaucratic rules where the discretion of officeholders must hold sway.

As discretionary decision making is recognized as inevitable, in effect, all bureaucratic decisions become subject to the discretionary will of the officeholder. Moreover, if one has a reason to look, vagueness and ambiguity can be found in any rule, no matter how carefully stipulated. And if ambiguity and vagueness are not sufficient to justify particularistic criteria being applied, contradictory rules or implications of rules can be readily located that have the same effect of justifying the decisions that, for whatever reason the officeholder wishes, can be used to enforce his position. Finally, as organizations characteristically develop their own set of common practices that take on the status of rules (whether written or unwritten), the entire process of applying rules becomes totally dependent on the discretion of the officeholder. The bureaucracy thus has its own set of precedents that can be invoked in cases where the articulated rules do not provide precisely the decision desired by the officeholder.

Ultimately the officeholder has license to apply rules derived from practically endless choices. Individual self-interest then depends on one's ability to ingratiate himself with officeholders at all levels to ensure that the rules most useful to him are applied. The bureaucracy therefore is not a rational institution with universal standards, but is, instead, irrational and particularistic. It is a kind of organization in which the organization's reason for being is displaced by a set of goals that often conflict with the organization's presumed purposes. This is precisely the consequence of the organizational response to the dilemma created by laws prohibiting the vices. Hence the bureaucratic nature of law enforcement and political organization makes possible the corruption of the legal-political bureaucracy.

In the case of Seattle, the goal of maintaining a smooth-functioning organization takes precedence over all other institutional goals. Where conflict arises between the long-range goals of the law and the short-range goal of sustaining the organization, the former lose out, even at the expense of undermining the socially agreed-upon purposes for which the organization presumably exists.

Yet, the law enforcement agency's tendency to follow the line of least resistance of maintaining organizational goals in the face of conflicting demands necessarily embodies a choice as to whose demands will be followed. Bureaucracies are not equally susceptible to all interests in the society. They do not fear the castigation, interference, and disruptive potential of the alcoholics on skid row or the cafe-owners in the slums. In fact, some residents of the black ghetto in Seattle and of other lower-class areas of the city have been campaigning for years to rid their communities of the gambling casinos, whore houses, pornography stalls, and bookmaking operations. But these pleas fall on deaf ears. The letters they write and the committees they form receive no publicity and create no stir in the smoothly functioning organizations that occupy the political and legal offices of the city. However, when the president of a large corporation in the city objected to the "slanderous lies" being spread about one of the leading members of the crime network in Seattle, the magazine carrying the "lies" was removed from newstand sale, and the editors lost many of their most profitable advertisers. Similarly, when any question of the honesty or integrity of policemen, prosecuting attorneys, or judges involved in the network is raised publicly, it is either squelched before it is aired (the editor of the leading daily newspaper in Seattle is a long-time friend of one of the network's leading members), or it arouses the denial of influential members of the banking community (especially those bankers whose institutions loan money to network members), as well as leading politicians, law enforcement officers, and the like.

In short, bureaucracies are susceptible to differential influence, according to the economic and political power of the groups attempting to exert influence. As every facet of politics and the mass media is subject to reprisals by network members and friends, exposition of the ongoing relationship between the network and the most powerful economic groups in the city is practically impossible.

The fact that the bureaucrats must listen to the economic elite of the city and not the have-nots is one important element that stimulates the growth and maintenance of a crime network. But the links between the elite and the network are more than merely spiritual. The economic elite of the city does not simply play golf with the political and legal elite. There are in fact significant economic ties between the two groups.

The most obvious nexus is manifested by the campaign contributions from the economic elite to the political and legal elites. We need not dwell on this observation here; it has been well documented in innumerable other studies. However, what is not well recognized is that the crime network is itself an important source of economic revenue for the economic elite. In at least one instance, the leading bankers and industrialists of Seattle were part of a multimillion dollar stock swindle, engineered and manipulated by the crime network with the assistance of confidencemen from another state. This entire case was shrouded in such secrecy that eastern newspapers were calling people at the University of Seattle to find out why news about the scandal was not forthcoming from local wire services. When the scandal was finally exposed, the fact that industralists and network members had heavily financed the operation (and correspondingly reaped the profits) was conveniently ignored in the newspapers and the courts; the evil-doers were limited to the outsiders who in reality comprised the front for the entire confidence operation.

In a broader sense, key members of the economic elite in the community are also members of the network. Although the day-to-day, week-to-week operations of the network are determined by the criminal–political–legal elite, the economic elite benefits mightily from the network. Not surprisingly, any threat to the network is quickly squelched by the economic elite under the name of "concerned citizens," which indeed they are.

The crime network is thus an inevitable outgrowth of the political economy of American cities. The ruling elites from every sphere benefit economically and socially from the presence of a smoothly running network. Law enforcement and government bureaucracies function best when a network is part of the governmental structure. And the general public is satisfied when control of the vices gives an appearance of respectability, but a reality of availability.

Vice in Seattle

The vices available in Seattle are varied and tantalizing. Gambling ranges from bookmaking (at practically every street corner in the center of the city) to open poker games, bingo parlors, off-track betting, casinos, roulette and dice games (concentrated in a few locations and also floating out into the suburban country clubs and fraternal organizations), and innumerable $2.00 and $5.00 stud-poker games scattered liberally throughout the city.

The most conspicuous card games take place from about ten in the morning—varying slightly from one fun house to the next—until midnight. A number of other 24 hour games run constantly. In the more public games, the limit ranges from one to five dollars for each bet; in the more select, around-the-clock games, there is a pot limit or no limit rule. These games are reported to have betting as high as $20,000–$30,000. During one game, the highest-stakes game witnessed in the six years of the study, the police lieutenant in charge of the vice squad was called in to supervise the game—not to break up the game or make any arrest—but only to ensure against violence.

Prostitution covers the usual range of ethnic groups, ages, shapes, and sizes of females. It is found in houses (with madams like the New Orleans stereotype), on the street through pimps, or in suburban apartment buildings and hotels. Prices range from five dollars for a short time with a street walker to $200 for a night with a woman who has her own apartment (which she usually shares with a male friend who is discreetly gone during business operations).

High-interest loans are easy to arrange through stores that advertise, "Your signature is worth $5,000." It is really worth considerably more; it may in fact be worth your life. The interest rates vary from a low of 20% for three months to as high as 100% for varying periods. Repayment is not demanded through the courts, but through the help of "The Gaspipe Gang," who call on recalcitrant debtors and use physical force to bring about payment. "Interest only" repayment is the most popular alternative practiced by borrowers and is preferred by the loan sharks as well. The longer repayment can be prolonged, the more advantageous the loan is to the agent.

Pinball machines are readily available throughout the city, most of them paying off in cash.

The gambling, prostitution, drug distribution, pornography, and usury that flourish in the lower-class center of the city do so with the compliance, encouragement, and cooperation of the major political and law enforcement officials in the city. There is in fact a symbiotic relationship between the law enforcement political organizations of the city and a group of local, as distinct from national, men who control the distribution of vices.

Corruption in Seattle

In the spring of 19— a businessman (whom we will call Mr. Van Meter) sold his restaurant and began looking for a new investment when he noticed an advertisement in the paper:

> Excellent investment opportunity for someone with $30,000 cash to purchase the good will and equipment of a long established restaurant in downtown area. . . .

After making the necessary inquiries, inspecting the business, and evaluating its potential, Mr. Van Meter purchased it. In addition to the restaurant, the business consisted of a card room that was legally licensed by the city, operating under a publicly acknowledged tolerance policy that allowed card games, including poker, to be played. These games were limited by the tolerance policy to a maximum one-dollar limit for each bet.

Thus, Van Meter had purchased a restaurant with a built in criminal enterprise. It was never clear whether he was, at the time of purchasing the business, fully aware of the criminal nature of the card room. Certainly the official tolerance policy was bound to create confusion over the illegality of gambling in the licensed card rooms. The full extent to which this purchase involved Mr. Van Meter in illegal activities crystallized immediately upon purchase of the property.

> We had just completed taking the inventory of the restaurant. I was then handed the $60,000 keys of the premises by Mr. Bataglia, and he approached me and said, "Up until now, I have never discussed with you the fact that we run a bookmaking operation here, and that we did not sell this to you; however if you wish to have this operation continue here, you must place another $5,000 to us and we will count you in. Now, if you do not buy it, we will put out this bookmaking operation, and you will go broke." "In other words," Mr. Bataglia continued, "we will use you, and you need us." I told Mr. Bataglia that I did not come to this town to bookmake or to operate any form of rackets, and I assumed that I had purchased a legitimate business. Mr. Bataglia said, "You have purchased a legitimate business; however, you must have the bookmaking operation in order to survive." I promptly kicked him out of the place.

The question of the legitimacy of the business Mr. Van Meter had purchased is not so simple as he thought. It was, to be sure, a licensed operation: There was a license to operate the restaurant, a license to operate the card room attached to the restaurant, and a license to operate the cigar stand (where much of the bookmaking operation had taken place before Mr. Van Meter's purchase. These licenses, although providing a "legitmate" business, also had the effect of making the owner of the business constantly in violation of the law, for the laws were so constructed that no one could possibly operate a "legitimate" business "legally." Thus, anyone operating the business was vulnerable to constant harassment and even closure by the authorities if he failed to cooperate with law enforcement personnel.

The card room attached to the business was the most flagrant example of a legitimate enterprise that was necessarily run illegally. The city of Seattle had adopted by ordinance a tolerance policy toward gambling. This tolerance policy consisted of permitting card rooms (then licensed by the city), pinball machines that paid off money to winners, and panorama shows. The city ordinance allowed a maximum one-dollar bet at the card table in rooms such as those in Mr. Van Meter's restaurant.

This ordinance was in clear and open violation of state law. The State Attorney General had publicly stated that the tolerance policy of the city was illegal and that the only policy for the state was that all gambling was illegal. Despite these rulings from higher state officials, the tolerance policy continued and flourished in the city, although it did so illegally.

This general illegality of the card room was not, however, easily enforceable against any one person running a card room without enforcement against all persons running card rooms. There were, however, wrinkles in the tolerance policy ordinance that made it possible discriminately to close down one card room without being forced to take action against all of them. This was accomplished in part by the limit of one dollar on a bet. The card room was allowed to take a certain percentage of the pot from each game, but the number of people playing and the amount of percentage permitted did not allow one to make a profit if the table limit remained at one dollar. Furthermore, as most of the people gambling wanted to bet more, they would not patronize a card room that insisted on the one-dollar limit. Mr. Van Meter, like all other card room operators, allowed a two- to five-dollar limit. The ordinance was written in such a way that, in reality, everyone would be in violation. It was therefore possible for the police to harass or close down whatever card rooms they chose at their discretion.

The health and fire regulations of the city were also written in such a way that no one could comply with all the ordinances. It was impossible to serve meals and avoid violation of the health standards required. Thus, when the health or fire department chose to enforce the rules, they could do so selectively against whatever business they chose.

The same set of cirumstances governed the cabaret licenses in the city. The city ordinances required that every cabaret have a restaurant attached; the restaurant, the ordinance stated, had to comprise at least 75% of the total floor space of the cabaret and restaurant combined. As there was a much higher demand for cabarets than restaurants in the central section of the city, this meant that cabaret owners were bound by law to have restaurants attached, some of whom would necessarily lose money. Moreover, these restaurants had to be extremely large to constitute 75% of the total floor space. For a 100-square-foot cabaret, an attached 300-square-foot restaurant was required. The cabaret owners' burden was further increased by an ordinance that governed the use of entertainers in the cabaret, requiring that any entertainer be at least 25 feet from the nearest customer during the act. Plainly, the cabaret had to be gigantic to accommodate any customers after a 25-foot buffer zone encircled the entertainer. Combined with the requirement that this now very large cabaret had to have attached to it a restaurant three times as large, the regulatory scheme simply made it impossible to run a cabaret legally.

The effect of such ordinances was to give the police and the prosecuting attorney complete discretion in choosing who should operate gambling rooms, cabarets, and restaurants. This discretion was used to force payoffs to the police and cooperation with the criminal syndicate.

Mr. Van Meter discovered the payoff system early in his venture:

I found shortages that were occurring in the bar, and asked an employee to explain them, which he did, in this manner: "The money is saved to pay the 'juice' of the place." I asked him what was the "juice." He said in this city you must "pay to stay." Mr. Davis said, "You pay for the beat-man [from the police department] $250.00 per month. That takes care of the various shifts, and you must pay the upper brass, also $200.00 each month. A beat-man collects around the first of each month, and another man collects for the upper brass. You get the privilege to stay in business." That is true; however, you must remember that it is not what they will do for you, but what they will do to you, if you don't make these payoffs as are ordered. "If I refuse, what then?" I asked. "The least that could happen to you is you will lose your business."

During the next three months, Mr. Van Meter made the payoffs required. He refused, however, to allow the bookmaking operation back into the building or to run the card room and bar with persons hired upon the recommendations of members of the organized crime syndicate and the police. He also fired one employee who he found was taking bets while tending bar.

In August of the same year, a man whom Mr. Van Meter had known prior to buying the restaurant met him in his office:

Mr. Danielski met with me in my office and he came prepared to offer me $500 per month—in cash deductions—of my remaining balance of the contract owing against (the restaurant) if I would give him the bookmaking operation, and he would guarantee me another $800 a month more business. He warned that if he wanted to give my establishment trouble, he would go to a certain faction of the police department; if he wanted me open, he would go to another faction. "So do some thinking on the subject, and I will be in on Monday for your answer." Monday, I gave Mr. Danielski his answer. The answer was no.

In June of 19—, a man by the name of Joe Link, who I found later was a second-string gang member of Mr. Bataglia's, made application to me to operate the card room because I had known him some 20 years ago when he was attending the same high school that I was. After I had refused the

offer of Mr. Danielski, Mr. Joe Link had received orders from Mr. Danielski and Mr. Bataglia to run my customers out and in any way he could,
cripple my operation to bring me to terms. I terminated Mr. Link on
November 6, 19—, and shortly after, after I had removed Mr. Link, Police
Officer Herb C. conferred with me in my office, and Officer Herb C. said
that I had better re-appoint Mr. Link in my card room; that his superiors
were not happy with me. If I did not return Mr. Link to his former
position, then it would be necessary to clear anyone that I wanted to
replace Mr. Link with. Officer C. felt that no one else would be acceptable.
He further stated I had better make a decision soon, because he would not
allow the card room to run without an approved boss. I informed Officer
C. that I would employ anyone I chose in my card room or in any other
department. Officer C. said "Mr. Van Meter, you, I think, do not realize
how powerful a force you will be fighting or how deep in City Hall this
reaches. Even I am not let know all the bosses or where the money goes." I
did not return Mr. Link, as I was ordered by Officer C., and I did select my
own card room bosses.

On November 7, 19—, I received a phone call stating that I soon would
have a visitor who was going to shoot me between the eyes if I did not
comply with the demands to return Mr. Link to his former position.

The crime network in Seattle (including police officers, politicians, and
members of the organized criminal syndicate), like the criminal law
that underpins it, relies on the threat of coercion to maintain order.
That threat, however, is not an empty one. Although Mr. Van Meter
was not "shot between the eyes" as threatened, others who defied the
network were less fortunate. Although it has never been established
that any of the suspicious deaths that have taken place involving
members of crime networks were murder, the evidence, nonetheless,
points rather strongly in that direction

Eric Tandlin, former county auditor for Seattle, is one of 13 similar
cases that occurred from 1955 to 1969. Tandlin had been county auditor
for 17 years. He stayed out of trouble, did the bidding of the right
politicians, and received a special gift every Christmas for his cooperation. In the course of doing business with the politicians and criminals,
he also developed extensive knowledge of the operations. Suddenly,
without warning or expectation, Tandlin was not supported by his
party for re-election as auditor, losing the nomination to the brother-
in-law of the chief of police. It was a shock from which Tandlin did not
soon recover. He began drinking heavily and frequenting the gambling houses; he also began talking a great deal. One Friday evening,
he made friends with a reporter who promised to put him in touch
with someone from the attorney general's office. On the following
night at 6:30, just as the card rooms were being prepared for the

evening, word spread along First Street that Tandlin had "been done in": "Danielski took Eric for a walk down by the bay."

The Sunday morning paper carried a small front-page story:

> Eric Tandlin aged forty-seven was found drowned in back bay yesterday at around 5:00 p.m. The Coroner's office listed the cause of death as possible suicide. Friends said Mr. Tandlin who had been county auditor for many years until his defeat in the primaries last fall had been despondent over his failure to be re-elected.

The coroner, who was the brother-in-law of a leading law enforcement officer, pronounced the probable cause of death as "suicide." The people of Miriam Street knew better. They also knew that this was a warning not to talk to reporters, sociologists, or anyone else "nosing around." In the last few years, the network has been responsible for the deaths of several of its members. Drowning is a favorite method of eliminating troublemakers, because it is difficult to ascertain whether or not the person fell from a boat by accident, was held under water by someone, or committed suicide. L.S., who was in charge of a portion of the pinball operations, but who came into disfavor with the network, was found drowned in a lake near his home. J.B., an assistant police chief who had been a minor member of the network for years, drowned while on a fishing trip aboard one of the yachts owned by a leading member of the network. In both instances, the coroner, who was the brother-in-law of one of the leading network members, diagnosed the deaths as "accidental drownings." Over the years, he has often made that diagnosis when network members or workers in the organization have met with misfortune.

Other deaths have been arranged in more traditional ways. At least one man, for example, was shot in an argument in a bar. The offender was tried before a judge who has consistently shown great compassion for any crimes committed by members of the network (although he has compensated for this leniency with network members by being unusually harsh in cases against blacks who appear before him), and the case was dismissed for lack of evidence. However, murder is not the preferred method of handling uncooperative people. Far better, in the strategy of the crime network, is the time-honored technique of blackmail and co-optation. The easiest and safest tactic is to "purchase" the individual for a reasonable amount, as was attempted with Mr. Van Meter. If this fails, then some form of blackmail or relatively minor coercion may be appropriate.

For instance, Sheriff McCallister was strongly supported by the network in his bid for office. Campaign contributions were generously provided, as McCallister was running against a local lawyer who was familiar with the operations of the network and had vowed to attack its operations. McCallister won the election—network candidates almost never lose local elections—but underwent a dramatic change of heart shortly thereafter. He announced that he would not permit the operation of gambling houses outside the city although he did not intend to do anything about the operations within the city limits because that was not his jurisdiction. Nevertheless, the county, he insisted, would be kept clean.

The network was as annoyed as it was surprised. The county operations were only a small portion of the total enterprise, but they were nonetheless important, and no one wanted to give up the territory. Further, the prospect of closing down the layoff center operating in the county was no small matter. The center is crucial to the entire enterprise, because it is here that the results of horse races and other sports events come directly to the bookmakers. The center also enables the network to protect itself against potential bankruptcy. When the betting is particularly heavy in one direction, bets are laid off by wiring Las Vegas where the national betting pattern always takes care of local variations. Clearly, something had to be done about McCallister.

No man is entirely pure, and McCallister was less pure than many. He had two major weaknesses: gambling and young girls. One weekend shortly after he took office, a good friend asked if he would like to go to Las Vegas for the weekend. He jumped at the opportunity. Although the weekend went well in some respects, McCallister was unlucky at cards. When he flew back to Seattle Sunday night, he left $14,000 worth of IOUs in Las Vegas.

Monday morning one of the network chiefs visited McCallister in his office. The conversation went like this:

Say, Mac, I understand you was down in Vegas over the weekend.
Yeah.
Hear you lost a little bit at the tables, Mac.
Uuh-huh.
Well the boys wanted me to tell you not to worry about those pieces of paper you left. We got them back for you.
I don't. . . .
Also, Mac, we thought you might like to have a memento of your trip; so we brought you these pictures. . . .

The "mementos" were pictures of McCallister in a hotel room with several young girls. Thereafter things in the county returned to normal.

Lest one think the network mercilessly exploitative, it should be noted that McCallister was not kept in line by the threat of exposure alone. He was, in fact, subsequently placed on the payroll in the amount of $1,000 a month. When his term as sheriff was over, an appointment was arranged for him to the state parole board. He was thus able to continue serving the network in a variety of ways for the rest of his life. Cooperation paid off much better than would have exposure.

Threats from outside the organization are more infrequent than are threats from within. Nevertheless, they do occur and must be dealt with in the best possible way. As no set strategy exists, each incident is handled in its own way. During Robert Kennedy's term as attorney general, the federal attorney for the state began a campaign to rid the state of the members of the network. People who held political office were generally immune, but some of the higher-ups in the operational section of the network were indicted. Ultimately, five members of the network, including a high-ranking member of local Teamsters' Union, were sentenced to prison. The entire affair was scandalous; politicians whose lives depended on the network fought the nasty business with all their power. They were able to protect the major leaders of the network and to avert exposure of the network politicians. However, some blood ran and it was a sad day for the five sentenced to prison terms.

Yet the network remained intact and, indeed, the five men who went to prison continued to receive their full share of profits from network enterprises. Corruption continued unabated, and the net effect on illegal business in the state was nil.

One reason Van Meter was not "shot between the eyes" was that, although not fully cooperative, he was nonetheless paying into the network $450 a month in "juice." Eventually he cut down on these payments. When this happened Van Meter became a serious problem for the network, and something more than mere threats was necessary.

No extortion was paid by me directly to them, but it involved a third party. Some time shortly after the first of each month, the sum of $250.00 was paid to (the above mentioned) Officer C., which he presumably divided up with other patrolmen on the beat. Two hundred dollars each month was given to (another bagman) for what the boys termed as "It was going to the upper braid." The $200.00 per month was paid each month from June 19— with payment of $200.00 being made in January 19—. After that I refused to make further payments. . . . After some wrangling back and forth, I just told them that I would not pay any more. They said, "Well, we will take $100.00 per month on a temporary basis. I paid $100.00 per month for the next twelve months. Early the next year I had planned to cut off all payments to the patrolmen. . . . About the 8th of July the explosion occurred. Police officers Merrill and Lynch conducted a scare program; jerked patrons off stools, ran others out of my establishment; Patrolman Lynch ordered my card room floorman into the rest room, and ordered my card room closed. When my floorman came out of the rest room, he left white and shaking and never to be seen in the city again.

Following this incident, Van Meter met with his attorney, the chief of police, and a former mayor. Although the meeting was cordial, he was told they could do nothing unless he could produce affidavits substantiating his claims. He did so, but quickly became enmeshed in requests and demands for more affidavits while the prosecuting attorney's office resisted cooperating.

The refusal of cooperation from the prosecuting attorney was not surprising. What Van Meter did not realize was that the prosecuting attorney was the key political figure behind the corruption of the legal and political machinery. He was also the political boss of the county and had great influence on state politics—coming from the most populous area of the state. Over the years his influence had been used to place men in key positions throughout the various government bureaucracies, including the police department, the judiciary, the city council, and relevant governmental agencies, such as the tax office and the licensing bureau.

There was, however, a shift in emphasis for a short time in the network's delaings with Van Meter. They offered to buy his business at the price he had paid for it. When he refused, the pace of harassment increased. Longshoremen came into his restaurant and started fights. Police stood around the card room day and night observing. City health officials came to inspect the cooking area during mealtimes, thereby delaying service to customers; the fire department made frequent visits to inspect fire precautions. On several occasions, Van Meter was cited for violating health and safety standards.

Finally, he was called to the city council to answer an adverse police report stating that he allowed drunks and brawling in his establishment. At the hearing, he was warned that he would lose all of his licenses if a drunk were ever again discovered in his restaurant.

During the next six months, the pressure on Van Meter continued at an ever-increasing rate. Longshoremen came into the restaurant and card room and picked fights with customers, employees, and Van Meter himself. The health department chose five o'clock in the evening to inspect the health facilities of the establishment. The fire inspector came at the lunch hour to inspect the fire equipment, writing up every minor defect detectable. Toward the end of Van Meter's attempt to fight the combination of the govermment, the police force, and the criminal syndicate, he received innumerable threats to his life. Bricks and stones were thrown through the windows of his building. Ultimately, he sold his business back to the man from whom he had purchased it at a loss of $30,000 and left the city.

The affair caused considerable consternation among the legal–political–criminal network that controlled and profited from the rackets in Seattle. In the "good old days" the problem would have been quickly solved, one informant remarked, "by a bullet through the fat slob's head." But murder as a solution to problems was clearly frowned upon by the powers that operated organized crime in Seattle. Although the syndicate had been responsible for many murders over the past ten years, these murders were limited to troublesome persons within the syndicate. As nearly as could be determined, no outsider had been murdered for a number of years.

Overall the gambling, bookmaking, pinball, and usury operations grossed at least 25 million dollars a year in the city alone. It was literally the case that drunks were arrested on the street for public intoxication while gamblers made thousands of dollars and policemen accepted bribes a few feet away.

Payoffs, bribes, and associated corruption were not limited solely to illegal activities. To obtain a license for tow-truck operations, one had to pay $10,000 to the licensing bureau; a license for a taxi franchise cost $15,000. In addition, taxi drivers, who sold bootleg liquor (standard brand liquors sold after hours or on Sunday) or who would steer customers to prostitutes or gambling places, paid the police officer on the beat who called the company when an accident occurred. As one informant commented:

> When I would go out on a call from a policeman I would always carry matchbooks with three dollars tucked behind the covers. I would hand this to the cops when I came to the scene of the accident.
>
> Q: Did every policeman accept these bribes?
>
> A: No. Once in a while you would run into a cop who would say he wasn't interested. But that was rare. Almost all of them would take it.

Most of the cabarets, topless bars, and taverns were owned either directly or indirectly by members of the organized crime syndicate. Thus, the syndicate not only controlled the gambling enterprises, but also "legitimate" businesses associated with night life as well. In addition, several of the hotels and restaurants were also owned by the syndicate. Ownership of these establishments was disguised in several ways, such as placing them formally in the name of a corporation with a board of directors who were really a front for the syndicate, or placing them in the names of relatives of syndicate members. It should be emphasized that the official ownership by the syndicate must be interpreted to mean by all of the members who were in the political and legal bureaucracies and simultaneously members of the syndicate, as well as those who were solely involved in the day-to-day operations of the vice syndicate.

The governing board of the syndicate consisted of seven persons, four of whom held high positions in the government and three of whom were responsible for the operation of the various enterprises. The profits were split among them. This is not a syndicate that paid off officials, but a syndicate that is part and parcel of the government, although not subject to election.

Conclusion

There are abundant data indicating that what is true in Seattle is true in virtually every city in the United States and has been true since at least the early 1900s. At the turn of the century, Lincoln Steffens observed that "the spirit of graft and of lawlessness is the American spirit." He went on to describe the results of his inquiries:

> In the very first study—St. Louis—the startling truth lay bare that corruption was not merely political; it was financial, commercial, social; the ramifications of boodle were so complex, various and far-reaching, that our mind could hardly grasp them . . . St. Louis exemplified boodle; Minneapolis Police graft; Pittsburgh a political and Industrial machine; Philadelphia general civil corruption. . . .[3]

In 1931, after completing an inquiry into the police, the National Commission on Law Observance and Enforcement concluded:

> Nearly all of the large cities suffer from an alliance between politicians and criminals. For example, Los Angeles was controlled by a few gamblers for a number of years. San Francisco suffered similarly some years ago and at one period in its history was so completely dominated by the gamblers that three prominent gamblers who were in control of the politics of the city and who quarrelled about the appointment of the police chief settled their quarrel by shaking dice to determine who would name the chief for the first two years, who for the second two years, and who for the third.
>
> Recently the gamblers were driven out of Detroit by the commissioner. These gamblers were strong enough politically to oust this commissioner from office despite the fact that he was recognized by police chiefs as one of the strongest and ablest police executives in America. For a number of years Kansas City, Mo., was controlled by a vice ring and no interference with their enterprises was tolerated. Chicago, despite its unenviable reputation, is but one of numerous cities where the people have frequently been betrayed by their elected officials.[4]

Frank Tannenbaum noted:

> It is clear from the evidence at hand—that a considerable measure of the crime in the community is made possible and perhaps inevitable by the peculiar connection that exists between the political organizations of our large cities and the criminal activities of various gangs that are permitted and even encouraged to operate.[5]

The frequency of major scandals linking organized criminals with leading political and legal figures suggests the same general conclusion. Detroit; Chicago; Denver; Reading, Pennsylvania; Columbus and Cleveland, Ohio; Miami; New York; Boston; and a hoard of other cities have been scandalized and cleansed innumerable times. Yet organized crime persists and thrives. Despite periodic forays, exposures, and reform movements prompted by journalists, sociologists, and politicians, organized crime has become an institution in the United States and in many other parts of the world as well.

Once established, the effect of a crime network on the entire legal and political system is profound. Maintenance of order in such an organization requires the use of extralegal procedures as, obviously, the law cannot always be relied upon to serve the interests of the crime network. The law can harass uncooperative people; it can even be used to send persons to prison on real or faked charges. But to make discipline and obedience certain, it is often necessary to enforce the rules of the syndicate in extralegal ways. To avoid detection of these procedures, the police, the prosecuting attorney's office, and the judiciary must be organized in ways that make them incapable of discovering events that the network does not want disclosed. In actual practice, the police, the prosecutors, and the judges who are not members of the network must not be in a position to investigate those things that the syndicate does not want investigated. The military chain-of-command of the police is, of course, well-suited to such a purpose. So, in fact, is the availability of such subtle but nonetheless important sanctions as relegating uncooperative policemen to undesirable positions in the department. Conversely, cooperative policemen are rewarded with promotions, prestigious positions on the force, and of course a piece of the action.

Another consequence is widespread acceptance of petty graft. The matchbox fee for accident officers is but one illustration. Free meals and cigarettes, bottles of whiskey at Christmas, and the like are practically universal in the police department. Television sets, cases of expensive whiskey, and, on occasion, new automobiles or inside information on investments are commonplace in the prosecuting attorney's office.

Significantly, the symbiotic relationship between organized crime and the legal system not only negates the law enforcement function of the law *vis-a-vis* these types of crimes, but actually increases crime in a number of ways. Perhaps most important, gradual commitment to maintaining the secrecy of the relationship in turn necessitates committing crimes other than those involved in the vices per se. At times, it becomes necessary to intimidate through physical punishment and even to murder recalcitrant members of the syndicate. Calculating the extent of such activities is risky business. From 1955 to 1969 in Seattle, a conservative estimate of the number of persons killed by the syndicate is 15. However, estimates range as high as "hundreds." Although such information is impossible to verify in a manner that creates confidence, it is virtually certain that some murders have been perpetrated by the syndicate in order to protect the secrecy of their operations. It is also certain that the local law enforcement officials, politicians, and businesspersons involved with the syndicate have cooperated in these murders.

The location of the vices in the ghettos and slums of the city may well contribute to a host of other types of criminality as well. The disdain that ghetto residents have for the law and law enforcers is likely derived from more than simply their own experiences with injustice and police harassment. Their day-to-day observations that criminal syndicates operate openly and freely in their areas with complete immunity from punishment, while persons standing on a corner or playing cards in an apartment are subject to arrest, cannot help but affect their perception of the legal system. We do not know that such observations undermine respect for and willingness to comply with the law, but that conclusion would not seem unreasonable.

It is no accident that whenever the presence of vice and organizations that provide the vices is exposed to public view by politicians, exposure is always couched in terms of organized crime. The question of corruption is conveniently left in the shadows. Similarly, it is not an accident that organized crime is inevitably seen as consisting of an organization of criminals with names like Valachi, Genovesse, and Joe Bonano. Yet the data from the study of Seattle, as well as that of earlier studies of vice, makes it abundantly clear that this analysis is fundamentally misleading.

The people who run the organizations that supply the vices in American cities are members of the business, political, and law enforcement communities—not simply members of a criminal society. Furthermore, it is also clear from this study that corruption of political–legal organizations is a critical part of the lifeblood of the crime network. The study of organized crime is thus a misnomer; the study should consider corruption, bureaucracy, and power. By relying on governmental agencies for their information on vice and the rackets, social scientists and lawyers have inadvertently contributed to the miscasting of the issue in terms that are descriptively biased and theoretically sterile. Further, they have been diverted from sociologically interesting and important issues raised by the persistence of crime networks. As a consequence, the real significance of the existence of syndicates has been overlooked; for instead of seeing these social entities as intimately tied to, and in symbiosis with, the legal and political bureaucracies of the state, they have emphasized the criminality of only a portion of those involved. Such a view contributes little to our knowledge of crime and even less to attempts at crime control.

NOTES

1. W.J. Chambliss and R. Seidman, *Law, Order and Power.* (Reading, Massachusetts: Addison-Wesley, 1971).
2. W.J. Chambliss, *On the Take: From Petty Crooks to Presidents.* (Bloomington: Indiana University Press, 1976). According to one informant: "Murder is the easiest crime of all to get away with. There are 101 ways to commit murder that are guaranteed to let you get away with it." He might have added that this was especially true when the coroner, the prosecuting attorney, and key policy officials were cooperating with the murderers.
3. L. Steffens, *The Shame of the Cities.* (New York: McClure, Phillips & Co., 1904), p 151.
4. National Commission on Law Observance and Enforcement, *Lawlessness in Law Enforcement.* (Washington, DC: Government Printing Office, 1931).
5. F. Tannenbaum, *Crime and the Community.* (Boston: Ginn & Co., 1978) p 128.

ORGANIZING CRIME IN EUROPE

III

History
and
Theory

6

Since the mid-1960s, American policy planners[1] along with a large segment of the academic world have been in a muddle in conceptualizing the phenomenon of organized crime. This was primarily caused by the tawdry romance Americans perennially enjoy with conspiracy theory as a method for explaining issues perceived as social problems. As we have noted, in various publications organized crime was characterized as both an alien conspiracy and a continually rationalizing phenomenon.[2] This terminological confusion that characterizes so much of the American effort at understanding the history and sociology of organized crime has had a rather perverse effect on European scholarship. As Mary McIntosh writes, "The best (indeed, the worst) of British criminology has usually been very dependent on ideas coming from America."[3] This has meant that the American obsession with organized crime as a social problem has altered, and indeed thwarted, European study of this phenomenon. The reason most often given for this inhibition is that "in Britain as in most other European countries, we simply do not have any 'organized crime' by American criteria."[4] The immediate problem in comprehending what she means lies, of course, in knowing what American criteria are being applied.

Even more telling than McIntosh's statements about organized crime in Europe are some of the problems found in John Mack's *The Crime Industry*, which sets out to survey European organized crime. In trying to define what he wishes to describe, Mack notes that "professional and organized crime has too many meanings."[5] He goes on to say that for the greater part of this century organized crime has been identified with the Al Capone or gangster imagery, which Mack maintains is distinctly American. In contradiction, however, Mack notes that it (presumably Al Capone-type crime) "has its analogues elsewhere." In fact, he continues, "something like it is to be found not only in Canada and other territories adjacent to the USA, but also, to a much lesser extent, in Europe and elsewhere."[6] This qualification is immediately followed by a baffling claim: "Whether it strictly speaking exists outside North America is a matter of dispute."[7] It is obviously unclear whether Europe has what we have, or for that matter whether we have what we are alleged to have, and so on.

It is pointless at this time to continue recounting the theoretical statements in Mack's work, which, nevertheless, does contain solid descriptive material on organized crime in selected areas of Europe. But it is profitable to return to Mary McIntosh's study for, after her initial rejection of the existence in Europe of organized crime by American criteria, she writes: "[I]f we free ourselves from the connotations that American usage has given the term 'organized,' we can start from the other end; we can accept that all crime involves social organization of some kind and raise questions about the nature of the organization and the way its nature is affected by the total social configuration."[8] In approaching the topic in this fashion, McIntosh suggests that the meaningful distinction to search for is that "between amateur crime and professional crime." She points out that her idea of professional crime is much broader than the type described by Sutherland in his classic work. Professional criminals, according to McIntosh, "are people whose major occupational role is a criminal one, though they may have another nominal occupation as well." Most importantly, she notes that in "professional crime there is organization around the criminal activity that would not be there but for crime and that is relatively independent of organization around other activities."[9] Continuing, she states that professional crime in this broad sense can be found in industrialized Western society as a distinctive social phenomenon. In addition, "there exist organizational patterns that are distinctively criminal and are not simply non-criminal organizations being put to marginal criminal use."[10] It is clear that there are criminal underworlds in Europe that are segregated to some degree from other social milieu.

The recognition by McIntosh that criminal underworlds exist in Europe is, it seems to us, a crucial point. It opens up a range of issues, both historical and sociological, that are ill served by concentrating solely on the structure of organized crime, which tends to remove the analysis of criminal organizations from its historical and political context. Unfortunately, it is almost impossible to find a coherent account of contemporary European underworlds or indeed of concrete examples of organizational patterns that are distinctively criminal in various European settings. As if that was not a sufficient handicap, it is also the case that little is known today about the rise and perpetuation of criminal underworlds in Europe, historically. McIntosh comments:

> Hobsbawm has hinted at some of the conditions in which urban underworlds replace what he calls "social banditry" and individualized crime. But there has been little comparative research on state formation in new nations, for instance, that would enable us to trace the processes involved. Historically, we need to know more about how the bourgeois revolutions in Europe that made professional crime as we know it possible, and more about the impact on professional crime of the changed situation of the state in late capitalism.[11]

Perhaps the best example of Hobsbawm's interest in the history of urban underworlds is found in his short discussion of the Camorra, appended to his chapter on the Mafia in *Primitive Rebels*. The Camorra, according to Hobsbawm, was and perhaps still is a criminal guild or fraternity reminiscent of "the underworld of Basel which had its own acknowledged court outside the town on the Kohlenberg."[12] Unlike the Mafia phenomenon in Sicily, at least prior to World War II the Camorra "represented no class or national interest or coalition of class interests, but the professional interest of an elite of criminals." The origin of the Camorra has been traced to the Neapolitan jails during the period from 1790 to 1830. Once the criminal fraternity was formed, its influence and power increased primarily because of the "goodwill of the Bourbons, who—after 1799—regarded the lumpenproletariat of Naples and all that belonged to it as their safest allies against Liberalism."[13] The Camorra, in league with the Bourbons' notion of the quiescent state, virtually dominated all segments of the life of Naples' poor through various extortion rackets, although it is reputed that gambling was its chief money-making enterprise. Hobsbawm claims that its peak of power was "reached during the 1860 revolution when the Liberals actually handed over the maintenance of public order to the Camorra."[14] This task was carried out with dispatch by the Camorra as it enabled them to reduce or eliminate free-lance crime, which was distinct from and probably competitive with Camorrist rackets. Following this period, the Camorra, for all intents and purposes, drops from the historical record. Hobsbawm does point out that something similar to the Camorra appears again during the 1950s in Naples, operating rackets in petrol, tobacco, and especially in the marketing of fruits and vegetables.[15]

It would, of course, be extremely valuable to be able to trace the development of the Camorra, as well as other elements of organized crime in Naples, from the Risorgemento through the post-World War II era, in order to know, "more about how the bourgeois revolutions in Europe made professional crime as we know it possible."[16] The social history of Europe's urban underworlds would also illuminate other aspects of state formation. Consider some of the material assembled by Gerald Brenan in his brilliant study, *The Spanish Labyrinth*. The portion of the exceptionally complex history of Spanish political and economic development in the late 19th and early 20th centuries that is of immediate interest concerns the Barcelona underworld and its involvement in labor and political struggles.

During World War I, Brenan writes that Barcelona became the "refuge of every sort of international criminal: a horde of spies, agents provocateurs, gangsters and *pistoleros* intervened in labour disputes and offered their services to anyone who might desire them."[17] For a variety of reasons, the year 1917 was a critical one in Spanish—as well as Soviet—history. Brenan writes: "The large industrialists of Spain, in alliance with the Socialists and other Leftwing parties, had come out in open revolution against the Government." It was when "what was to be decided was whether factory owners of the north or the large landowners of Castile and Andalusia should have the chief share in governing the country." The manner in which this division was worked out was a "pact by which Castile became the economic tributary of Catalonia whilst Catalonia remained the political tributary of Castile."[18]

One of the keys to accomplish this division was for the Catalan manufacturers to have a docile labor force. And it is in the struggle between capital and labor in Barcelona in the immediate post-war years that professional criminals played leading roles. The battle was between the anarchist trade union, called the Confederacion Nacional del Trabajo, and the manfacturers who were collected in several employer federations. The Barcelona situation was further aggravated by a split between the civil and military authorities, in which the military sided with the employers. Brenan contends that the Army's position was taken to be: "win over the Catalan bourgeoisie to their camp." This meant that at least a portion of Barcelona's underworld would be "organized from the Captain General's headquarters."[19] The floating terrorist gangs of Barcelona recruited from its swollen underworld "grew up in close association with the police." As Brenan writes:

The Spanish political police or Brigada Social, formed in the nineties to investigate the anarchist bomb outrages, was, as one would expect, a lazy, incompetent body without any technical training and therefore very badly informed. It relied upon private denunciations for its information and as it had few scruples it seldom took the trouble to investigate them on its own account. Thus there grew up in close touch with it and indeed under its orders various gangs of professional *confidentes* or informers, who were paid for their information. These gangs also cooperated with specially interested bodies, such as the Federation of Employers. When a crime occurred, they gave information as to the supposed authors—and, as it was usually easier to inculpate an innocent man than to find the criminal, they became adept at faking evidence and at planting bombs or incriminating material upon innocent people. For this purpose they would of course choose workmen whose activities as strike leaders or as propogandists of anarchism made them objectionable to the owners and to the police, and from this it was not a long step to incriminating such people as were officially indicated to them.[20]

Brenan claims that the situation in Barcelona in 1918 was especially conducive to the expansion of gangs drawn from the above milieu, to which should be added the uncounted criminals from all over Europe who, for unexplained reasons, found Barcelona a refuge. Undoubtedly one of the reasons for Barcelona's attractiveness was the marketability of skills of violence: a market that, it should be noted, had been enriched by German money during the last years of World War I, which was supposed to be spent for the purpose of closing munition factories supplying the Allies.

Inevitably, the workmen also had gangsters in their ranks, if not their employ. Without much explanation, Brenan notes that beginning in 1916 membership in the CNT had increased enormously. Part of this growth was attributable to a large number of what he terms "doubtful characters, including many professional criminals."[21] Such were the conditions in Barcelona that finally came to a boil in 1919. Gangs of *pistoleros* representing both sides were let loose and violence engulfed Barcelona.

There were several attempts at conciliation, but none of them was effective, and during the winter of 1919–1920, "rival gangs of terrorists roamed the streets and assassinations took place every week." One of the attempts to arrange peace in Barcelona deserves some comment, however. In March, 1920, a new government came to power in Spain under the Conservative leadership of Eduardo Dato, who appointed as Civil Governor of Barcelona a moderate, Carlos Bas. It was Bas's mission to reconcile peacefully the dispute between workers and employers in Barcelona. One of his actions was to dissolve one of the most offensive gangs employed by the manufacturers' federation. What is instructive about this particular gang is that, while working for the employers and assassinating as many CNT leaders as possible, they were also killing employers who had refused to be blackmailed. Bas's mission was a failure primarily because of the obdurateness of the military and the employers, and he was dismissed.[22]

In place of Bas, the Government appointed, at the King's insistence, General Martinez Anido, who was given complete authority to end the strife in Barcelona. Anido chose three related methods to bring order to the city. First, he reorganized and armed a small *company* trade union, the *Sindicato Libre*, which already had a high proportion of professional criminals, and "gave them a list of the syndicalist leaders whom they were to shoot on sight." In less than two days they murdered 21 CNT leaders. The second method was simply to have the Barcelona police arrest labor leaders and then have them shot. Anido's third approach was to have workers arrested and than released: "a gang of *pistoleros* would be waiting for them outside the prison and they would be killed before they could reach the comparative safety of the workers' districts."[23] The methods of Anido were met in kind by the gunmen of the CNT. The result of all this fighting, which was finally ended in 1923 with the coming of the dictatorship, was over 700 assassinations in Catalonia, with the great majority taking place in Barcelona.[24]

It is a strange fact that scholarship dealing with Europe's urban underworlds, scant as it is, is far stronger on certain 19th century cities than it is on any contemporary ones. It is as if the very notion of the urban underworld has been bequeathed to either historical study or to that branch of criminology that is solely concerned with juvenile crime. Undoubtedly, the latter point is one of the effects of the continuing influence of the Chicago school of social ecology on European academics. There are several solid studies of the London underworld in the 19th century,[25] Chevalier's enigmatic work dealing with Paris,[26] as well as other important studies, all of which suggest in one manner or another both the presence of criminal organizations in concrete urban environments and the connections between them and various urban or state institutions.

To be sure, there are snippets of information about organized crime and/or the urban underworld in post-World War I European cities, which can be found in scholarly works whose focus is the police or some other criminal justice agency. One example of the kind of research we mean can be seen in Hsi-Huey Liang's *The Berlin Police Force in the Weimar Republic*. In the chapter on the Detective Force, Liang notes that the majority of the "detective inspectors who grumbled about the Republic were in charge of fighting Berlin's organized underworld."[27] Commenting on the Berliners' fascination with stories about criminals, Liang holds that the underworld clubs, the *Ringvereine*, were seen as the "classical milieu of professional crooks." But he states that the word *Ringvereine* only applied to regional associations that controlled local underworld clubs. In Berlin during the Weimar period there were three underworld associations: the *Freier Bund*, the *Grosser Ring*, and the *Freie Vereinigung*. These three acted in the interest of a larger syndicate, known as the *Mitteldeutscher Ring*. Liang writes that "they imposed rigid statutes on the local clubs, controlled their activities, and exacted money tributes for the syndicates."[28]

It is unclear, according to Liang, how many of these underworld clubs were operational during the 1920s in Berlin. A conservative estimate was about 85. Their total membership is also unknown, although there are claims from as few as 1,000 to almost all the criminals in Berlin. "One journalist maintained," Liang states, "that Berlin-Mitte at night was virtually in the hands of criminal gangs: doormen, bootblacks, street vendors, prostitutes, and toilet attendants were all paying members in one of the underworld clubs."[29] If accurate, the representatives are a fascinating and revealing cross section of the associational life of Berlin's organized criminals. Among the functions that these clubs performed were the exchange of information for teams of thieves and securing financial help and fake witnesses for jailed members. One other revealing tidbit mentioned by Liang concerns objections that were raised to the habit of police detectives "negotiating deals with confidence men in 'licensed burglars clubs.' "[30]

It is, of course, inconceivable that the flourishing underworlds of Europe's major cities simply dried up during the cataclysm of World War II. In fact, with the exception of those cities that were destroyed during the war, there is every reason to believe that at least certain organized illicit activities boomed under wartime conditions and the immediate aftermath. It also seems highly likely that in those European cities that were located in neutral states, the range and influence of the local underworlds would have grown during the years of chaos. With the incredible rise in general violence, the rampant instability of government, the various commodity shortages, the problems of identity papers and currency, the opportunities for stealing, smuggling, counterfeiting, black marketing extortion, and so on, were enormous.

There is no adequate history or sociology of organized crime or indeed illicit activities either during World War II or during the immediate postwar period in Europe. But we would hazard a guess that the following passage taken from Graham Greene's *The Third Man* had innumerable real-world analogues.

> The war and the peace (if you can call it peace) let loose a great number of rackets, but none more vile than this one. The black marketeers in food did at least supply food, and the same applied to all the other racketeers who provided articles in short supply at extravagant prices. But the pencillin racket was a different affair altogether. Penicillin in Austria was only supplied to the military hospitals: no civilian doctor, not even a civilian hospital, could obtain it by legal means. As the racket started, it was relatively harmless. Penicillin would be stolen and sold to Austrian doctors for very high sums—a phial would fetch anything up to £70 . . . .
>
> This racket went on quite happily for a while. Occasionally someone was caught and punished, but the danger simply raised the price of penicillin. Then the racket began to get organized: the big men saw big money in it, while the original thief got less for his spoils, he received instead a certain security. If anything happened to him he would be looked after . . . .
>
> This, I have sometimes called stage two. Stage three was when the organizers decided that the profits were not large enough. Penicillin would not always be impossible to obtain legitimately: they wanted more money and quicker money while the going was good. They began to dilute the penicillin with coloured water, and in the case of penicillin dust, with sand.[31]

A more scientific example of the illicit activities that blossomed after World War II can be found in Marshall Clinard's *The Black Market* under the rubric white-collar crime. He notes that black marketing in Europe after the war was exceptionally extensive. Among the commodities traded in the black markets were cigarettes, coffee, foodstuffs, and currency, including, naturally, occupation scrip in Germany. Clinard adds that "Reichmarks were traded for occupation francs, Swiss francs, pounds and the like. Except for the barest necessities of life the black market was all-pervasive,"[32] especially in the defeated countries. It must be noted that Clinard also holds that black marketing was conducted on an individual basis, although this conclusion in no way precludes either considering some of it as organized crime or suspecting that organized criminals were deeply involved in many of its manifestations.

Without intentionally trying to make this too tedious, let us return for a moment to John Mack's work on contemporary European organized crime. In marshalling his material on Europe, Mack notes several degrees of difference between the European varieties of organized crime and that in America. What Mack considers the most significant divergence has to do with the supplying of illegal goods and services. He begins with the assumption that at the core of syndicated crime activities in America is the supply function. He continues by asserting that this is simply not the case in contemporary Europe: The mobs, as he calls them, "may engage in some incidental illicit trafficking, but they fill no major role of middleman supplying powerful economic demands for forbidden goods and services."[33] The role the European mobs do fulfill, according to Mack, is one described as parasitical. He does not define parasitism, although an example of it is given—"the enforcement of 'protection' payments."[34] Parasitism, then, appears to be a form of extortion. What Mack is really attempting to describe and distinguish are some differences between local urban underworlds, composed primarily of stealing gangs who also terrorize local merchants, and those inter-European "criminal organizations" that exist, as he acknowledges, in the form of flexible and changing networks whose principal role is the supply function. Mack therefore must believe that American organized crime is only approachable in scope and structure by those overarching continental syndicates.

There are a number of criticisms that can be made of these assumptions. First, the notion of American organized crime harkens back to what we earlier called the mistaken idea of the Monolith. In fact we assert that the bulk of organized criminal activity in America is much closer to what Mack describes as parasitism—small extortion and stealing rings fairly limited in range. Instead of considering the notorious criminals of New York and Chicago, consider the probable scope of illicit activities in Baltimore, Omaha, Fresno, Tucson, St. Louis, Pittsburgh, Richmond, or Memphis. To be sure, there is and has been contact between local urban underworlds in the less glamorous American cities and various criminals from New York and Chicago, which supposedly represent the nerve centers of syndicate crime. In all likelihood, this is no more than the contacts between the local underworlds in a score of European cities and organized criminals from such capitals as London, Paris, and Rome. A more common-sense approach would be to view America as a federation composed of smaller states similar in many ways to the European Common Market, or what is called Western Europe. This would bring into sharper focus the probable similarities between cigarette smugglers in America—who purchase cigarettes inexpensively in such states as North Carolina, and then sell them for a profit in New York and Connecticut, thus avoiding the taxes in the northern states—and the cigarette smuggling endemic to Scandinavian countries and Poland: both are organized crime. It is apparent that if one wants to make an interesting and significant comparison of organized crime between America and Europe, one must surely have more dynamic notions of geography and political structure.

Second, and equally important, Mac's view is severly ahistorical. It denies even the little we do know—and the great deal we suspect—about the history of Europe's urban underworlds which displays on numerous occasions criminal organizations founded on the supply of forbidden goods and services. Perhaps most misleading in this quasi-definition is the lumping together of goods (commodities) and services (behavior). This is so because the overwhelming service performed by professional criminals (in McIntosh's sense) is one form or another of extortion, which for Mack is the cutting edge distinguishing parasitic organized crime from American syndicated crime. But it is precisely the selling of services that characterized the function of the Barcelona underworld during the years of turmoil as well as the history of the Mafia so brilliantly developed by Anton Blok (1974). In addition, there is little reason to accept as significant the distinction between criminal organizations structured around the supply function and those structured around parasitism. In fact, when Mack writes that the "existence of the two kinds of large-scale full-time crime is generally agreed," and follows that by doubting "whether the two kinds of crime are practised by two distinct sets of criminals,"[35] one wonders what these distinctions are supposed to convey. Certainly they are not based upon research into the changing functions of organized crime or professional criminals over the last one hundred years. Clearly they are not grounded upon knowledge of the interplay between patterns of criminality and the articulation of different political economies on the European continent from, let us say, the Congress of Vienna to the Great Depression.

This brings us to a third crucial point concerning contemporary work on organized crime in Europe. Viewing European organized crime through the distorted lens of a flawed American model has led to this conclusion: "The general inference to be drawn from European experience is that syndicated crime does not possess that capacity to win friends and influence people in power which is the most striking feature of its U.S. counterpart."[36] The study of organized crime has, it appears, reversed a rather old theme—American innocence versus European decadence. The symbiotic relationship between representatives of American politics, including criminal justice agents and professional criminals, is missing in studies of Europe.

Can this be the case? In what sense can this be accurate, given what so many scholars have discovered about politics and crime in Italy, for instance?[37] Or, for that matter, what we know about the interplay between professional criminals and politicians in Marseille during most of this century.[38] Clearly, the inference quoted above rests first upon a very restricted meaning or definition of Europe. Real Europe, good Europe, decent Europe is somewhere north of the Alps and west of the Elbe. The claim of European propriety, then, rests upon the belief in the integrity of politics and politicians in northwestern Europe.

There is a second assumption built into the inference that also must be considered: How does one account for such a stunning phenomenon as the heroin traffic in Amsterdam and related drug trafficking in Copenhagen and Stockholm?[39] The manner in which the acknowledged trafficking is discussed, especially in Holland, reveals several themes. In The Netherlands, the heroin traffic is seen to be controlled by Chinese syndicates whose major function is the transshipment of heroin to other countries. In other words, very little heroin is consumed locally, so the standard account runs, and thus there is no real Dutch drug problem. At the same time, what little local consumption there is, it is argued, is confined to immigrant and migrant worker communities. Although the Chinese, Mollucan, and Surinamese communities are often deeply involved in narcotics, both as racketeers and consumers, the "real" Dutch are clean. The integrity of the indigenous northern Europeans is maintained by both government and police officials. Nevertheless, it is still true that Amsterdam is probably the major heroin center of Europe. In addition, there is little effort by either law enforcement agencies or Government bureaucracies in stopping the traffic. The Dutch are, it seems, content to let it continue as long as it is perceived to be a foreign or nonwhite problem. As long as this attitude prevails, Chinese heroin racketeers will enjoy—for free—the same kind of immunity that has supposedly been so costly for American racketeers. Heroin racketeering would then be much more expensive in New York than Amsterdam. Indeed, this may account for the fact that the street price for heroin is significantly cheaper in Amsterdam than in New York. A function of corruption for racketeers is to neutralize people who have the power and will to interfere with illegal activities. In The Netherlands, at this time, it has either happened, or it is unnecessary.

If nothing else, the point of the inference is lost. It is simply not the case for vast areas of Europe (Italy, Spain, the Balkan countries). In other places, such as The Netherlands and Denmark, the scope of law enforcement may be so circumscribed as to make corruption an unnecessary expense. What might we conclude, after all this, about the

state of research on organized crime in Europe? It is, in the main, theoretically weak and disorganized, receiving almost no foundation or
governmental support.[40] It is permeated with a kind of chronic ra-
cism. It is confused about the state and nature of American organized crime. And finally, it lacks historical perspective and shows little
sign of merging the insights of contemporary social urban historians
with the views of critical criminology.

But it is not sufficient merely to carp about shortcomings in the study
of European organized crime. Let us see if we can suggest a proper
frame around which future studies can be constructed. We begin by
noting that in an explicit sense the manifestations of organized criminality are always the expression of something else. Organized crime
and criminality are analagous or synonymous with what Marx calls
"legal relations" that could not be understood by themselves because
"they are rooted in the material conditions of life, which are summed
. . . under the name of 'civil society'; the anatomy of that civil society is
to be sought in political economy."[41] Organized crime is not a modern,
urban, or lower class phenomenon: it is a historical one whose changes
mirror changes in civil society—the political economy.

This is, of course, what McIntosh means when she calls for studies
dealing with the impact of the bourgeois revolutions on professional
crime. Stated in a slightly different fashion, what needs to be done is to
explore the impact of the Industrial Revolution on patterns of organized criminality. Before turning to that, however, one point must be
clear: European cities had organized criminality that pre-dated the
Industrial Revolution. As historian Jeffrey Kaplow writes in an elegant
study of the Parisian laboring poor in the 18th century: "The picture of
Parisian crime that emerges is that of a pre-Industrial Revolution urban
center in which crimes against property far outweigh crimes against
persons and where personal violence is a means to an end but not an
end in inself."[42] Parisian crime was carried out by an amalgam or
conglomeration of amateur and professional criminals whose differences were often marginal. Kaplow states that the "laboring classes
and the dangerous classes lived in constant communion with one
another, and the passage of individuals between them was doubtless a
gradual process more than the result of a conscious decision to lead a
life of crime."[43] It is, of course, no more remarkable to locate organized
criminality within the ranks of the urban poor in a pre-Industrial
Revolution city than it is to find a pre-Industrial Revolution proletariat.
As historian David Landes points out, the first true industrial proletariat was not the creation of the Industrial Revolution: "the bluenails of
medieval Flanders and Ciompi of the Florence of the quattrocento are

earlier examples of landless workers with nothing to sell but their labour."[44]

What Kaplow finds characteristic of Parisian organized crime is notable. There were stealing gangs with established fences, criminal families, a particular argot, numerous varieties of prostitution, arsonists, and pimps. There were organized criminals who preyed upon both Paris and the countryside and others who worked only Paris— some "even remaining in a single quarter, like the environs of the Pont Neuf, a notorious center of mischief." There were also some identifiable patterns of police toleration and/or protection as "only clandestine prostitution was punished while the organized variety was allowed to go on undisturbed."[45] The inducements to crime were many, but they can be reasonably reduced to some combination of poverty and opportunity. Crime, organized and disorganized, was an outgrowth of the wretched conditions of the laboring poor.

There is one distinction between organized and disorganized urban criminality that is not emphasized by Kaplow but which is significant to us as noted earlier. It is suggested by the term "le milieu," which should be taken to mean both concrete urban environments and behavioral subcultures. "Le milieu" connotes areas rich in links between organized criminals, merchants, owners and managers of certain types of urban real estate, and representatives of municipal and state power, especially the police. This is what Richard Cobb has in mind when he comments:

> The words horse dealer and horse thief were largely interchangeable, and . . . the legislation concerning the purchase and sale of horses at a fair or market was actually to facilitate the disposal of stolen horses. The horse market was thus to provide the most valuable link between the faubourg Saint-Marceau and the left bank in general and the various bandit groups that operated with such success in the rural communes south of Paris, in the neighborhood of Montlhery and Arpajon, during the Directory.[46]

"Le milieu," in other words, is what we mean by an urban underworld. Real areas where the business of crime is planned, where contacts are made, where some crimes are carried out, where the fruits of crime are often enjoyed, where aspects of the associational life of the urban poor are played out, and where the methodologies for the integration of organized criminals into civil society are established.

Just as crucial as recognizing the historicity of such urban enclaves is noting their transformations, which is the point of our suggested framework. Many of the urban underworlds of pre-industrial Europe must have been enormously augmented during the first stages of industrialization, their growth roughly corresponding to the increase of the urban laboring poor and the rookeries that housed them.[47] There were, however, immense differences in Europe in the extent and timing of industrialization, and certainly in the connections between population growth, urbanization, and industrialization. The three developments derive at least in part from what Landes calls "autonomous origins" and "subsequent interaction." This means that the civil societies of European cities would differ markedly even under the blooming and encompassing culture of modern capitalism. And it is the quantitative and qualitative differences in urban economies, along with the structural changes of Europe's cities,[48] which account for different patterns of organized criminality in the 19th and 20th centuries.

Nevertheless, the growth in sheer numbers of the urban poor, especially in the years 1750–1850, must have put a great burden on the vast majority of urban underworlds. Until these increases could be accommodated by legitimate employment or welfare systems, the stability of many European underworlds would be undermined. After all, how many thieves, whores, pimps, arsonists, fences, and others could be active without destroying the economics of these enterprises? The law and order crises that struck so many European cities in the first half of the 19th century were not simply a surfeit of crime, but equally the inability of many European underworlds to incorporate great numbers rapidly. The integrative functions of these areas were inadequate to the task.

The crises were largely stemmed by the timely help of the bourgeoisie. First, they were instrumental in developing state and municipal welfare systems that rescued some from crime and, just as importantly, rescued others from so much unwanted criminal competition. In addition, the bourgeoisie was largely responsible for the growth of criminal justice agencies and instututions that increased state capacities for controlling the unorganized criminal while creating new patrons for the organized. More significantly, modern capitalism itself came to the rescue by creating lucrative new enterprises for criminals.

> Mass production and urbanization stimulated, indeed required, wider facilities for distribution, a larger credit structure, an expansion of the educational system, the assumption of new functions by government. At the same time, the increase in the standard of living due to higher productivity created new wants and made possible new satisfactions, which led to a spectacular flowering of those businesses that cater to human pleasure and leisure: entertainment, travel, hotels, restaurants, and so on.[49]

As specialists in vice, violence, and corruption, urban organized criminals were able to penetrate segments of the licit pleasure businesses while also monopolizing the illicit ones.

It is one of the ironies of bourgeois culture that its dedication to pleasure is severely circumscribed. The pleasurable commodities (their production and distribution) and leisure businesses are endlessly regulated by the state—thereby satisfying the moral community—which at the same time creates the climate for criminal conspiracies whose purpose is the systematic avoidance of regulation. In fact, the varieties of criminal conspiracies in the tertiary sector of modern capitalism devoted to pleasure and leisure enterprises (narcotics syndicates, linen suppliers to hotels and restaurants whose forte is monopoly though violence, trade associations in small capital enterprises specializing in price fixing and labor discipline, sports entrepreneurs connected to gambling syndicates with interests in call-girl rackets, vending machine operatives who specialize in terror, and so on) represent the most significant expansion of organized criminality in the last two centuries. In so many ways, contemporary organized criminality is a creature of the bourgeois pattern of life: a merging of "possessive individualism" with the demands of the regulatory state mediated by violence and corruption."[50]

Organized crime always reflects the structure and tension in civil society, the opportunities for profit and power, and the contradictions in political economy. And if the "mark of the modern world is the imagination of its profiteers and the counter-assertiveness of the oppressed," as Immanual Wallerstein suggests,[51] then surely aspects of contemporary organized criminality play a powerful role within that drama. The criminal conspiracies, which highlight so many of the licit enterprises in the tertiary sector as well as the totally illicit ones, clearly reflect the imagination of profiteers and the place modern capitalism and the bourgeois state have reserved for the sellers of goods and services whose specialties are extortion and corruption. And insofar as they operate as labor disciplinarians in the interests of owners and managers, organized criminals thwart to some degree the counter-assertiveness of the oppressed. In these respects, contemporary organized crime is a method of integrating segments of the urban poor—whether in Amsterdam, Hamburg, London, Paris, or Barcelona—into the often rapacious political economy of capitalism. Naturally the modes of integration differ according to the size and ethnicity of the urban poor, the structure of law enforcement, the power of trade unions, and the economies of particular European cities. To expect less complexity and diversity would be exceedingly foolish. And to search for the nature of contemporary organized criminality outside the social history of capitalism in Europe, as Mack does, is more foolish still.

NOTES

1. For the lamentable confusion, see again GAO, *War on Organized Crime Faltering.* (Washington, DC: U.S. Government Printing Office, 1977).

2. The level of discussion on rationalization and organized crime would be radically altered if more attention were paid to D.C. Tipps's Modernization Theory and the Comparative Study of Societies: A Critical Perspective, *Comparative Studies in Society and History.* (1973), p 199–226. Tipps writes: "When modernization is conceptualized in terms of a single variable such as rationalization or industrialization it functions merely as a synonym for other, already well-defined concepts, thus tending to be not only superfluous, but obfuscating. . . .Perhaps the most damaging argument comes from those who have challenged the systematic character of modernization by showing that many processes of change associated with modernization may occur in isolation from other such processes, that some of these processes of change may be incompatible with others, and that because of differences in timing and initial setting processes of institutional change associated with modernization in one context need not be recapitulated in others. . . .The attempt by modernization theorists to aggregate in a single concept disparate processes of social change which rather should have been distinguished has served only to hinder rather than facilitate their empirical analysis." p 221–223.

3. M. McIntosh, New Directions in the Study of Criminal Organization, in H. Bianchi, M. Simondi, and I. Taylor (eds.) Deviance and Control in Europe: Papers from the European Group for the Study of Deviance and Social Control. (London: John Wiley and Son, 1975).

4. Ibid., p 144.

5. J. A. Mack with H. Kerner, *The Crime Industry.* (Westmead: Saxon House, 1975).

6. Ibid., p 5.

7. Ibid.

8. M. McIntosh, op. cit., p 144.

9. Ibid., p 147.

10. Ibid., p 148.

11. Ibid., p 153.

12. E. J. Hobsbawm, *Primitive Rebels: Studies in Archaic Forms of Social Movement in the 19th and 20th Centuries.* (New York: W. W. Norton, 1959).

13. Ibid., p 54.

14. Ibid., p 55.

15. Ibid.

16. M. McIntosh, op. cit., p 148.

17. G. Brenan, *The Spanish Labyrinth: An Account of the Social and Political Background of the Spanish Civil War,* (Cambridge: Cambridge University Press, 1960).

18. Ibid., p 63–66.

19. Ibid., p 67–68.

20. Ibid., p 68; see also R. Cobb, *Paris and Its Provinces, 1792–1802.* (London: Oxford University Press, 1975).

21. G. Brenan, op. cit., p 70.

22. Ibid., p 72–73.

23. Ibid., p 73.

24. Ibid., p 74.

25. K. Chesney, *The Victorian Underworld*. (New York: Schocken Books, 1970). J.J. Tobias, *Urban Crime in Victorian England*. (New York: Schocken Books, 1967).

26. L. Chevalier, *Laboring Classes and Dangerous Classes in Paris During the First Half of the Nineteenth Century*. (New York: Howard Fertig, 1973).

27. H. Liang, *The Berlin Police Force in the Weimar Republic*. (Berkeley and Los Angeles: The University of California Press, 1970).

28. Ibid., p 145.

29. Ibid., p 146.

30. Ibid., p 147.

31. G. Greene, *The Third Man*. (New York: Bantam Books, 1950).

32. M.B. Clinard, *The Black Market: A Study of White Collar Crime*. (Montclair, New Jersey: Patterson Smith, 1969).

33. J.A. Mack, op cit., p 36.

34. Ibid., p 6.

35. Ibid.

36. Ibid., p 36.

37. G. Servadio, *Mafioso: A History of the Mafia from Its Origin to the Present Day*. (New York: Stein and Day, 1976).

38. A.N. McCoy, *The Politics of Heroin in Southeast Asia*. (New York: Harper & Row, 1973).

39. Information on the current scene in Amsterdam and Copenhagen was collected in January 1977, January 1978, and the first two months of 1979, during a research trip to both countries. Among the individuals interviewed were Police Inspector Ruub Petow in The Hague, Professor Albert Hauber of Leiden University, Professor Preben Wolf of the University of Copenhagen, Chief Constable Soren Sorenson of the Danish Police, and Police Inspector P. M. Gaugin who is head of the Copenhagen narcotics squad.

40. The lack of governmental support for research on organized crime in Holland was discussed with us by various members of the Research and Documentation Centre, Ministry of Justice, The Hague. The same point was repeated in Copenhagen.

41. L. S. Feuer (ed.), *Basic Writings on Politics and Philosophy: Karl Marx and Freidrich Engels*. (Garden City, New York: Doubleday, 1959).

42. J. Kaplow, *The Names of Kings: The Parisian Laboring Poor in the Eighteenth Century*. (New York: Basic Books, 1972).

43. Ibid., p 143.

44. D. Landes, *The Unbound Prometheus: Technological Change and Industrial Development in Western Europe from 1750 to the Present*. (Cambridge: Cambridge University Press, 1969).

45. J. Kaplow, op. cit., p 148–149.

46. R. Cobb, *Paris and Its Provinces, 1792–1802*. (London: Oxford University Press, 1975).

47. See T. Beames, *The Rookeries of London*. (London: Frank Cass and Company, 1852). A. Lees and L. Lees (eds.), *The Urbanization of European Society in the Nineteenth Century*. (Lexington, Massachusetts: D.C. Heath, 1976). E. Weber, *A Modern History of Europe: Men, Cultures, and Societies from the Renaissance to the Present*. (New York: W.W.

Norton, 1971). A.F. Weber, *The Growth of Cities in the Nineteenth Century: A Study in Statistics*. (Ithaca, New York: Cornell University Press, 1963).

48. E.J. Hobsbawm, *Revolutionaries: Contemporary Essays* (New York: New American Library, 1973).

49. D. Landes, op. cit., p 9.

50. See the magnificent work by C.B. MacPherson, *The Political Theory of Possessive Individualism: Hobbes to Locke*. (London: Oxford University Press, 1962).

51. I. Wallerstein, *The Modern World-System: Captialist Agriculture and the Origins of the European World-Economy in the Sixteenth Century*. (New York: Academic Press, 1977), p 357.

Organizing Crime in Sweden

7

There is a paradoxical relationship between legal and illegal business enterprises in capitalist countries. The paradox is that the seeds of the illegal business that is so pervasive in these societies are sown in the nature of business enterprises that are legal. This is why we begin our discussion of illegal businesses with, paradoxically, a discussion of some of the legal businesses in Sweden that engage in activities that are illegal in other countries and that have facets that are illegal in Sweden as well.

In 1975, when this research took place, some forms of gambling were legal in Sweden: slot machines, horse race betting, roulette, and bingo.* Our discussion begins with these legal enterprises by way of introduction to the organization of business activities that are illegal.

Gambling

One of the most important companies organizing, operating, selling machinery, and running legal gambling in Sweden today is an American-based firm: the Bally Manufacturing Corporation.

The Bally Corporation was incorporated in the State of Delaware in the United States in 1952. Although incorporated in Delaware (because of that state's liberal laws concerning required reports of who owns the corporation's stocks and how the business is run), it is actually based in

*The material in this chapter was collected in field interviews and observations by the authors and Goran Elwin, Stina Holmberg, and Lisa Reeve Stearns in Sweden in 1975–1976.

Chicago, Illinois. The company was founded in 1946 by three men who manufactured and sold pinball machines. It was a small company with unknown profits. One of the employees at the time was William O'Donnell. The men who began the corporation were all people connected with America's very large, very profitable gambling businesses. One of the founding members was a notorious underworld figure known as "Doc" Stacher—a man who had for many years been a prominent figure in illegal gambling. He was eventually deported to Israel, at which time he sold his interest in Bally to Jerry Catena—a high-level official in one of the larger crime cartels in America, which at that time was headed by Vito Genovese. During this early period the company was affiliated with a company appropriately (and legally) registered as "Runyon Sales," having taken the name of one of America's most famous writers about the criminal underworld, Damon Runyon.

During these years the man who would eventually become the head of the company, William O'Donnell, was working as a pinball and slot machine salesman. In 1955, he became the head of sales. In 1958, the firm changed its name as a result of adverse publicity stemming from a Federal investigation that clearly linked the operation and ownership of the company with "organized crime" figures.

In 1963, a consortium was put together, consisting of two different groups, each owning 50% of the stock. One group consisted of William O'Donnell and several people who represented or were themselves heavily involved in illegal businesses; the other group consisted of people who were closely affiliated with one of the strongest and most corrupt unions in the United States: the International Brotherhood of Teamsters. Over $250,000 was raised as capital for further investment.

The name of the company was changed to Bally Manufacturing. The company went public and was listed on the American Stock Exchange. Investors buying stock at this time were in for some welcome news in the next ten years. One dollar invested in Bally stock in 1964 was worth ten thousand dollars ten years later. Crime pays extremely well.

The growth of the company was phenomenal, even in comparison with other fast-growing U.S. corporations. Most of the machines sold by the company were transported and sold illegally. By American law it is illegal to transport and sell gambling machines that are illegal in the state where they are to be shipped. Nevada is one of the few states in the United States where pinball and slot machines can be legally sold and operated. Despite this, Bally sold machines to virtually every state in the United States, where they were subsequently operated at very high profits by local crime cartels.

In 1964, Bally controlled 90% of the American market for slot machines. They had a monopoly that was unchallenged by either competitors or legal reprisals. By law in the United States, a corporation that controls over 50% of a given market may be forced to sell part of its corporation in order to encourage competition. This did not happen to Bally.

Many of the people to whom Bally sold machines were themselves connected either directly or indirectly with the corporation. For example, the Fremont Hotel in Las Vegas purchased all of its slot machines from Bally. The Fremont Hotel was owned by Jerry Catena's brother (probably as a front for Catena who owned much of the stock).

In 1974, the Teamsters Union loaned Bally $12 million from the infamous Teamsters' Pension fund. For this service the President of the Teamsters, Frank Fitzsimmons, was given 900 shares of Bally stock. With this capital, Bally purchased a leading slot machine manufacturer in West Germany. The purchase of the West German company enabled Bally to become international in scope and practice. Like other businesses in the capitalist world of the 1950s and 1960s, Bally expanded into international markets as quickly as its capital and its contacts with public officials and private entrepreneurs permitted.

Sweden was one of the countries chosen by Bally for extensive investment and development as a potentially high-profit endeavor. The move into Sweden began in the late 1960s even before the purchase of the West German firm.

In 1967, Jan Peterson, with an investment of $2,000, founded a small company called Nordick Automat. Peterson and his wife were sole directors of the company. In October, 1969, Bally International purchased Nordick Automat from Peterson. A new board of directors was then appointed, which included Mr. and Mrs. Peterson, Commander Nilsson Lundberg, and Alex Wilms, the Belgian representative of Bally International (and European Director of the company). As we will see, Wilms has been implicated in a number of questionable practices in connection with Bally business and people associated with Bally Corporation. In August, 1971, the name was changed to Bally Scandinavia; at this time Bally became the parent corporation of what until then had been several local companies, such as Bally Norkorping.

The gambling business in Sweden in which Bally was interested consisted of the sale, distribution, and serving of slot machines, roulette tables, and bingo parlors. Their business strategies and policies are those that have been tried and found successful in other countries where Bally has operated: obtaining political support through the hiring and enteraining of politicians; using innocent front organizations (such as sports clubs or charities) to give the appearance of legitimacy and to provide as wide a base of political support and economic dependence upon gambling as possible; and, finally, to be willing to compromise in the face of conflict in order to protect profits. The latter point is crucial: the history of Bally in Sweden, as elsewhere, is the history of a company determined to maximize profits for the shareholders—a not unseemly quality for a capitalist enterprise. This often means that the company must move and dodge like a boxer to deflect an attack here and slip in a punch there in order to win the fight, not just a single round.

Thus it was that when Bally was attacked in the early 1970s by the Swedish press for being a foreign-owned company with "Mafia" and "organized crime" ties, Bally quickly moved to dispel this impression in every way it could. It hired as consultants some of the leading business and political figures in Sweden to lend credibility to the corporation's name. It employed public relations firms to counterattack the accusations made in the press. And, finally, it sold 80% of its bingo stock.

Bally obtained oral testimony from some of Sweden's leading business and political figures to the effect that the company was sound, reliable, and engaged only in legal enterprises. These statements are surprising to anyone familiar with Bally's history in the United States and Australia, where the company's involvement in illegal businesses and illegal techniques of doing "legal" business are beyond a shadow of a doubt. Armed with these "testimonials," the Bally Corporation then sent testimonial-tapes from Hans Wetter, General Manager of the state-owned Railway Restaurant System, and Per Axel Bronnsbonn, General Manager of the state-owned Scandinavian Airlines (SAS) Hotels, plus rather expensive tape recorders to the leading members of Parliament. The MPs were allowed to keep the tape recorders. In addition, Bally gave several leading politicians and law enforcement people a free trip to see its "headquarters and operations" in Chicago and Las Vegas. An all-expense-paid vacation to Las Vegas under the smoke screen of inspecting company operations doubtless made the public relations campaign among the parliament considerably easier than it might otherwise have been. Those who could not take the long trip, or who were not important enough to warrant the expenditure, were treated to luxurious meals at expensive restaurants as the guest of Bally. Bally even went so far as to offer one of the news reporters who—pursuing allegations of organized crime connections between Bally and American "gangsters"—a trip to the states to "see the operation."

The co-optation of management from the state-owned Railway Restaurants and The SAS Hotels is significant in that it reflects the extent
to which these people as career bureaucrats and these organizations as
state-owned enterprises operating within a capitalist economic system
are susceptible to precisely the same kinds of pressures and considera-
tions that private industries are. The profits these agencies make from
slot machines and roulette wheels are a substantial asset in their
operations. Without these profits, it would be considerably more difficult for the management of these "state-owned" agencies to show a
profit at the end of the year. Their support for Bally, particularly, and
legalized gambling, generally, is thus a predictable result of their own
positions both in the state and the economy. The net profits to Railway
Restaurants and SAS Hotels from gambling devices are not available to
us; however, we were able to determine that the Sheraton Hotel in
downtown Stockholm receives $100,000 a year from its gambling
devices.

Indeed, the entire history of legalizing various types of gambling in
Sweden can be seen as ever-increasing dependence of the state upon
these revenues. The most direct link is, as we have just pointed out,
between the agencies of government that share directly in the profit.
However, the tax revenues are substantial and cannot be gainsaid by
any government. Keeping in mind that there is a distinction between
the government (the politically elected and appointed officials) and the
state (the permanent bureaucracy that lingers on from one election to
the next regardless of changes in government), it is clear that the
government's tenure in office is dependent in part upon placating a
wide range of conflicting and competing interests. A government that
can solve the problem of how to increase tax revenues for expenditures
on defense, welfare, education, and policing without simultaneously
taxing the rich beyond their tolerance limits is a government likely to
stay in power for a very long time. So long as the economy is expanding at a fairly rapid rate, this can be accomplished without great
difficulty. Once the economy begins to decline in its rate of growth,
however, the government in power is pressed between conflicting
forces that make its hold on the reins of power tenuous. One solution,
though not a totally adequate one, is to legalize gambling, thereby
providing a quick and fluid source of added tax revenues. Thus, it was
not surprising to find that the controversy over Bally, particularly, and
gambling, generally, created considerable consternation within the
government of the late 1960s. In 1972, after much controversy, the
State Lottery Committee was appointed to investigate gambling in
Sweden and to make recommendations to the government. In March,

1975, the Committee reported that the present situation was fraught with potential danger and inequities; it recommended that gambling be taken over by the state—nationalized, as it were. The Minister of Finance, at the time, refuse to make a proposal to the government consistent with the Committee's recommendations. In the traditional procedures of Swedish government, a recommendation from a committee would usually be proposed by the appropriate minister for legislative action, whether or not the Minister agreed with the proposal. The Lottery Committee's proposal was, however, "sat on" by the Minister of Finance. The threat of nationalization of gambling was over—at least for the moment.

As a final gesture of sincerity, Bally offered to sell 80% of its stock in the bingo parlors to sports clubs—those organizations that support amateur football clubs and other sports activities. This gesture was approved and relieved Bally of much criticism, as now ostensibly the "profits" from the bingo parlors went directly to the sports clubs with Bally retaining only a token share of the stock. The stock in these clubs was sold for $300,000—a considerable profit over Bally's initial investment. Furthermore, Bally retained the most profitable aspect of the bingo parlors—the management and servicing of the slot machines. And, finally, Bally negotiated a contract with the clubs by which Bally was paid 15%–25% of gross for running the machines and parlors, plus a 5% profit. All of this in the end was more of a profit boondoggle than a sacrifice. It was a perfect illustration of how a conflict generated by contradictions leads to a resolution that, on the surface, establishes the legitimacy of the entire operation while at the same time enhancing the profits of the corporation.

By the end of the 1960s, there were slot machines in hotels, motels, restaurants, coffee shops, gas stations, boats (ferries), sex clubs, social clubs, and cinemas throughout Sweden. Furthermore, there were slot machines in private clubs, sport clubs, places where people worked, and in shops. According to figures produced by the slot machine industry, there were over 10,000 slot machines in Sweden at the end of 1968. Most of these machines were imported from the United States, with smaller numbers coming from Great Britain and Australia. The importation of slot machines was highest during the years 1967–1969. In 1965, slot machines were imported for a total of $1 million; 1966, $700,000; 1967, $1 million; 1968, $4 million; and 1969, $10 million. These numbers do not reflect the entire market for slot machines because some are imported and sold illegally. In fact, the number of slot machines in Sweden at the end of 1968 was not 10,000, as the official reports claim, but more nearly 20,000.

Generally, the slot machines are owned by a few corporations that put the machines in the place of business. The machines are leased by the owner of the establishment. There is then a contract between the owner of the business and the owner of the slot machines in which it is specified how the profits should be shared.

The slot machine owners are organized in the "National Branch of the Swedish Slot Machine Owners." At the end of the 1960s, there were approximately 60 members of that organization.

It is difficult to estimate profits and income from slot machines, given the nature of the business and the illegal character of it. But some estimates are possible. The slot machine owners give data that suggest that a slot machine, on the average, gives $2,000 a year in profit. Some men in the business have stated that this estimate is ludicrously low. Indeed, one manager of a club in central Stockholm estimates that each machine in his club takes in $3,000 *daily*. Investigations made by the Swedish police have invariably shown that the profits must be much higher than $2,000 a year.

According to the most conservative estimates, it was in the late 1960s, nonetheless, a very large business. Taking the annual $2,000 per machine estimate provided by the owners themselves means the gross volume of business was nearly $100 million a year. The profits from the total of 10,000 machines would have been $14 million a year. These figures assume that: (a) there were only 10,000 machines in Sweden at the end of the 1960s; (b) these machines paid back to the owners only an average of $2,000 per year; and (c) that the machines were set to pay to the players 80% of the money put into them. Each of these assumptions is undoubtedly false, but even accepting them it is clear that the market in slot machines and their use was very large indeed in Sweden in the late 1960s.

Slot machines were not the only legal gambling market in Sweden at this time. Bingo was also very big business. At the end of the 1950s the bingo business began in Sweden. At that time sports clubs, especially in southern Sweden, began arranging to have bingo games. After that, bingo spread across the Swedish plains. At the end of 1968 (less than ten years later), there were over 10,000 licenses issued by the State granting clubs or individuals the right to organize and operate bingo parlors. The total turnover of bingo games that took place under these licenses were about $90 million. But, in addition to these licensed bingo games, there were unlicensed games estimated to have taken in about the same amount as the licensed ones—that is, another $90 million. If you look at these figures from a slightly different perspective, you could say that by the end of the 1960s there were over 60,000 bingo players daily throughout Sweden. The number of persons interested enough in bingo to play it at some time during the year was in excess of 300,000.

Who were the people who organized, invested in, and ran the bingo market? At first the games were arranged by the local sports clubs, but gradually, especially in the larger cities, companies grew up specializing in the arrangement of bingo for sports clubs (for a percentage of the profits of course). Bingo cards and the prizes given to those who won were supplied by these companies. In some areas there were also some privately owned places used only for bingo owned by these entrepreneurs. In these privately owned places everything from the machinery to personnel was arranged for by the entrepreneur. The sport club in whose name these private businesses were arranged received a share of the profits. The officially admitted profits of the bingo operations were claimed to be around 13% of the turnover.

Roulette

During the 1950s, roulette began appearing in a few restaurants in Sweden. It was generally a complement to other forms of entertainment: dancing, floor shows, music, and such. By the end of 1968, there were 268 restaurants with licenses permitting them to have roulette. Besides the licensed roulette places, there was a great deal of illegal roulette playing (as well as other gambling) in so-called private clubs—that is, in clubs that claimed to be open only to "members," but which were, in fact, open to the public providing one could pass the superficial test at the door designed to determine that the prospective customer was not a hostile police officer (friendly police officers were, of course, always welcome.)

Roulette playing was usually arranged by a company that specialized in the equipment and personel necessary to run the games. There were 30 such companies at the end of the 1960s, but the lion's share of the business was controlled by ten companies.

The roulette companies shared the profits—negotiated on an individual basis—with the owners of the restaurants and the like. Official estimates were that the roulette companies took about one-third of the profits: this is probably too low even for the percentage existing in the official agreements between the roulette companies and the restaurant owners. It is certainly a gross underestimate of the profits actually taken.

Roulette, like bingo, slot machines, horse racing, and, indeed, any form of gambling, is an enterprise that is open to "the skim" to an extraordinary degree. For it is absolutely impossible to estimate accurately the amount of money that the roulette table is making in profits. The roulette table that runs ten, twelve, or even six hours a day runs with people constantly placing bets in varying amounts and the "croupier" giving back chips to those who win and shoveling into a box the chips of the people who lose. The chips are purchased at the tables and at central cages in the establishment. Only those who count the money at the end of the evening can possibly know how much has been taken in. If those who count the proceeds slip some of it into a bag or a parcel before the total is reported to the owner, no one is the wiser—except perhaps the roulette company with records from many other establishments to go by. The point is that an enterprising roulette company can easily skim 20%–30% of the profits off the top of the winnings before the restaurant or club owner ever sees the tally. This profit, then, is hidden not only from the owner of the establishment, but from the tax collector as well.

If the restaurant owner is a suspicious type who insists on being around at the final tally of each night's proceeds (unlikely, given the length of time the owner would need to perform this check), then the people who take the money in the cages or the croupier can simply be instructed to take the skim before it ever reaches the bag from which the final count is made. The roulette company protects itself against "crooked" personnel by having one of the managers work in the cage from time to time to be sure that the skim is as large as it should be and that the profits are counted in accordance with the instructions that the company has given to its employees.

Skimming profits from bingo operations is accomplished similarly. The manufacturers of bingo cards are suspiciously willing to provide cards with duplicate numbers, with serialized figures that are used to disguise the number of cards purchased and the number sold in the course of a day's, week's, month's, or year's operation. Thereafter, the only problem for those running the bingo operations is how to transfer physically the money collected from the customers to the pouch of the company that organizes the play. That sleight-of-hand trick is not at all difficult to accomplish.

Skimming from slot machines (one-armed bandits) involves a rather more complicated process. By Swedish law, a slot machine must pay back to the customer 80% of the money put into the machine. Naturally, it is not required that this be true for each customer who plays. It is only required that it be true over the long haul. This can be accomplished quite simply because all slot machines are manufactured with a mechanism that can be set to return whatever percentage of the amount put in that the owner wishes. A machine can be set to give back nothing, or it can be set to give back 100%. The "chance" or "gamble" in the machine is not how much of what is put in will be returned, it is only when the amount to be returned will be returned and whether it is returned in the form of jackpots, small payoffs, or large ones.

The machines are also constructed with a counter that records every coin that is put into them. In the machines legally available in Sweden, this counter is enclosed in such a way that it cannot be changed or altered without an inspector being able to tell that this has been done. Finally, the machines record how much money is paid out. Thus, an inspector can theoretically enter a machine, see how much has been put into the machine since the last inspection, see how much has been paid out, and thereby know (a) what the total amount of the machine's business has been, and (b) whether the machine has paid off its required 80%. Naturally, the chance element in the game means that for any given six-month or six-week period, the machine might only pay off 70% but during another period it should then pay off 90%. There is, then, a range of acceptable payoff percentages that would not arouse suspicion. But, if a machine constantly paid off 10%, or even 40%, then the inspector would, of course, suspect that the machine had not been correctly set.

One technique for skimming from the one-armed bandits is for the owner (or one of his employees) to "service" the machine by opening it and holding the jackpot line (three baboons in a row or three orchids diagonally, for example) while pulling the arm of the machine down. This has the effect of emptying the machine of all of its receipts, setting the official record on the counter to indicate that the machine has paid off its required 80%, assuring that the machine will not pay off for the next week or so because its payoff percentage will already have been consumed by the establishment, and, finally, keeping almost all of the receipts in the form of profit for the company.

Where the machine is taking in more money than the owners wish to admit for tax purposes, then it is necessary to set the number of plays recorded on the machine. This can be accomplished by having the machine record every other or every fourth coin rather than every coin. An inspector checking the machine would find it virtually impossible to realize this but there is always a chance that the inspector might become suspicious. It is, therefore, wise for the company that leases the machines to have either in its employ or in its complicity, some of the inspectors who are responsible for checking the machines. In some cases, that is precisely what has happened. Inspectors are not always above the temptations offered by such easy profits from such an "innocuous" source. We will return to this later; first, we should look briefly at some relevant legislation.

Horse Racing

Legal horse racing in Sweden is limited to licensed tracks with competition between nonthoroughbred horses. Betting is restricted to betting at the track with official bet-takers. The legal restrictions are easily circumvented and circumvention enhances profits substantially.

Thoroughbred horses are substantially faster than nonthoroughbreds. By introducing a thoroughbred into a race, the owner not only has a guaranteed winner whenever it is desired, the owner, trainer, or, for that matter, the jockey can hold the horse back and lose whenever it is advantageous. Given the large amounts of money bet on horse races, it is not surprising to find that this practice has been fairly widespread over the years.

There is also considerable off-track illegal betting connected with the races. Indeed, Sweden is the only place we know of where illegal bookmakers take bets *at the track*. In the clubhouse of the Manor Race Track outside Stockholm, several bookmakers set up tables every Sunday and conduct business, paying the same odds that the track pays. In addition, there is considerable off-track betting, most of which takes place in the card clubs and "social clubs" sprinkled throughout the country, and especially in the major cities. Obviously, these bookmaking activities serve those who wish to bet on the horses, but do not want to go to the track.

One of the more subtle illegal activities connected with horse racing is the sale of winning betting tickets. This, too, is connected with tax evasion. People whose incomes are derived largely or significantly from illegal enterprises must have a way of demonstrating to authorities that they can reasonably account for a standard of living in excess of the income they claim for personal taxes. Winnings from gambling on horses are *not* part of personal income for tax purposes—the tax being paid presumably at the time of winning the bet. Thus, people who wish to demonstrate that their incomes are justified will pay 20%–30% of the price of a large winning ticket in order to have this as a record for the tax authorities to show their earnings. Someone who wins a large amount can thus sell his winning ticket worth, say $2,000, for $2,400. The purchaser will then cash it in for $2,000, thus "losing" $400, but in fact gaining a legitimation for money earned illegally, or money, although earned legally, that has not been reported as taxable income.

The police estimate that illegal betting on horses in Sweden amounts to one-third of the total amount bet. The official records of the race tracks show that each year there is $300 million bet at race tracks; using the police estimate of one-third this means that illegal betting constitutes a business enterprise amounting to $100 million a year. Needless to say, the profits of those who finance and manage these illegal betting activities are not taxable, thus making the profit even greater. Given that the tax structure on personal incomes earned from business range from 50% to 90%, this means that the real value of this illegal business is astronomical.

Usury

Until now, we have been exploring what are basically legal businesses, but which by their nature are involved in many illegal acts as well—some of which are endemic, others are simply spin-offs. We turn now to an examination of businesses that are wholly illegal, but which at least in part grow up as services to legal businesses. Usury is an example of such an enterprise.

People who own or manage gambling clubs, even legal ones, must occasionally obtain large amounts of cash at odd hours. The very nature of the business makes it necessary to have usurers. No one can always tell how much a casino will lose in a given evening, or for that matter, how much it will make. Over time, of course, the probabilities favor the casino such that it will make substantial profits, but on any given evening the manager may have to have several hundred thousand dollars available. Large organizations can provide sufficient security to allow keeping that much capital, but smaller operators may not have so much capital readily available, and even if they could, the risk of theft makes it dangerous to keep large amounts on hand. Thus, the usurer becomes an integral part of the business. A casino operator in Sweden tells the following story:

> Whenever I need extra money I have two or three people I can go to anytime: day or night and they will loan me very quickly a hundred or two hundred thousand kronor. I don't know where they get it from but I had heard it was from [Mr. X]. I ran short in the casino one night and needed forty thousand kronor. I kould not find any of the people I usually dealt with so I called [Mr. X]. He agreed to make the loan and I went to his house to get the money. I agreed to pay him back fifty thousand kronor the next day, which I did.

This is strictly illegal, of course. The maximum rate of interest that can be charged on loans is set by law, but not everyone who wants or needs money can obtain the necessary capital from lending institutions; they must then seek it elsewhere. Sometimes, as in the above case, the nature of their business leads them to seek assistance from private lenders. These private lenders, in turn, can charge much higher than legal interest rates. Other businesses requiring large amounts of capital are themselves illegal—drug importation, for example. The financier is also a critical link in this chain of endeavors. Banks will not loan money for illegal transactions, such as drugs, but private citizens with capital they wish to increase can and do. They become knowledgeable about the drug business in which they are investing and they develop mechanisms of controlling people who might otherwise refuse to pay back the loans, jeopardize their business, tell the police, or whatever might threaten the security of their investments and their profits. Everyday business people protect themselves in such matters through legal contracts and the threat of the law to force people to pay their debts. People in illegal business cannot formally request and obtain such protection by state intervention in disputes. People engaged in illegal businesses must essentially duplicate this process with their own "police force" (often referred to as a group of "enforcers"), their own investigators, and their own collectors. In this way the involvement of someone in usury connected with illegal or legal businesses necessarily involves the person in other illegal acts, such as the use of violence, threats of the use of violence, and intimidation to force cooperation.

Once established, this organization of violence and potential violence generally takes on a life of its own. Just as police bureaucracies inevitably create their own peculiar logic and form independent of the intentions of the legislative and judicial enactments that created them, so too do those parts of illegal businesses concerned with enforcing the rules and interests of those at the top become self-generating and may be profitable in ways that were not originally anticipated. For example, the same people who have become specialized in the use of violence as a means of collecting gambling debts, repayment of loans, and the high interest can be employed in ways that increase the degree to which one group of financiers and business people have a monopoly over a particular market.

An illustration of this in Stockholm has occurred in connection with the issuing of licenses for liquor sales and the development of a "protection" racket that is under the control of the same people who are generally financing and organizing illegal gambling and the illegal importation of drugs. The protection business works rather easily. By law, a restaurant owner or cabaret owner who sells liquor can have his or her license removed if fighting or rowdiness occurs on the premises.

One restaurant owner reports that when he refused to pay protection to a group of men who came and demanded such payment, he discovered very shortly that every evening there were fights breaking out in his business establishment. For several nights, the police had to be called to come and restore order, and he was threatened with losing his license. He was also contacted simultaneously by the same men who had come to see him before. He agreed this time to pay this group of men a monthly fee to see that fights and such things did not disrupt his business. Had he not agreed to make this payment, the owner is quite sure that these disturbances would have continued, he would have lost his liquor license, been forced to sell the restaurant, and lost much money. The new owners, he believes, would have been the same group of financiers who were forcing him to pay protection.

Of course, one can argue that this man could have gone to the police and sued in court to have this stopped. But such allegations are almost impossible to prove. Furthermore, it might have stopped these particular men from starting fights, but there are others who would replace them. In the end the choice will be between making payments for protection or going out of business. This particular man made the payments and has had "no further trouble."

This case also illustrates how people engaged in one illegal enterprise branch out into others. A man referred to by Swedish press as "Mr. X" and reputed, we believe erroneously, to be the main figure in "organized crime" in Sweden, is one of the principal usurers for gambling casinos, drug traffickers, brothels, and sundry other illegal enterprises. He is also closely allied with an associate with whom he personally has forced some restaurants and casinos to pay protection to avoid being "closed down." It is a startling fact that someone whose income is easily in the millions of dollars a year would stoop to "strong arming" restaurant owners for what must be only small change to his income. The evidence suggests, however, that such profit aggrandizement is not uncommon among business people whether they be engaged in legal or illegal businesses. It is no more a surprise than to discover that International Telephone and Telegraph hires illegal aliens for their restaurants in order to avoid paying what in comparison with ITT's profits must amount to a miniscule contribution to their employee's welfare benefits.

Usury is, of course, not limited to loaning money to gambling casinos after hours. There are individuals and organizations dependent on obtaining large sums of money in a short period of time for illegal purposes: buying for example, some stolen automobiles that have suddenly appeared and must be "unloaded" immediately; purchasing a large shipment of heroin, cocaine, or amphetamines. These illegal transactions cannot be predicted and planned for in the same way that "normal business" can. People trafficking in illegal commodities, be they stolen paintings or blackmarket cigarettes, must adhere to a very flexible schedule of operations. They must be able to decide at the last moment to fly the goods over the border rather than take them by boat. Furthermore, because secrecy is imperative, these business people cannot afford to communicate with those interested in purchasing the ill-gotten goods. As a result there is a built-in, structural demand for usurers who will loan large amounts of money on short notice and who will do so with absolute discretion. The same people, in other words, who have learned how to make illegal loans to legal businesses are also in a position to make illegal loans to illegal businesses. In time, bankers tend to become managers. Just as the Swedish National Bank places people on the board of directors of major corporations, so usurers become more and more involved in the day-to-day operations of the illegal businesses that they underwrite. This comes about as a way of increasing profits by cutting out middlemen and as a way of minimizing risks by reducing the number of people involved. The secret, of course, is to be as closely involved in the illegal businesses as one can be without jeopardizing the safety one has by being a "back man" for the operation.

Illegal Drugs

In the last ten to fifteen years, Sweden has become one of the most important markets for illegal drugs in Europe. It is a market of very great potential in a nation where unemployment among youth runs close to 20% of the population between 18 and 25; where alienation from work is consistent with the alienation of workers throughout the capitalist world; where welfare payments and unemployment benefits are sufficient to guarantee that even the unemployed youth will have some money to spend in support of his or her drug habit.

That drug abuse is rampant can be observed by anyone who walks slowly throught the Central Terminal (T-Centralen) of Stockholm's underground. Little groups of people buying and selling dope abound. The blatancy of some of these transactions is truly surprising in view of the legal sanctions that might be imposed. One afternoon, a man stepped out of a toilet cubicle with a hypodermic needle filled with blood in his hand. He casually washed the needle in the washbasin, nonchalantly put the neddle in his shirt pocket so that it protruded clearly for all the world to see, and sauntered out of the washroom, across the foyer of the terminal where several policemen were standing observing the crowd.

For all of the openness of the drug scene in Stockholm, it is still difficult to establish very precise estimates of the extent of the market. There are basically three major markets in drugs: heroin, amphetamines, and hashish. There is a smaller, but rapidly expanding market in cocaine, but at the time of our study, the cocaine market was only beginning to see its growth period; we therefore concentrate on the others.

It is estimated by social workers and state officials in drug rehabilitation services that there are only 2,000 heroin addicts in Sweden low. People "closer to the action," that is, those engaged in the sale and distribution of heroin, put the number of "addicted heroin users" at closer to 5,000. In addition, these people insist that there are many other people who are sometime-users of heroin who make the market much larger than the 5,000 figure reflects. There is also the fact that on several occasions very large shipments of heroin have been discovered coming into Sweden from abroad—shipments that are too large to be accounted for by too small a number of addicts. For example, in 1975 a satchel containing heroin valued at 130 million kronor was "found" by customs agents at the airport in Linskorping.

Nevertheless, even if we take as accurate the very conservative estimate of 2,000 heroin addicts in Sweden, we are still talking about a very large import industry. It is estimated that the average heroin user spends $100 a day to support his or her habit. This means that the gross volume of business in heroin in Sweden is $40 million a year. If we accept as accurate a more realistic estimate of 5,000 addicts in Sweden, then the volume of business in heroin goes up to $100 million a year.

It is often alleged by people involved in attempts to work with heroin addicts that the heroin market is principally supplied by personal contacts. The "typical" supply route was described by one person thusly:

> One of the addicts will get together with his friends and put together enough money to buy a small amount of heroin. Then he will go to Amsterdam, purchase the stuff and bring it back and split it amongst his friends.

Although it may be true that some of the heroin in Sweden is supplied by this route, it is clear that most of it is not. No people involved in the supply of heroin themselves nor any of the addicts to whom we talked felt that this route was an important source of heroin. These people— those closer to the scene and the action—all told of suppliers who had to be contacted by a circuitous route. The police confirmed that this was the more typical procedure for the distribution of heroin:

> If you want some dope, heroin or hash or amphetamines, you let it be known to someone who knows you, even if you've just met them. They will in all likelihood introduce you to someone else who says he knows another person who lives at such and such an address. Then you go to that address, probably 24 hours later, meet someone there who says he doesn't have the stuff but that if you give him the money he can get it for you. After you give him thee money, or some of it—say, half the cost—then he will give you a phone number to call, and a meeting will be arranged where you can pick up the stuff you want and pay the other half of the money.

This procedure, it was said, helps to maintain the secrecy of the people selling heroin and provides them maximum protection from police detection. Others, people who had bought heroin for their own use, described the process as more straightforward, involving only contacting a "friend" who sold the drug.

There is substantial other evidence that the heroin supply is a highly organized affair involving the investment of substantial amounts of money that could not be raised among a group of addicts. The police have captured shipments of heroin coming into Sweden that totaled several hundred million kronor. Furthermore, it is difficult to simply "go to Amsterdam or Munich" and buy a supply of heroin. Wholesalers are suspicious and cautious business people who sell only when they are relatively certain that the purchaser is not in the employ of the police. Given that in Europe these wholesalers must contend not only with local police whom they may know and therefore be in a fairly good position to identify, but also with Interpol and police from other countries as well, they are extremely cautious. An addict, who is by virtue of addiction bound to be a poor risk (susceptible to police pressure to inform in return for a supply of free drugs), is high on the list of suspicious people from the perspective of the wholesaler.

Finally, we talked at length with informants who have themselves been engaged in the drug business. These people invariably tell the same story: that the drug business is financed by a relatively small group of people who arrange for the purchase of drugs from international sources and hire local people to import the drugs and to distribute them to selected agents. The experience of one of our informants, who was involved in the business of supplying illegal drugs for several years, is illustrative:

> I had borrowed and saved enough money from my work to open a small sex club. We had a few slot machines, some pornographic movies and drinks. It was a pretty good business. It was all legal; all according to law.

One weekend I was visiting friends in Malmö and I met a man I had known before I bought the club. We began drinking beer and talking about different things. Toward the end of the evening he asked me if I would like to make some quick money. I asked him how and he said by helping him smuggle some drugs from West Germany to Sweden. He told me that it was all arranged; all we had to do was go to West Germany and pick up a car and drive it back to Sweden.

We went that very night to West Germany where we met a man in a parking lot just across the border. He gave us the keys to a car which I then drove back to Sweden and the man who had set this up drove my car back. Everything went smoothly and after that I began making frequent trips to Germany to do the same thing.

At first the drugs were turned over to this guy who had first introduced me to the business. But then we began hiding them in the slot machines in my club. Then people I knew or people who were sent to me by this guy would come in and I would sell them a hundred or two hundred capsules—it was mostly amphetamines; or if it was heroin I'd sell them two or three grams. But I wasn't selling to people who were using them. I was a wholesaler and I sold them to people who retailed them. I'd pay 20 kronor ($4.00) for a capsule of amphetamines and sell them for 40 kronor ($8.00). The people who bought them from me then sold them for 60 kronor ($12.00) and sometimes they would be resold at the "street price" of 80 kronor ($16.00). I think the people I bought them from paid 5–10 kronor ($1.00–$2.00) apiece for them. I did this for several several years; I made lots of money. I had a new Mercedes Sports car and good clothes. My kids had lots of money and so did my wife. Then I got arrested for taking drugs; I had begun taking them during this time too. So, I was arrested for taking them and sent to prison for eight years.

The cost of heroin in 1972 breaks down in a similar fashion. One kilo of heroin was worth $2 million on the retail market. Wholesale, this kilo would cost approximately $200,000. A hekto (1/10 of a kilo) cost about $30,000. The addict payed about $70 for a fix, which consists of 0.2 to 0.3 grams of heroin.

The Structure of Illegal Business in Sweden

The social organization of illegal businesses in Sweden is by now becoming quite clear. The mainstay of these businesses are the three horsemen of usury, gambling, and illegal drugs. Usury consists of short term, high interest, illegal loans to gambling casinos, drug traffickers, and others engaged in illegal or semilegal businesses who for whatever reasons do not qualify for loans from state-sanctioned lending institutions, such as banks. Gambling is varied and has both legal and illegal manifestations. The legal gambling consists of slot machines that are licensed and taxed, gambling casinos with slot machines, roulette tables, and on-track betting on horses. Illegal aspects of these enterprises consist of "skimming" profits from slot machines and roulette tables, borrowing money illegally, and the selling of "protection" to avert trouble for the owners of casinos. Illegal gambling, which is widespread, takes many forms: bookmaking which is spread throughout the country in social clubs, sex clubs, and card clubs—as well as at the race track; card games where gambling is involved; and the widespread distribution of illegal slot machines and gambling casinos.

The illegal drug industry involves many of the same social and structural relations as gambling and usury. Financing large transactions on short notice requires usurers: sex, social, and card clubs are often the transmission point for smuggled drugs. Both the suppliers and users of these various illegal activities tend to move in and out of the various transactions. This is not difficult to explain; the kinds of skill and social connection necessary for one illegal activity are easily carried over to others. To be sure, some people (especially at the lower level) specialize and have little to do with "other people's hustles," but the more general pattern seems to be to move freely in and out of various illegal hustles.

There is a high degree of consensus among police, newspaper reporters who have investigated various aspects of illegal business, and people engaged in the illegal businesses themselves that there are between 7 and 13 "Swedish millionaires" who are the principal financiers and organizers of illegal businesses in Sweden. The precise number varies. The best informed officer in the Stockholm police says that there are ten such millionaires. A newspaper reporter, who has concentrated on the comings and goings of one of the more infamous of these men, thinks there are only six or seven major "back men," and that one person, the aforementioned "Mr. X," is *the* major "Godfather" in Sweden's organized crime. From our data, this seems highly unlikely. Indeed, it is more likely that "Mr. X" is a go-between for some other high level financiers rather than that he is "Mr. Big" in Sweden's illegal businesses. For our purposes, whether we are talking about 6, 7, or 15 "back men" is of little consequence. It is important to understand the *structure* of social relations created by these illegal enterprises, not the particulars of the people involved.

At the very top are the financiers: these are the people who supply the large amounts of capital necessary to open, operate, and deal in illegal services of commodities. For the sake of convenience, we will set the number of these people in Sweden at 15. These 15 people all have ready access to large amounts of liquid capital. In addition, most of these people also invest heavily in real estate—especially in properties that rely on illegal or quasi-legal activities for their income. One of the main financiers of illegal businesses, for example, owns several hotels and apartments where prostitution, drugs, illegal liquor sales, and gambling take place. Another financier owns hotels that are distribution points for drugs. Yet another is involved in horse racing as an owner of racehorses. Several of the major financiers of illegal businesses also have heavy investments in perfectly legal businesses: one owns a factory that employs several hundred people; another owns restaurants that are principally concerned with serving food (although these restaurants along with many others in the city, participate in the "gray labor" market that illegally hires aliens, but does not pay the workers either their minimum wage or the social security benefits they are supposed to receive).

Attached to the financiers and supporting illegal businesses of professional people (sometimes acting themselves as investors in various enterprises) necessary for the survival of *any* business—legal or illegal. Lawyers advise them on how to hide their money for the tax accountant; how to appear to be earning money legally while living luxuriously; how to deal with police and administrative hassles; and how to write contracts with legal businesses. The lawyer becomes the manager of the illegal empire. These lawyers tend to be relatively few in number; several known financiers use the same lawyer. Like financing illegal business, counseling illegal business people is a highly specialized task. In addition, there are accountants who are hired to give a smooth surface to the financing and architects who are instructed to design buildings that will afford the owners the maximum protection from police while enhancing the use of space for profit.

Immediately below the financiers are the gamblers, restaurant owners, sex club owners, and automobile dealers. Many of the people whose principal occupation is illegal business are engaged in several of these enterprises at the same time, hence we find considerable overlap between these key categories. Nonetheless, it is useful to isolate these different roles in order to get an understanding of the social relations involved.

Next are the wholesalers who purchase drugs, operate bookmaking, or serve as a go-between for the person getting the loan and the usurer. These people tend to be fairly transient—moving in and out of various illegal hustles and into and out of illegal business entirely.

Finally there are the retailers, the croupiers at the roulette tables, the people who maintain and operate the slot machines, and others. These lower-level people are the ones who sell the drugs to the users, who skim the profits off the machines or the roulette tables, who help the financiers and wholesalers collect debts owed them, who drive the cars that bring in the illegal drugs, and so on. Ironically, it is these people who are most often arrested and sent to prison as "criminals." Indeed, it is a fair generalization that the arrest and prosecution rate of people whose livelihood derives from illegal business activities is inversely related to their position in the hierarchy. The rich get richer and the poor go to prison.

Protecting Illegal Enterprises

As with any business, the central problem facing illegal business entrepreneurs is to maximize profits and minimize risks. One risk, shared by businesspeople everywhere, is that an investment will not pay off: a drug shipment is confiscated by the police; a loan is not repaid on time; a bookmaker absconds with the week's receipts; a "fixed" horse race does not stay fixed. For businesses with the appearance of operating within the law (no matter how many illegal acts they may commit in the course of doing business), the state stands as a protective cover, reducing some of these risks. People who do not pay their debts may be forced to by threat of having the state transfer some of their personal property to the person to whom they are indebted; shipments of goods that do not arrive on time can result in the state forcing the recalcitrant party to pay damages to the receiver; an employee who absconds with company money is liable to imprisonment and repayment of the stolen money. The illegal businessman has few of these protections provided by the state; thus, his risks are doubtless greater. In addition, illegal business faces the constant threat of exposure.

To protect themselves against the risk of straying shipments, unpaid debts, or monies misappropriated by employees, the illegal business establishes its own law enforcement system. The system lacks a judge and jury, but in other respects it closely resembles the state's legal apparatus. There are those who specialize in tracing people who have violated the rules, punishing them for their transgressions, forcing them to pay debts or return stolen property, and applying penal sanctions—not only to keep wayward members from repeating their offenses (special deterrence), but also as a warning to others who might contemplate such actions that their actions will not go unpunished (general deterrence). To accomplish their desired enforcement, the illegal business entrepreneurs develop the use of informants to tell them whether anyone is violating the rules; they repay these informants with special privileges (jobs, money, drugs, women) just as the police reward their informants. It is possible that this system of "justice" works considerably more efficiently than the state's, and it is probably no less "just."

The illegal entrepreneur faces one major problem not faced by legal business: the threat of exposure. This problem is ubiquitous and omnipresent for illegal business. Much of the resources of the industry are spent to reduce the likelihood of this risk. The problem, it must be noted, is *not* that the police will discover what is going on. The police know who is involved in these illegal businesses, and for the most part the police know where and when the activities are being conducted. The problem is that if the police are forced to act through public pressure or political machinations, they will have to interrupt the business. In part, this is simply a problem of keeping the police from getting sufficient evidence to arrest and convict people. But that is not unconnected to the greater problem of keeping the business from public scrutiny or political chicanery so that the police are not forced to do something.

Thus it is that illegal businesses are constantly wary of newspaper reporters, television newspeople, and others who might bring public attention to their endeavors. Indeed, there is a considerable amount of evidence that the potential of exposure by reporters is a problem that receives a good deal of official attention among those who deal in illegal services and commodities.

One Swedish reporter, Berndt von Corswandt, conducted an extensive investigation into the illegal drug business in Sweden. This was at a time when the official line of the police and the government was that there was no substantial "drug problem," nor was there an "illegal drug industry" in Sweden. Von Corswandt found out differently. People close to him said that he had information that linked political figures, law enforcement officials, and drug traffickers into a criminal cartel. What von Corswandt knew we will never know—he died under suspicious circumstances before he was able to publish all of his findings.

In the midst of his investigation into the illegal drug business in Sweden, von Corswandt was sent to London as a correspondent for the weekly newsmagazine, *Se*. Shortly after he arrived in London, he was found dead in his apartment. The cause of death was an overdose of pills. No package for the pills was found in the apartment. There was no suicide note. According to the photographer with whom Corswandt worked, he did not drive the car home himself on that evening. The London police did not exclude murder, but they gave little thought to why this man might have killed himself from an overdose of drugs. Such deaths are not uncommon, and visitors are by definition beyond the pale of immediate concern to local police. For this or some more sinister reason, the London constabulary handled the matter routinely and without fanfare. They notified the Swedish authorities, but made no particular point of the fact. They did not investigate further to see if the man had a history of drug abuse.

The police in Sweden also showed little interest. The incident had occurred far from home shores; there was no great pressure to investigate. There was no reason to doubt the validity or the appropriateness of the interpretation provided by the London officials. The case was quickly "closed."

People close to the reporter were, however, shocked, not only at this death, which is, of course, shocking in any event, but because of the alleged cause of death. Berndt von Corswandt was not known to have ever taken drugs of any kind. He was, in fact, known by friends and associates as a person who was deeply concerned with physical fitness. He skied regularly and even took part in amateur competition. His fiancee swore that she would have known had he ever taken drugs; she said he never did. So, too, did his colleagues on the newspaper where he worked.

Rumors to the effect that Sweden had a highly developed narcotics business were often heard among journalists and others interested in criminality. As a result, several journalists began independent investigations of narcotics. Each time, these investigators were warned to stop their inquiry. One reporter for a weekly newsmagazine, assigned the task of investigating rumors of a narcotics ring in Sweden that was connected with other types of organized crime, received an anonymous telephone call. The caller told the reporter: "It only costs 800 kronor to get you. We just import a Turk and he flies back to Turkey on the same day." The reporter believed that this threat was made at the behest of one of Sweden's most notorious criminal figures.

People who have tried to investigate the narcotics traffic have not only been threatened by anonymous phone calls, they have often been discouraged from their investigation by government officials. One newspaper reporter, who was gathering evidence linking police officers and the narcotics traffickers, was quietly summoned by a police officer and warned that he would be in serious danger if he did not stop his investigation. The police officer indicated quite clearly that the danger would be from police action, not solely from the possible reprisals of narcotics traffickers.

There is good reason for the police and the government to attempt to suppress an exposure of organized crime. Sweden had an amazingly stable political situation for over 40 years. The Social Democrats came to power during the depression, ostensibly as the party to represent labor interests in opposition to the interests of capitalists. Over the years the leaders of government have consistently maintained this image to such an extent that they have, until 1970, managed to win national and local elections with only minor opposition. In recent years, however, perhaps as the ability to sustain the illusion of serving the interests of labor has become more difficult, the political power of the Social Democrats has begun to wane. Certainly, if it could be shown that Sweden is not the harmonious, crime-free society that the Social Democrats have managed to convey as the image of contemporary Sweden, then the blame for the less-than-utopian reality would necessarily be born by the party that has held power for most of these past 40 years. Given the emerging threat to its power from other sources, the fact that a major organized-crime system might be exposed as existing in Sweden would certainly be a serious blow to the image of the government.

This is true above and beyond the fact that some people in the government and among the police are profitting from the existing organized criminal activities and therefore wishing to protect the system for their own personal benefit. It is indeed in this coalescence of interests between the political leadership, the state, and the personal interests of individual bureaucrats that we find the key to understanding why criminal organizations emerge, why economic crimes are tolerated, and why relevant laws are systematically enforced with nothing like the vigor of enforcement that characterizes other crimes.

There are good theoretical and some empirical reasons for thinking that all this organized illegal activity cannot and does not go on without the complicity and cooperation of government and police officials. Theoretically, it is inconceivable, with all the profits being made and the clear necessity for reducing personal risks as much as possible, that people at the top levels of illegal business in Sweden would not *try* to co-opt government and police officials through bribes and favors. Obviously, help from politically important people, bureaucrats in key positions in government and, of course, police officials would be investments that would vastly increase not only the predictability of the profits and investments but would assure an ongoing and less variable business enterprise. It is also clearly the case that the people involved in Sweden's illegal business organizations know of the very great advantage American illegal businessmen have experienced as a result of using bribes and favors.

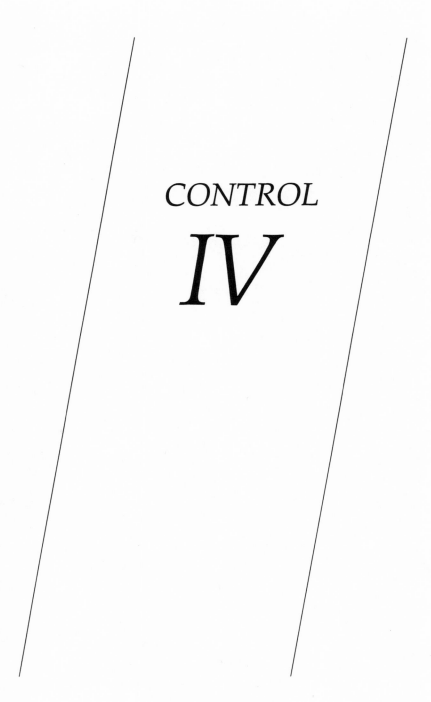

CONTROL
IV

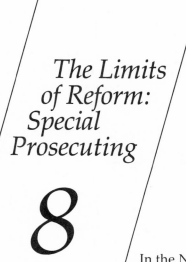

The Limits of Reform: Special Prosecuting

8

In the National Advisory Committee on Criminal Justice Standards and Goals' *Report of the Task Force on Organized Crime*, it is noted that the "influence of organized crime in the political sphere . . . permits all of its operations—the legitimate and the illicit—to flourish." Indeed, the *Report* continues that "the final explanation offered for the growth of organized crime and corruption concerns the structure of government in the United States—particularly at the State and local levels."

> The American pattern of fragmentation of governmental authority . . . tends to guarantee that attacks on crime syndicates or other corrupters will be fragmented, that results will be delayed, and that most reform movements can be outwaited.
>
> Although it might be argued that this fragmentation at least protects the public from a systematic tyranny by a corrupt leader, that the same public must be prepared to pay the price of inefficient and protracted law enforcement efforts. Furthermore, in a nation divided into thousands of local governments, a crime syndicate that can buy control of key officials in just one police department can thereby secure for itself a base of operations for a gambling or drug network spanning an entire metropolitan area.[2]

One of the linchpins in the social system of organized crime, recognized and discussed by the Committee on Standards and Goals, is the local prosecutor. Several of the recommended Standards deal exclusively with the office of prosecutor. One example is Standard 1.3, which comments that "Where the prosecutor's office is corrupt, the efforts of the most dedicated police agencies can be destroyed. To separate the prosecutor's office from corrupting influences, all members of that office should be barred from partisan political activity."[3] Much more significant than the above recommendation, however, is Standard 7.2 "Statewide Authority for Supersession," which calls for the establishment of procedures to authorize "the statewide organized crime prosecutor to supersede a local prosecutor in a specific ase of investigation."[4] What is notable about the Committee's suggestion in this case is the merging of supersession, an important but relatively unknown response to local corruption,[5] with the call for a statewide organized crime prosecutor.

The recommendations of the Task Force and the attendant assumptions that changes in law can successfully suppress organized crime networks (for example by depoliticizing the prosecutor's office) contradict the explanation for the emergence and persistence of organized crime suggested in the preceding chapters. If, as we argue, crime networks are likely (albeit not inevitable) consequences of contradictions, conflicts, and attempted resolutions that are linked to the structure of capitalist democratic political economies, then tinerking with law and law enforcement practices will have little effect on the pattern of organized crime. We may ask, then, whether there is any evidence that previous attempts to supress organized crime through changes in law have been effective.

Attempts at legal supression form a part of the political history of many metropolitan communities vexed by the social system of organized crime. Despite this fact, there has been no systematic attempt to evaluate the effectiveness of these programs through an analysis of historical data. Without historical discussion and evaluation, there is no way of knowing if proposed remedies, such as those made by the Task Force, will have any utility at all. Moreover, beyond questions of utility lie the issues of the law-creation process itself and its alleged ability to remove criminal justice from its political nexus as an antidote to corruption, and hence organized crime. Can the nexus be broken, as it were, by some structural tinkering under the fiat of an abstraction like "depolitization?" If so, to what extent and for how long? There is no sense in pursuing these rhetorical interrogatories until we contextualize the phenomena by discussing a case study of supersession and several closely related incidents that spanned the decade of the 1930s in New York City.

Corruption in New York: The 1930s

Throughout the decade of the 1930s, a vigorous reform movement attacked the entrenched democratic machines, especially in Manhattan and Brooklyn, characterizing them as venal and corrupt. Charges against the Democratic party centered on the criminal justice bureaucracies that, in a series of investigations, were shown to be marked by a variety of criminal conspiracies. Criminal justice in New York was a system composed of "officials, such as the police, prosecutors, judges, bailiffs, and probation officers; mediators between the legal system and criminals, such as bail bondsmen, criminal lawyers, fixers and politicians; and finally, criminals."[6] This system, which operated through "diverse informal relationships and mutual obligations," developed through frequent contact between these groups. Racketeers linked with businesspeople and trade union leaders were also tied to politicians, police, prosecutors, and judges through complex patron–client networks; it was a "social system held together by friendships and favors." In fact, after surveying New York's criminal justice system during the early part of the decade, Constance Marshall wrote that the category of racketeer should be extended to incorporate bondspeople, lawyers, police, and prosecutors.[7]

New York's criminal justice bureaucracies were politicized: the various positions such as judge, court officer, district attorney, assistant district attorney, etc., were the rewards of successful politics.[8] The criminal justice bureaucracies were part of the patronage of municipal politicians; the authority of the bureaucracies was subordinate to the power of politicians and their patrons and clients, who included organized criminals. One of the results, therefore, was the protection of organized criminals.

The first crack in this fortress of corruption opened in the summer of 1930 when Samuel Seabury was appointed referee in an inquiry into the magistrates courts of New York City.[9] Initially, the investigation centered on police corruption and a vice ring. The work of Seabury and his staff uncovered a "racket in which innocent women were framed as prostitutes by an alliance of police officers, bondsmen, lawyers, assorted court clerks . . . magistrates and . . . politicians" who were in charge of political appointments to the lowest criminal courts.[10] Next, Seabury gathered testimony that indicated that some people working in or having connections with the criminal courts, including assistant district attorneys and certain favored lawyers, were receiving a share of the payoffs in the vice cases, as well as in cases resulting from gambling arrests. As a consequence of his findings, Seabury censured the magistrates for their lack of action "in the face of palpably perjurious testimony" by the vice squad. He also decided to inquire into the affairs of every magistrate in the city, calling them in one at a time and questioning them in private about their competency and honesty. Subsequently, when some of the judges were requested to disclose their testimony in public session, there was a sudden rush to resign by a number of them. Part of the evidence uncovered by Seabury disclosed that the positions as magistrates were obtained by crooked and inept attorneys: the positions were handed out by the political parties for services rendered.[11]

Writing about this first stage of the Seabury investigation, Charles Garrett commented that it was established that the judiciary was only one of many branches of government involved in corruption. Also revealed as grafters and crooks were members of the police department and an assistant district attorney. Most significantly, the scandals uncovered in the magistrates' courts created enormous pressure for other investigations into municipal government. As examples of official misconduct accumulated during the inquiry, the public began to "wonder how deep the corruption went." Soon it was asked why a special referee had to be appointed to lead this investigation. Finally this question was posed: "Where had the District Attorney been all this time?"[12]

Responding to the growing public clamor, on March 10, 1931, Governor Roosevelt selected Seabury, who was still conducting his inquiry into the magistrates' courts, to investigate charges against New York County District Attorney Thomas C. T. Crain. Seabury's inquiry into the activities of District Attorney Crain was revealing in two areas: first, it established Crain's neglect and incompetency; second, it gave New Yorkers a picture of extensive racketeering. It was concluded that both the district attorney and the police department had abjectly surrendered to racketeers.[13]

The third and last of the Seabury investigations began at the same time as his inquiry into charges against the District Attorney and before he completed the investigation of the magistrates. This time he was appointed counsel to the Joint Legislative Committee to Investigate the Affairs of the City of New York, headed by State Senator Samuel Hofstadter. It is reported that Seabury, while concerned with the activities of district leaders and minor municipal officials, had as an overall purpose the prosecution of Mayor James Walker.[14]

Beginning with the district leaders, Seabury established that Thomas M. Farley, Sheriff of New York County, Michael J. Cruse, City Clerk, Harry Perry, Chief Clerk of the City Court of New York, and James A. McQuade, Register of Kings County, had all been involved with professional gamblers, allowing them use of political clubhouses for gambling headquarters. Seabury also revealed that Farley, Cruse, Perry, and McQuade had accumulated a great deal of money within a short period of time on relatively small salaries. The case of Sheriff

Farley was instructive: Seabury asked the sheriff, who also was president of the Thomas M. Farley Association, and leader of the Fourteenth Assembly District, how it was that on a yearly salary of $8,500 he had in six years accumulated almost $400,000. Farley's explanation added a new phrase to the lexicon of American politics. He attributed his financial success to the mysterious qualities of a "wonderful box of tin." Farley was eventually removed from office by order of Governor Roosevelt.[15]

Other disclosures of malfeasance, misfeasance, and neglect followed. For example, it was found that Democratic politicians had used the $10,000,000 city relief fund of 1931 as a fund to reward cooperative politicos. Spectacular scandals also developed when the Hofstadter Committee inquired into the granting of franchises, leases, and permits by the city. Seabury next focused his attention on several Brooklyn politicians, including the Honorable Peter J. McGuiness, assistant commissioner of public works, and John H. McCooey, known for over two decades as Brooklyn's Democratic boss. Their stories were remarkably similar to Farley's.[16]

Finishing his excursion into the political machine in Brooklyn, Seabury finally turned to Mayor James Joseph Walker. After spending months in an intensive search of Walker's financial records in an attempt to locate *his* "tin box," Seabury's staff finally succeeded. The information they uncovered implicated Walker in the efforts of the Equitable Coach Company to secure a citywide bus franchise. For his services, which included helping the Equitable secure a franchise from the city's Board of Estimate, Walker received secret payments. Other facets of Walker's financial and administrative deals were also discovered. For example, Walker received $26,000 worth of bonds that were supposedly the mayor's profit from a stock deal in which he had not invested; the bonds had been sent by J. A. Sisto, a banker interested in one of New York's large taxicab companies. After the gift of the bonds, a Taxicab Control Board was founded, whose effect of limiting entry into the taxi business was an obvious help to the larger companies. Walker had other benefactors, such as Paul Block, a newspaper publisher, who started a joint brokerage account with Walker which in less than two years gave the mayor about $250,000. Following his interrogation of Walker, Seabury forwarded to the governor charges holding Walker unfit for office. Beginning on August 11, Roosevelt conducted public hearings in which he personally questioned the mayor. Finally, on September 1, 1932, Walker resigned.[17]

So ended what has been called the "greatest investigation of city corruption in this century." Clearly established was the pervasive and extensive corruption throughout the ranks of city government. With the venality of the political machine and the criminal justice system exposed, reform energies moved to the issue of the governance of the city. Within the reform movement, Seabury had assumed a dominant position and, as Arthur Mann ably reported, was instrumental in the selection of Fiorello La Guardia as the Fusion nominee for mayor. In 1933, La Guardia won a plurality in a tight three-way race. Beside the mayorality, Fusion won the other citywide races and three of the five Borough presidencies, thereby winning control of the Board of Estimate. Tammany did, however, hold onto the New York County office of district attorney. But soon this success turned sour as the lack of accomplishment by District Attorney William Copeland Dodge resulted in the appointment of Thomas E. Dewey as a special prosecutor.[18]

The process that led to the appointment of Dewey began with the revelations stemming from an investigation of a bail-bond racket, held before Commissioner Blanshard, who was La Guardia's newly appointed Commissioner of Accounts (New York's Department of Investigation). The evidence had stimulated a number of civic organizations, including the Society for the Prevention of Crime, led by the Reverend George Drew Egbert who was the pastor of the First Congretational Church in Flushing, New York, to initiate another drive against organized crime. The activities of this society, along with the continuing inquiry by the Commissioner of Accounts and statements by Mayor La Guardia to the effect that he had evidence for a number of indictments, would all turn into a famous dispute beginning in March, 1935, with District Attorney Dodge in the middle. Soon other groups and individuals entered the controversy that centered on the allegation that Dodge was reluctant to press an investigation into the bail-bond situation. Early in May, the grand jury investigating policy, bail-bonds, and vice, began withholding evidence from Dodge and his staff. Subsequently, the foreman of the grand jury, Lee Thompson Smith, announced that the meager success of the jury was directly attributable to legal barriers. A week after Thompson's statement, the Reverend Egbert suggested that Governor Lehman appoint a special deputy attorney general to supersede Dodge. Other interested parties joined the demand for the supersession of Dodge.[19]

Finally, in June, 1935, Governor Lehman odered Dodge to appoint a special prosecutor from a list of the Governor's choosing. Lehman made it clear that if Dodge did not accept this plan, he would supersede the district attorney. Recommended as candidates by the governor were Charles Evans Hughes, Jr., George Z. Medalie, Thomas D.

Thacher, and Charles H. Tuttle. Dodge accepted the plan. However, Lehman's choices for special prosecutor all announced they were unable to serve. In a joint statement, they strongly urged the appointment of Thomas E. Dewey, who was also supported by the local bar association. At the end of June, Lehman recommended Dewey to the district attorney with assurances of his confidence in Dewey's acceptance.[20]

Among Dewey's numerous and impressive accomplishments as special prosecutor and later as District Attorney of New York County (Manhattan) were the prosecutions of Lucky Luciano, Tammany Hall, politician James Hines, restaurant racketeers formerly headed by Dutch Schultz, and finally, gangsters Louis Buchalter and Jacob Shapiro. One might well argue that Dewey's efforts against Buchalter and Shapiro were his most important, and not simply because they were eventually convicted of various crimes, including murder. The activities and events constituting the criminal careers of Buchalter and Shapiro furnished Dewey with a continuing source of material that he masterfully utilized in his campaign for district attorney. In addition, Dewey's investigation of their usurpation of the flour trucking industry provided evidence that the criminal justice system in Brooklyn needed as much reform attention as Manhattan.[21]

Special Prosecutor Thomas E. Dewey's active interest in the affairs of Buchalter and Shapiro, which was sufficient to drive them into hiding in the summer of 1937, was evident as early as October, 1935, only a few months after Dewey had taken office. On October 11, 1935, Dewey's investigators raided the Perfection Coat Front Manufacturing Company and Leo Greenberg & Shapiro, Inc., seeking information about racketeering in the garment industry. At the same time, Dewey was also pursuing an inquiry into Buchalter's involvement in the flour trucking industry. Late in the year, Dewey's men seized the books and records of the Flour Truckmen's Association. Dewey also let it be known that he was seeking Max Silverman, the labor adjustor for the Association.[22]

The next clear indication of Dewey's concern with Buchalter and Shapiro came in the spring of 1936, when Oscar Saffer, a garment manufacturer, was charged with filing a fraudulent state income tax return in 1933. Saffer was described as a Buchalter associate who had channeled over $150,000 in illegal payments to Buchalter and Shapiro. In the fall of 1936 Dewey released information on his investigation into the bakery and flour trucking racket. Max Silverman was identified as Buchalter's front man in the closely related rackets. In January 1937, Dewey closed in on the bakery racket—an offshoot of the flour trucking racket—arresting David Elfenbein, president of a baking company, attorney Benjamin N. Spevack, William "Wolfie" Goldis, president of Teamster Local 138, and Samuel Schorr, an official of Local 138. Barent Ten Eyck, a Dewey assistant, gave an indication of the scope of the flour trucking and bakery rackets when he stated that the 1934 murder of William Snyder, former president of Local 138, was tied to these rackets.[23]

The trial in the bakery racket opened in the summer of 1937. The defendants included Goldis, Schorr, Spevack, and Harold Silverman, the son of Max Silverman, who was a fugitive. It was charged that they formed and dominated an employer association that controlled the cake and pastry branches of the industry. The purpose of the association was to restrain competition and regulate prices. The trial ended on July 20 with Spevack, Goldis, Schorr, and Harold Silverman found guilty. Following the conviction of Goldis and Schorr, Morris Diamond, a "member of the executive board of Local 138," issued a public statement that both men had the "complete confidence" of all elements of the union. Newspapers commented on Diamond's statement, reminding their readers that Goldis only became president of the union upon the murder of William Snyder in a restaurant on the lower East Side, where, among others, Max Silverman, Harold Silverman, Benjamin Spevack, William Goldis, and Samuel Schorr were present. The four convicted men were each sentenced to terms in the city penitentiary which were not to exceed three years.[24]

Dewey's victory in the bakery case, added to his already impressive list of victories as special prosecutor, made him a formidable candidate for district attorney in Manhattan. The bakery racket also provided a key issue for his campaign in the unsolved murder of William Snyder. Dewey had been selected by Fusion as their candidate during the summer of 1937. On September 23, Samual Seabury announced for Dewey, calling his election "the keynote of the municipal campaign." The day after the Seabury endorsement, Dewey announced the arrest, in Los Angeles, of Max Silverman, wanted for extortion in flour trucking and complicity in the Snyder murder. Dewey disclosed, at this time, that Morris Goldis, the younger brother of William Goldis, was being held as a material witness in both cases. It was also revealed that Morris Goldis had been arrested and charged with the murder of Snyder back in 1934, but had been released when none of the witnesses could identify him.[25]

On September 27, the special grand jury turned in an indictment of 11 counts, charging Silverman with extortion. Both Buchalter and Shapiro were included in the indictments. To make matters worse for

Buchalter and the others. Dewey stated that a superseding indictment, containing possibly 50 more counts and several additional defendants, would be returned before Silverman's trial began. Besides the indictment in the flour trucking racket, Buchalter and Shapiro also faced charges of extortion from garment manufacturers that had been voted by the grand jury in the summer of 1937.[26]

Only a few days after these legal proceedings, Max Rubin, the business agent for the Clothing Drivers and Helpers Union, Local 240 of the AFL and an important Buchalter associate, was shot and seriously wounded. The next day, at Silverman's arraignment, Dewey explained why Rubin was shot: "When William Snyder was shot and murdered, . . . Rubin was sent into Local 138, which was Snyder's union, as the agent of Lepke and Gurrah, and the partner" of Max Silverman. Dewey noted that he had been searching for Rubin for almost a year in connection with the investigation of Buchalter. Finally located, Rubin had testified before the grand jury. Dewey added that police protection had been offered Rubin, but he had turned it down.[27]

The immediate significance of Rubin's shooting, along with the unsolved murder of William Snyder and the capture of Max Silverman, was evident in Dewey's campaign for district attorney. Beginning with a radio address on October 3, Dewey molded these events into the rhythm of his campaign. Calling the attempted murder of Max Rubin "the frightened act of a desperate criminal underworld," Dewey chronicled the careers of Buchalter and Shapiro, describing their dominance of industrial rackets. He stated that, as a result of Buchalter's operations in flour trucking, employers paid over $1,000,000 to the racketeers. Once in control of flour trucking, they added the pastry and pie division of the baking industry to the racket. Dewey also attacked the machine-controlled and corrupt district attorney in Manhattan, describing Dodge as a man who "would not, dare not and could not lift a finger" to stop these rackets. Finally, rolling out his own record, Dewey reminded his listeners that he had broken the cake and pie part of the racket and had sent Goldis, Schorr, Harold Silverman, and Benjamin Spevack to jail. He also pointed out that Max Silverman had been captured by his men and that Silverman, Buchalter, and Shapiro were all under indictment.[28]

Dewey developed his campaign from primarily an attack on racketeers to an assault on the politicians who acted in collusion with gangsters. In a radio broadcast at the end of October, Dewey accused Albert Marinelli, Tammany leader of half of the Second Assembly District and County Clerk of New York County, of being an associate of thieves, drug pushers, and racketeers. It was with Marinelli's aid, according to Dewey, that James "Jimmy Doyle" Plumeri, Dominick "Dick Terry" Didato, and Johnny "Dio" Dioguardi had taken over the trucking industry in downtown Manhattan. Dewey also noted Marinelli's connection with "Lucky Luciano" and pointed out that 32 men appointed by Marinelli as either members of the county committee or as election inspectors in the Second Assembly District had police records.[29]

Dewey's expsoure of Marinelli was only the prelude to his attack on Charles A. Schneider, an Assistant Attorney General and the Tammany Hall leader of the Eighth Assembly District. Apparently, Schneider had played an important role in the cover-up following the murder of William Snyder, which Dewey described in great detail. The most significant aspect of his story related how efficient police work produced the outline of a strong case against Morris Goldis. There were, for instance, two witnesses who recognized a picture of Morris Goldis as the killer. But, in trying to locate Goldis the police found that he had disappeared. Goldis did not turn up for seven weeks when he was surrendered by his lawyer to the district attorney. The point Dewey was establishing with all this detail was obvious: during the time Goldis was a fugitive, the corrupt criminal justice system of New York, under the leadership of its Tammany district attorney, creaked along doing nothing except providing an opportunity for the racketeers to work on their defense, which included terrorizing the witnesses. Schneider, it turned out, was the attorney for Goldis. Dewey stated his case: "Now it's not a crime in the State of New York for an assistant attorney general to represent a man accused of murder. But it's a shocking betrayal of the people of New York." Dewey accused Schneider of accepting money from racketeers in taking the case and withholding Goldis until the prosecution witnesses had been silenced.[30]

On November 2, the election was over and Dewey was in. He had defeated his opponent by over 100,000 votes, a plurality that exceeded Mayor La Guardia's margin in Manhattan. For the first time in 20 years, Tammany had lost control of the district attorney's office in New York County.[31]

With Dewey as district attorney, the pressure on the fugitives, Buchalter and Shapiro, intensified. And then, in the spring of 1938, Jacob Shapiro surrendered to federal authorities. After the federal authorities finished with Shapiro, he was prosecuted by the New York District Attorney for extortion in the garment industry. Convicted, Shapiro died in prison. It took over a year from the time of Shapiro's surrender before Buchalter finally turned himself over to J. Edgar

Hoover and Walter Winchell, thereby ending one of the largest man-hunts in New York City history. Buchalter faced three separate trials beginning with a federal conviction for narcotics, followed by conviction in Manhattan for extortion in flour trucking, and ending with a guilty verdict in Brooklyn for murder. He died in the electric chair in 1944.[32]

Focus on Brooklyn

The 1930s' reform attack on machine politics in the city, which had primarily concentrated on criminal justice and organized crime in Manhattan, soon moved across the river to Brooklyn. In the space of a few years, the district attorney of Kings County would be twice superseded amid charges of bribery, obstruction of justice, and other crimes in the administration of justice. The first scandal, which involved members of the Flour Truckmen's Association, concerned the handling of a homicide by the district attorney's office; the second involved the whole issue of official corruption in Brooklyn and resulted in the retirement of the incumbent district attorney.

The trouble in Brooklyn began on the night of March 3, 1935, when a call was received at police headquarters telling of a disturbance at a garage in the Williamsburg section of Brooklyn. Arriving at the garage, the police found a man running and arrested him. Inside the building, the police spotted a pool of blood and a trail of drops leading to a parked car inside of which was the still warm body of Samuel Drukman. Drukman had been bludgeoned with a sawed-off pool cue and strangled with a rope. Two men were caught hiding in the building: Fred Hull and Harry Luckman, a nephew of Meyer Luckman who had been arrested outside. The police noted that Harry Luckman's hands and clothing were heavily stained with blood. Hull was also found to have traces of blood on him. Near the car, police located the murder weapon, which had blood stains on it. Finally, in Meyer Luckman's pocket there was more than $3,000 in cash. The arrested men were taken to the police station where they were questioned. It was learned that the Luckmans were flour truckers who appeared to enjoy a virtual monopoly in Brooklyn. Drukman was Meyer Luckman's nephew and was employed by the Luckman trucking company as a shipping clerk.

The accused were brought to Homicide Court for arraignment and then held for the grand jury. In court, the State's exhibits, including the bloodstained clothing, the "affidavits of toxicologists as to the blood stains," Meyer Luckman's $3,000, and a number of checks that were supposed to establish a motive for the murder, were displayed to the grand jurors, along with the testimony of police. Despite this evidence the grand jury voted not to indict, and the checks, clothing and other evidence were released to the accused and they were discharged.[33]

As far as the Luckmans, Hull, and the district attorney's office were concerned, the case was closed. But this was an election year and opposing District Attorney William F. X. Geoghan[34] was the Republican-Fusion nominee Joseph D. McGoldrick. The theme of McGoldrick's campaign was "murder is safe in Brooklyn." In October, McGoldrick, speaking at a Methodist Church in Brownsville, reopened the Drukman case alluding to some bizarre maneuvers in the district attorney's office. The first response to McGoldrick's statements came not from his opponent, but from Police Commissioner Lewis J. Valentine, who said that four Brooklyn detectives would face department trials in connection with the Drukman affair. Valentine's statement, which came after a conference with Mayor La Guardia and Captain John McGowan of the Homicide Squad in Brooklyn, held that the "Drukman case is a live, active case in the Police Department and has never ceased to be anything else from the night the murder was committed." Valentine added that the case would not be tried during the political campaign. Valentine's and presumably the mayor's disinclination to press on immediately with an investigation matched an earlier decision of Governor Lehman. The governor had been asked by McGoldrick to supersede Geoghan, but he had refused to take action until the election was over.

As the campaign intensified, McGoldrick hammered at the district attorney for failure to secure an indictment. On November 2, McGoldrick received the support of Samuel Seabury who charged that Geoghan was another in the long and dismaying list of Tammany district attorneys. He added that whenever there was anything difficult to accomplish, the governor appointed someone to do the job for the district attorney. The allusion to Manhattan's special prosecutor could hardly have been lost on many of his listeners.

On November 5, the voters in Brooklyn turned back the Republican-Fusion challenge to machine politics and re-elected District Attorney Geoghan by a substantial margin; McGoldrick carried only one assembly district. Geoghan's victory was part of a sweep scored by the Democratic organization that, it was reported, "rivaled those of the days preceding the Seabury investigation."Commenting on the Drukman case, the triumphant district attorney said that as far as he was concerned it was closed unless there was new evidence. Almost simultaneously with Geoghan's statement, however, the grand jury minutes of the Drukman case were turned over to Police Commissioner Valentine.

During the last week in November, Governor Lehman requested both Commissioner Valentine and District Attorney Geoghan to meet with him to discuss the case. By now constant rumors or allegations of bribery surrounded the affair. In addition, Geoghan had re-submitted the case to the grand jury in November and they had announced they were investigating bribery as well as murder. The day after the governor's request for a meeting, the grand jury indicted Meyer and Harry Luckman and Fred Hull for murder. During this same week, Lehman asked that all records, including those of the grand jury that had failed to indict the Luckmans and Hull, be delivered to him. It was also reported that influential civic organizations were pressuring the governor to replace Geoghan. Dewey made his presence felt on December 4 by seizing the records and books of the Flour Truckmen's Association, of which Meyer Luckman was a director. Dewey denied that he was interested in the Drukman murder, however.[35]

In the first week of December, Governor Lehman announced that he had decided to supersede Geoghan. Also, an extraordinary term of the supreme court would be called and a special grand jury drawn. There were three distinct areas, Lehman held, which must be effectively and thoroughly investigated: first was the murder; second, charges of police bribery; and third, bribery in the district attorney's office. A few days later, Attorney General John J. Bennett Jr. appointed Hiram C. Todd a deputy attorney general and placed him in charge of the investigation.[36]

Within six weeks, the murder trial of the Luckmans and Hull was underway. The state's case began with the motive for the murder. Drukman, it was held, stole thousands of dollars from his uncle's flour and produce trucking business for gambling. When Meyer Luckman discovered the thefts he "openly threatened" to kill his nephew, and also "tried to choke his bookkeeper, Harry Kantor," whom he suspected of helping Drukman. Kantor fled to Chicago, where he either fell, was pushed, or jumped from a window in a sanitarium and died.

The state presented a number of witnesses who testified that Drukman was a heavy gambler and loser. Money was given Drukman that was supposed to reach his uncle, but that was never turned over. Defense counsel called no witnesses. In their summations, the best they could offer was a defense of District Attorney Geoghan, asking for a "verdict that will be an answer forever to these interlopers that we have a prosecutor who investigated the case thoroughly." The three defendants were found guilty of murder in the second degree and sentenced to 20-years-to-life in Sing Sing.[37]

With the question of murder solved, Deputy Attorney General Todd proceeded with the other phases of the case. By the middle of March, Todd's work on the question of bribery became evident: indicted for attempting to influence members of the April (1935) grand jury were James J. Kleinman, the father of William W. Kleinman, an assistant district attorney on Geoghan's staff, and Carmine Anzalone, a Republican State Committeeman from the Fourth Assembly District, Brooklyn, chief of the clerical staff of the Assembly. Several days later, Todd brought charges of bribery and attempted bribery against Henry G. Singer, a former United States assistant attorney active in Republican politics in the Sixth Assembly District, Brooklyn. In subsequent weeks Todd announced that he was seeking Max Silverman of the Flour Truckman's Association in connection with bribery. Silverman, who at that time was still a fugitive, was described as a close friend of William W. Kleinman, the assistant district attorney, whose father had been indicted. Eight more indictments were handed down by the middle of May. Heading the new group and charged with obstruction of justice was Assistant District Attorney Kleinman. Joining him was Detective Giuseppe F. L. Dardis, a partner of Detective Charles S. Corbett, the man who was first responsible for charging bribery when the case seemed forgotten in the summer of 1935. Also charged were Carmine Anzalone, James J. Kleinman, and Henry G. Singer. The last three men charged were Max Silverman, Jack Silverman (not related), and Meyer Luckman's brother, Isaac. Other people named in the conspiracy but not indicted included Leo P. Byk, who was characterized as a former Brooklyn slot machine czar, Detective Charles Hemendinger, who committed suicide days before he was scheduled to appear before the grand jury, the three convicted murderers, and two members of the March grand jury predecessor to the one that had dismissed the Luckmans.[38]

At the same time, the grand jury demanded that the governor remove District Attorney Geoghan. They accused Geoghan of gross negligence and demonstrated incompetence in failing to investigate the scandal, and with associating with undersirable persons, specifically Leo P. Byk and Frank Erickson, known as a professional gambler and bookmaker. It was alleged that these two men contributed to Geoghan's reluctance to investigate the murder. Governor Lehman responded, however, that he would not act until the whole investigation was completed. This was interpreted as an indication to

Todd that he must prove at least some of the allegations before the governor would proceed against Geoghan.[39]

Todd had five of the eight men indicted for bribery and conspiracy on trial soon after the public disclosure of the charges against Geoghan. Isaac Luckman and Max Silverman were still missing, and Carmine Anzalone had pleaded guilty to conspiracy, becoming an important state's witness. During the trial, Anzalone implicated former Chief Assistant United States Attorney Henry G. Singer in the scheme. Anzalone testified that Singer, whom he had known for several years while an assistant United States marshal, and Singer, a federal prosecutor, asked him to contact a grand juror and offer him a bribe of $100 to vote against an indictment. The state's major witness was Detective Charles S. Corbett. He took the stand on June 11 and implicated William W. Kleinman, Leo P. Byk, and Detective Dardis in the conspiracy. In his free-wheeling manner, Corbett also damned District Attorney Geoghan. The defense tried to counter his testimony by demonstrating he was mentally incompetent. As the prosecution neared the end of its case, other witnesses were called who stated the roles played by Jack Silverman and Max Silverman. On June 18, the defense presented its version of the bribery, claiming that Detective Corbett had actively solicited money in return for throwing the case. Earlier, the defense had charged Anzalone with being one of the conspirators.

Near the end of June, the jury returned its verdict. Convicted of conspiracy to interfere with justice, a misdemeanor punishable by a maximum fine of $500 and one year in prison, were Singer, James Kleinman, and Jacob Silverman. The jury was deadlocked, supposedly at ten to two for conviction, in the cases of William Kleinman and Dardis. The three convicted men were sentenced to one year in prison. Tentative plans were made for retrying Kleinman and Dardis.[40]

Todd must have had feelings of accomplishment and deep satisfaction: he had successfully prosecuted the Drukman killers, and had convicted four out of the six men, counting Anzalone, indicted for bribery and conspiracy. However, one year later, Todd's convictions were reversed by the Appellate Court. Concerning James J. Kleinman, the Court stated there was simply no proof that he had joined with any persons to further any conspiracy. In reviewing Singer's conviction, the court found serious reservations in the testimony of Anzalone. As to Jacob Silverman, accused of influencing an April grand juror and of conspiring with Leo P. Byk to obstruct justice, the court found a great deal of innuendo but little proof. Some of the innuendo, however, was most interesting. For example, in a conversation taking place the day the Luckmans were released from jail, secured by tapping Silverman's telephone, the defendant said: "Those two fellows will be out in 15 minutes." In return he was asked if he had called "that fellow to tell him about it." Silverman answered no and then added: "Listen, those fellows won't believe what I can do so I had Frank Costello's brother, Eddie, with me and I told him to sit there and listen so that he would know that I took care of it." Silverman was also described as an associate of Lucky Luciano. The convictions were reversed and new trials ordered for Silverman and Singer. In Kleinman's case the indictment was dismissed.[41]

Following the conspiracy and bribery trial, public interest turned to District Attorney Geoghan, who had been ordered by Governor Lehman to defend himself at a public hearing. The charges were prosecuted by Todd, and Geoghan was defended by Lloyd Paul Stryker. Governor Lehman, on September 17, reached his decision: Geoghan was completely exonerated of all charges. Lehman held there was no evidence that important information was "willfully or corruptly withheld from the April grand jury or that the District Attorney should have known that an attempt had been made to tamper with the April grand jury." Concerning Corbett, the governor stated that his testimony was "completely discredited." And as far as Geoghan's friendships with Byk and Erickson, Lehman said that they were "manifestly ill-advised," but that there was no evidence that corruption and neglect of duty resulted.[42]

In the spring of 1938, an apparently relaxed Geoghan jokingly stated that he was worried because Brooklyn criminals did not seem to be committing serious crimes anymore. That was probably one of his last jokes: within five months Governor Lehman again found it necessary to supersede the district attorney.

The origin of this supersedure began with the work of the Citizens Committee on the Control of Crime in New York, Inc., which was founded in 1936 through the initiative of the special New York County grand jury impaneled to hear evidence gathered by Dewey and his staff on organized crime. Dismayed by the scope of racketeering and the fearfulness of potential witnesses, the grand jury called for a citizens committee that would assure protection to witnesses and monitor the criminal courts and activities of prosecuting officials. The grand jury recognized that the proposed committee would have to function citywide. Mayor La Guardia responded to the suggestion by forming the Citizens Committee and appointing Harry F. Guggenheim, the former ambassador to Cuba, as chairman.[43] In July, 1938, the committee presented to Mayor La Guardia evidence of large-scale irregularities in the administration of justice in Brooklyn. In the early autumn of 1938, the committee's negative attitude toward the criminal justice system in Brooklyn was reinforced when rumors were circulated charging obstruction of justice in two criminal cases by members of Geoghan's staff.[44]

The first case centered on Joseph Mauro who was charged with perjury. Mauro, released on bail, failed to appear and was rearrested. In explaining his action, Mauro claimed that he had paid $100, through an intermediary, to Assistant District Attorney William F. McGuinness to fix his case. The second criminal case involved Isidore Juffe, supposed ringleader of a fur racket in Brooklyn, who after his arrest was freed when Assistant District Attorney Baldwin claimed that he was unable to find witnesses. The newspapers reported that Juffe stated that he had paid for his release. District Attorney Geoghan's response to the news stories was that he was conducting an investigation. New York newspapers were quick to point out that this amounted to an investigation carried on by the accused.[45]

At this point, Mayor La Guardia announced that the inquiry conducted by the Citizens Committee had followed thousands of cases in Brooklyn and had found innumerable irregularities. La Guardia added that the commissioner of investigations had been ordered to examine charges of police and prosecutorial corruption in Brooklyn. On October 10, the commissioner submitted a petition to Governor Lehman asking for the supersession of Geoghan. Three days later, the governor superseded the district attorney. Named by Lehman to carry on the inquiry into official corruption in Brooklyn was John Harlan Amen.[46]

Amen's first investigation was a probe into the fur racket. The most important indictment in this phase of Amen's investigation was the one charging Assistant District Attorney Alexander R. Baldwin with accepting an $800 bribe from Isidore Juffe to prevent his prosecution in one of the fur swindles. The incidents related by Amen reveal Juffe, desperate to avoid prosecution as he already had 25 arrests and three felony convictions, shopping around for a man willing to cooperate. According to Amen, when Juffe was brought to Baldwin in the District Attorney's office for interrogation, the search for a solution to his problem ended. At his trial, Baldwin characterized the whole affair as part of a diabolical plot to have Geoghan superseded. He explained his lenient treatment of Juffe by noting that Juffe was an informer who had proven helpful to the district attorney's office. Having to choose between Baldwin's explanation and Juffe's accusation, the jury went with Baldwin: he was acquitted and subsequently reinstated as an assistant district attorney. Following this victory, however, Baldwin's license to practice law was suspended by the appellate division.[47]

The second major official of the district attorney's office to be prosecuted by Amen was William F. McGuinness. McGuinness faced four charges, two of which related to an abortion racket. The portrait of McGuinness drawn by Amen depicted him as actively pursuing bribes of a consistently paltry nature: $50 to fix a suspected abortion case; $100 to have a perjury charge dismissed in the grand jury where the foreman was a friend; $50 to have an extortion charge against three members of Teamsters Local 138 dropped (Local 138 was, as mentioned earlier, an integral part of Buchalter's flour trucking racket); and $200 to undermine an investigation of a suspected abortionist. Amen presented other instances of McGuinness hustling money that were not included in the indictment. McGuinness pleaded guilty and was sentenced to Sing Sing for no longer than three years.[48]

The phase of Amen's work that seems to have received the greatest public attention was his inquiry into bail bond rackets. Public interest was first aroused with the disclosure in mid-October, 1938, several days before Amen was authorized to begin his investigation, that six arrest books containing data on 7200 prisoners had been stolen from a Brooklyn police station. Under the personal supervision of Police Commissioner Valentine an intensive investigation was started which implicated Police Lieutenant Cuthbert J. Behan. A few days later, Amen took over the investigation from Valentine.[49]

In his report to Governor Lehman, Amen described, in general terms, how the bail bond racket operated. "A person who owns real estate may pledge it as security to obtain the release of a prisoner." In a felony case, a judge determined the amount of bail necessary and whether or not the security offered was sufficient. However, in certain misdemeanor cases "where no court is open at which bail can be offered" an alternate system was sanctioned, which became the area of greatest exploitation. In these cases the "desk officer in a police precinct stationhouse" was allowed to accept bail—"the amount of bail being fixed as a matter of law." Amen added that "to qualify as a surety a person must be the owner of property in the county in which the bail is offered"; and a person who goes bail more than twice in one month, "or for a fee, is engaged in the bail-bond business," and must secure a license. Amen stated that there had been so many violations of both these requirements and others that a blacklist was drawn up by the chief city magistrate and circulated to all police stations and magistrates' courts. Unfortunately, it was totally ignored.[50]

Amen continued: "In the Magistrates' Courts, members of the racket would approach a defendant's relatives and offer to arrange bail for a fee." None of the racketeers were licensed nor did any of them own property, but they did have the names of property owners who were willing to pledge their real estate as bail for a percentage of the fee. The only area of risk for the person who pledged his property concerned the appearance of the defendant in court. However, as Amen pointed out, this was hardly a risk in Brooklyn: "although $300,000 in judgments on bail forfeitures had accumulated in Kings County between 1930 and 1940, none of the property involved had been sold." With cooperation between police officials and racketeers, the process was simplified. In many instances the "desk officer knew that the person who appeared before him as surety was using a false name, or that the deed offered was made out to someone other than the person presenting it." According to testimony taken during the investigation, "these officers received a percentage of the fee obtained by the bondsman" in return for accepting the phony bonds and releasing the prisoners.[51]

The first case reported on by Amen concerned Police Lieutenant Cuthbert J. Behan charged with stealing the arrest records from the police station because they could have implicated him in the bail bond racket. Amen's case against Behan rested partly on the testimony of two patrolmen, Edward J. Lawler and James Sweeney. Patrolman Sweeney, after appearing against Behan at a hearing, committed suicide "worried that his career in the department would be ruined by his testifying against a superior." Behan was removed from the force, although acquitted on criminal charges.[52]

Amen's investigation into the bail bond racket moved from police corruption to the bench. In the autumn of 1938, Amen probed the affairs of racketeer Louis Kassman. Kassman's importance to the overall investigation lay in his testimony, which formed part of the basis for charges of bribery and corruption against Magistrate Mark Rudich. Testimony against Rudich was also given by Jacob Nathanson, a former member of the New York State Assembly and a partner of Kassman's in his bail-bond racket. Rudich was paid by Kassman for exercising judicial restraint. In the early spring of 1939, the apellate court removed Rudich from the bench. This decision was unprecedented in Brooklyn: It was the "first time since its establishment as a judicial department in 1897 that the Appellate Division had removed from office a judge from the inferior courts under its jurisdiction."[53]

Following the Rudich affair, Amen turned to other bail-bond rackets and uncovered some of the activities of Abe "Kid Twist" Reles and his associates. Reles and the others were closely associated with Buchalter and were among the most notorious racketeers and, indeed, killers, in New York. On May 4, 1939, Mrs. Rose Gold, "69 years of age, decrepit and unable to read or write English," was charged with 17 counts of perjury. Rose Gold was the proprietor of a candy store that was Reles's headquarters. According to Amen, Gold's involvement with Reles and his associates was fairly complex. She made frequent appearances in Brooklyn police stations posting bond for gamblers protected by Reles and the others. More importantly, Gold was the banker for Reles' extensive loan shark operation. How extensive was detailed by Amen, who found in the space of a year about $400,000 deposited and withdrawn from Gold's bank account. Amen also established that all the bank transactions were carried out by Gold's daughter, Shirley Herman, whose husband worked for Irwin Steingut, the leader of the Democratic minority in the State Assembly and considered one of Brooklyn's most powerful politicians. Gold was permitted to plead guilty to perjury in the second degree, a misdemeanor, and received a suspended sentence.[54]

During the course of his four-year-long investigation, Amen uncovered some of Abe Reles's more durable enterprises. While gathering evidence on the gambling racket—including lotteries, bookmaking, crap games and such, which flourished with the knowledge and help of corrupt police officers—Amen found, as noted above, Reles's loan shark racket. In charge of Reles's operation were Sam "The Dapper" Siegel and Louis "Tiny" Benson. Siegel managed the local neighborhood lending service, which operated out of the Brownsville candy store owned by Rose Gold who, it turned out, was Siegel's mother. Benson handled the shylock racket at the dice games. Benson met with Reles "each night before the games" to receive money that was to be lent to needy participants. Benson had as much as $10,000 in cash to use at the games. By the time Amen had gathered sufficient evidence to indict Benson and Siegel on nine counts of violating the banking law, Reles had already been indicted for murder. Benson and Siegel pleaded guilty, and they received suspended sentences.[55]

The Amen investigation covered such areas as the Probation Department of the Kings County Court, the Department of Corrections, and the Office of the Commissioner of Jurors—in addition to the bail bond, fur, gambling, and abortion rackets. In elaborating on the results, Amen placed high on the list of his accomplishments the forced retirement of District Attorney Goeghan.[56] In fact, within six months of the time the Amen investigation started, powerful political interests in Brooklyn requested Geoghan's resignation. More than half of Brooklyn's Democratic leaders met with Frank V. Kelly, the so-called boss of the county machine, to devise a strategy to remove Geoghan. But Geoghan resisted, stating that he would not be the scapegoat for the crooks he had hired at the insistence of the district leaders. The future of the district attorney's office was finally resolved that summer. Geoghan would retire at the end of his term, which was over that year. In his place, Brooklyn Democrats nominated County Judge William O'Dwyer, who enjoyed an untarnished reputation. Unlike Manhattan, the reform forces in Brooklyn were weak and disorganized, and O'Dwyer had an easy time winning.[57] It is important to note that even with a new district attorney in Brooklyn, the Amen investigation continued for two more years.

Evaluation

Supersession and allied tactics are methods to circumvent the "normal" political system of municipalities at one of their most critical points: the criminal justice system, especially the office of prosecutor. As we have seen, New York City from 1935 to 1942 was the scene of three supersession incidents, including Dewey's appointment as special prosecutor, which was not technically a supersession. The question now, of course, is how to evaluate them. First of all, it is clear that these particular developments were part of a broad reform movement that attempted—with some spectacular successes—to wrest political control of the city from the Democratic machines. As such, New York's suspersessions are a part of the political history of the city. The prosecutors' offices were an integral unit in a web of corruption and racketeering that permeated all levels of city government as well as much of the political economy of New York.

Nothing was quite as telling in this regard as the Seabury investigations which led, one is tempted to say inexorably, to all the rest. Taking all his investigations together, Seabury and his staff implicated the range of city government in a tangled mass of mis-, mal-, and nonfeasance as well as in several discrete criminal conspiracies that had all the characteristics of long-term rackets. Broken down by position, the totals are: one mayor; 26 district leaders, including a borough president; four assistant district attorneys; 13 magistrates; one state supreme court justice; six sheriffs; three aldermen; 20 commissioners; and six members of the police department, including one inspector. Added to this list are a large number of businesspeople and corporations along with attorneys involved in numerous shady deals and 32 individuals whose careers appear to have been totally criminal: bootleggers and gamblers. In one way or another, in small and large conspiracies, all these people were veritable engines of crime and corruption.[58]

It was this display of public venality that paved the way for La Guardia's election and Dewey's appointment. Unlike Seabury, Dewey's work was totally focused on organized crime as it is commonly understood. He was out to get the infamous racketeers, to show the kind of job a real prosecutor could do if freed from the corrupt grip of the political machine. That his own political ambition was apparent in no way lessened his effectiveness as special prosecutor. From 1935 to 1938, when he took office as Manhattan's district attorney, Dewey convicted Luciano and his associates for compulsory prostitution; convicted "Tootsie" Herbert and others for an industrial racket in the kosher chicken industry; convicted several remnants of Dutch Schultz's restaurant racket mob; convicted James Plumeri and Johnny "Dio" Dioguardi for extortion among garment truckers; convicted the bakery racketeers and solved the murder of William Snyder; indicted J. Richard "Dixie" Davis and others for gambling; and finally, indicted Buchalter and Shapiro for extortion in the garment industry, the bakery racket, and flour trucking. But Dewey's work must be viewed within a radically different or changed context than Seabury's and the later supersessions. Dewey took office in the wake of very substantial political changes; behind him stood the revelations of Seabury and the power of a new adminsitration whose mission was at least partially the uprooting of the social system of organized crime. Within this climate, Dewey chose to prosecute racketeers and to expose their political protectors. Through his sensational prosecutions and timely exposés, Dewey placed Dodge and the official district attorney's office into limbo. Dewey's election in 1937 only confirmed the situation.

Brooklyn was, as usual, another story. Much more limited in scope and certainly in accomplishment was the supersession of Geoghan by Hiram Todd. In this instance, the universe of crime and corruption was centered on 14 principals, including District Attorney Geoghan, Assistant District Attorney William Kleinman, one former assistant U.S. attorney, one former U.S. marshal, two police officers, and assorted truckers. There were no other public officials named or charged. Aside from the three men convicted of murder, the only others to serve prison time were Max Silverman, sentenced to a year for becoming a fugitive, and Jack Silverman, who pleaded guilty to obstruction of justice at his second trial. Todd's major effort, which centered on removing Geoghan from office, was a failure. But like Dewey's, Todd's work must be seen in the light of the political history of both the state of New York and the borough of Brooklyn. Governor of New York at this time was Democrat Herbert Lehman, who could almost daily see the havoc wrought upon New York's Democratic party by an ambitious special prosecutor (Dewey). Lehman was surely in no mood to launch another Dewey, this time in Brooklyn, which was solidly Democratic. In addition, Brooklyn had little of the reform ethos that animated Manhattan. Lehman went so far as superseding Geoghan, but he would not sustain Todd's charges unless there was unavoidable and unimpeachable proof of his guilt. With such tenuous support at the state level and almost no support locally, Todd's investigation into corruption was severely circumscribed. Unable to connect his efforts to broader segments of reform or to effectively penetrate the power of Brooklyn's politicos, Todd's major contribution was historical—he materially weakened Geoghan's political power, thus making him a potential liability for the Brooklyn machine. Geoghan's weakness was graphically displayed first in 1938 by the swiftness with which Lehman again superseded him (this time, scandal overwhelmed political expediency) and then a short time later when the machine forced him into retirement.

This brings us to the last supersession, one that lasted longer than any of the others and one that is much more difficult to judge. The reason for its somewhat enigmatic character has to do with the change in the district attorney's office after the election of O'Dwyer. As the new district attorney, O'Dwyer was immediately involved in a series of sensational murder cases that sent seven men to the electric chair, including Buchalter and most of Reles's associates. From 1940 to 1942, it appeared that the regular district attorney was on his way to smashing organized crime in the most spectacular manner—prosecutions for murder. Indeed, while Amen uncovered Reles's loan shark racket, O'Dwyer had Reles informing on Buchalter, Joe Adonis, Albert Anastasia, and other infamous racketeers. In the midst of these prosecutions, the Amen forays into police corruption and problems with Brooklyn's Raymond Street jail seemed mild if not inconsequential. To most observers, it appeared that the regularly elected prosecutor was doing an exceptional job. There was no chance then for either Amen's work or that of Brooklyn's quasi-special prosecutor to become institutionalized within the formal structure of the borough's criminal justice system. Unlike Dewey, who took over the office, the Amen forces had less and less to do with the prosecutor's office as time went on.

This meant that the educational and political value of Amen's investigation was short-circuited by O'Dwyer's successes. The vigor of the initial murder prosecutions suggested that the endemic corruption rampant throughout Brooklyn's criminal justice system had been met and overcome through the regular electoral process. How foolish this conclusion was would not become evident until at least the mid-1940s, when allegations of corruption about O'Dwyer and members of his staff would be seriously investigated.[59] Long before, however, Amen had finished his investigation, which resulted in indictments and grand jury presentments charging primarily bribery against five members of the district attorney's staff, three Brooklyn judges, 48 police officers, 39 corporations, and 94 individuals. Amen's conviction record was, outside of the private citizens who pleaded guilty and received suspended sentences and the corporations that pleaded guilty and were lightly fined, rather dismal. In fact, as one surveys the results, moving from indictments and presentments down finally to departmental actions, the impression is one of a series of acquittals, dismissals, and departmental disciplinary actions. Although unfolding with deadly accuracy the social structure of corruption and the social system of organized crime, the Amen investigation had little effect on either the structure or the system.

Conclusion

What finally can we say about supersession in general? First, there is no doubt that it has had some success against aspects of organized crime and corruption or particular personalities in New York City, at least up to the tenure of Maurice J. Nadjari (special prosecutor 1973–1976).[60] But it is also quite clear that major victories against professional criminals and their patrons and clients in the criminal justice system do not simply follow supersession. Special prosecuting is most effective when it is part of a broadly based reform movement; it is least effective when it stands alone as the culmination or climax of reform as it did in Brooklyn. Perhaps even more significant in this regard is to consider supersession as part of a continuing struggle against the political structure of select municipalities. As it circumvents the elected prosecutor, it stands apart and indeed often against many of the innumerable arrangements developed by political power brokers that have been institutionalized within the criminal justice bureaucracies. Special prosecuting reveals the true nature of city politics and one of its major patronage fields—criminal justice.

But this brings us to one of the ironic contradictions of supersession and special prosecuting: as its effectiveness in one sense is proportional to reform in general, the stronger the reform movement, the more likely will it seek to totally overwhelm the corrupted. Not only are the rascals to be prosecuted, but they are to be replaced within the regular criminal justice system by the reformers through traditional political processes. When and if that happens, however, it opens to the new officers and politicos the range of extralegal and informal channels of influence and accommodation. The only force to combat corruption, then, is personal morality—which is always a fragile defense. The irony is that the most effective form of special prosecuting leads reformers into the traditional web of city politics where civic virtue is continuously assaulted. The point, it would appear, is whether special prosecuting can be made effective without its moving into the mainstream of city politics.

And clearly, that is what the various standards dealing with supersession and special prosecuting, as proposed by the National Advisory Committee on Criminal Justice Standards and Goals, seem to deal with. The recommended standards in this area are keyed to depoliticizing the prosecutor's office or to a combination of local supersession directed by an *apolitical* statewide special prosecutor. What is not clear, of course, is the manner by which the statewide special prosecutor would be depoliticized. Surely state politics has been and is as political, indeed as corrupt, as local politics. In fact, the lack of clarity and direction in the recommended standards indicates that there is no way for criminal justice agents to be permanently removed from the normal political processes, whether on the state or local level. Additionally, citizens should be extremely wary of any recommendations that attempt to depoliticize law enforcement agents and institutions. Typically, at the core of such recommendations is the desire for efficient if not zealous professionalism, which has its own vast potential for abuse. Finally, it should be clear that the law creation process itself is inherently political and that the invocation of any of its attributes, even a so-called apolitical special prosecutor, is and must be a political act.

As our case study has shown, each concrete manifestation of supersession and special prosecuting displays significant limitations on their effectiveness, whether in the form of extraordinarily limited targets, minimal convictions, tyrannical prosecutions, or some other fall from grace. Supersession and special prosecuting are, in practice, expressions of the political culture of certain cities at certain times as well as sign posts detailing political relationships between municipal and state politics. They reflect the tenacity, resolve, and limitations of both reform and reformers. To advance them as something more than they are or have been—reform devices limited in accomplishment, duration, and extent—is to misunderstand the nature of the symbiotic relationships at the core of organized crime, and the contradictions and conflicts of law creation. The real-world accomplishments of supersession and special prosecuting are individualistic, not structural, even though they are invoked to overcome structural abuses and problems.

NOTES

1. National Advisory Committee on Criminal Justice Standards and Goals, *Report of the Task Force on Organized Crime* p 29. (Washington, DC: Government Printing Office, 1976).

2. Ibid., p 29.

3. Ibid., p 38.

4. Ibid., p 144.

5. For what there is, see E. Johnson, Jr., Organized Crime: Challenge to the American Legal System, *Journal of Criminal Law, Criminology, and Police Science* (1963), especially Part 2: The Legal Weapons . . . and Part 3: Legal Antidotes . . . Also see: Legal Methods for the Suppression of Organized Crime (A Symposium), *Journal of Criminal Law, Criminology and Police Science* (1957–1958), especially M.E. Aspen, The Investigative Function of the Prosecuting Attorney (1957–1958). There is one study concerned with supersession, which includes material on New York City. M. Ploscowe and M.H. Spiero, The Prosecuting Attorney's Office and the Control of Organized Crime, in M. Ploscowe (ed.), *Organized Crime and Law Enforcement.* (New York: The Grosby Press, 1952).

6. M.H. Haller, Urban Crime and Criminal Justice: The Chicago Case, *The Journal of American History* (1970), p 620–622.

7. The statement made by Marshall can be found in J.L. Albini, op. cit., p 30–31.

8. See W.S. Sayre and H. Kaufman, *Governing New York City: Politics in the Metropolis,* p 522–557. (New York: W.W. Norton, 1965). Sayre and Kaufman point out that the relationship "between the parties and all elected officials and employees" is one of mutual benefit and accommodation." p 548.

9. For differing accounts of the Seabury investigation, see H. Mitgang, *The Man Who Rode the Tiger: The Life of Judge Samuel Seabury and the Story of the Greatest Investigation of City Corruption in This Century.* (New York: Viking Press, 1963). C. Garrett, *The LaGuardia Years: Machine and Reform Politics in New York City.* (New Brunswick, New Jersey: Rutgers University Press, 1961). N. Thomas and P. Blanshard, *What's the Matter with New York: A National Problem.* (New York: MacMillan, 1932). R. Moley, *Tribunes of the People: The Past and Future of the New York Magistrates' Courts.* (New Haven: Yale University Press, 1932).

10. Mitgang, op. cit., p 181.

11. Ibid., p 189–194. For a discussion of the influence of district and county leaders see R.V. Peel, The Political Machine of New York City, *American Political Science Review* (August 1933).

12. Garrett, op. cit., p 70–71. Mitgang, op. cit., p 203–205. Specifically, a call for governmental action issued from the City Club of New York, which charged the district attorney with conduct "incompetent, inefficient and futile," with failure to expose graft and other crimes and with an overall failure of purpose and activity. Joining with the City Club was the City Affairs Committee of New York whose members included John Dewey of Columbia, Bishop Francis J. McConnell, and Rabbi Stephen S. Wise.

13. *The New York Times,* (September 1, 1931) Text of Seabury's Report, p 14.

14. Garrett, op. cit., p 72–73.

15. Mitgang, op. cit., p 216–217.

16. Garrett, op. cit., p 74–75; Mitgang, op. cit., p 232–239.

17. Garrett, op. cit., p 76–78; Mitgang, op. cit., p 247–249.

18. See Arthur Mann, *La Guardia Comes to Power, 1933*, (Chicago: University of Chicago Press, 1965); Garrett, op. cit., p 78–79, 112–113.

19. *The New York Times* (March 1, 1935), p 1; (March 14, 1935), p 1; (March 16, 1935), p 1; (April 2, 1935), p 1; (May 8, 1935), p 40; (May 13, 1935), p 11; (May 16, 1935), p 1; (May 19, 1935), p 1.

20. *The New York Times*, (June 25, 1935), p 1; (June 28, 1935), p 15. At the time Dewey was Chairman of the Committee on Criminal Courts, Law and Procedure of the Bar Association, chairman of the Committee on Penal Law and Criminal Procedure of the State Bar Association, and a member of the Committee of the Columbia Law School Alumni Association. His first exposure to national prominence came in the spring of 1931 with his appointment as an assistant Federal attorney. Dewey prosecuted an income tax case against Arthur "Dutch Schultz" Flegenheimer and another against Irving "Waxey Gordon" Wexler.

21. For the best summary of Dewey's efforts as special prosecutor, see R. Campbell (ed.), *T.E. Dewey, Twenty Against the Underworld*. (Garden City, New York: Doubleday, 1974).

22. *The New York Times*, (October 16, 1935), p 48; (December 5, 1935), p 1. Also see FBI, op. cit., p 9.

23. *The New York Times*, (April 30, 1936), p 44; (October 22, 1936), p 1; (January 16, 1937), p 1.

24. *The New York Times*, (June 29, 1937), p 1; (July 7, 1937), p 48; (July 21, 1937), p 3; (August 3, 1937), p 7. Diamond's confidence in the racketeers was short-lived and ill-rewarded. He was shot to death in 1939 for giving information to Dewey about Buchalter's trucking racket in the garment industry. B.B. Turkus and S. Feder, *Murder, Inc.: The Story of the Syndicate*, p 459–493. (New York: Farrar, Straus, and Young, 1951).

25. *The New York Times*, (August 29, 1937), VIII p 7; (September 24, 1937), p 1; (September 25, 1937), p 1; (September 26, 1937), p 3.

26. *The New York Times*, (September 28, 1937), p 1. Also indicted with Buchalter and Shapiro were Benjamin Levine, Samuel Weiner, Irving Feldman, Joseph Miller, Abraham Friedman, Herman Yuran, Harry Greenberg, Sol Feinberg, Henry Teitelbaum, Paul Berger, David Horn, Joseph Amoroso, Joseph Rocconbone, and Leon Scharf. At least four of these men were murdered before Buchalter's surrender to the FBI. FBI, p 20.

27. *The New York Times* (October 2, 1937), p 1; (October 3, 1937), p 1 and 41. Also see Turkus and Feder, p 363–407.

28. *The New York Times* (October 4, 1937) p 1; the text of Dewey's radio address is on p 2.

29. *The New York Times* (October 25, 1937), p 1.

30. *The New York Times* (October 28, 1937), p 1; the text of Dewey's radio address is on p 17.

31. *The New York Times* (November 3, 1937) p 1. Several days after Dewey's victory, Morris Goldis was indicted for the first degree homicide of Snyder. Seven months later, a superseding indictment naming Max Silverman, Samuel Schorr, William and Morris Goldis was handed down. By this time Silverman was serving a sentence for his part in another case while William Goldis and Schorr were in prison for their participation in the bakery racket. At long last, on the first of July, it was reported that Morris Goldis had confessed that he was the gunman in the killing. Both brothers were allowed to plead guilty to first-degree manslaughter. See Court of General Sessions of the County of New York—Part IV, *The People of the State of New*

York Against Max Silverman, Samuel Schorr, William Goldis, Morris Goldis, Indictment #221026.

32. FBI, p 34, 44–45.

33. *The New York Times,* (November 17, 1937), p 11.

34. Geoghan was born in Philadelphia in 1882, where he attended St. Joseph's College receiving a BA in 1903 and an MA in 1905. From there he went to Georgetown Law School while at the same time teaching English and History at Gonzaga College. He passed the Bar in 1906 and then went to New York as an instructor in English at the College of the City of New York. He practiced law at the same time. On January 1, 1923, he was appointed an assistant district attorney of Kings County. He became the district attorney on January 1, 1931. Geoghan took office in a special election held after the incumbent resigned to become a justice of the supreme court of New York. In the fall of 1931, Geoghan was elected to a full term of four years. "Charges Made to Governor Herbert H. Lehman with Respect to the Removal of William F.X. Geoghan from the Office of the District Attorney of Kings County, May 19, 1936, in the *Public Papers of Herbert H. Lehman, Forty-Ninth Governor of the State of New York,* Second Term, 1936, (1940).

35. *The New York Times* (October 23, 1935), p 1; (November 3, 1935), p 1; (November 6, 1935), p 1; (November 7, 1935), p 16; (November 25, 1935), p 1; (November 27, 1935), p 1; (November 29, 1935), p 1; (December 5, 1935), p 1.

36. Todd, born in Saratoga Springs, New York, and admitted to the bar in 1900, had long experience as a special prosecutor. He had served as one of the counsels for the Board of Impeachment, which removed Governor Sulzer in 1913, and was appointed a U.S. attorney by President Harding in 1921. He resigned that position one year later and went to work for Attorney General Harry M. Daughtery as a special assistant working to prosecute striking western railway workers. Todd served in the same capacity in 1924, this time prosecuting Gaston B. Means and Colonel Thomas B. Felder for conspiring to obstruct justice. In 1929, Todd was appointed a special assistant district attorney and took charge of the cases resulting from the failure of the City Trust Company. Subsequently, he was appointed a special assistant attorney general and worked on the case of former Magistrate George E. Ewald, Tammany leader Martin J. Healy, and Thomas K. Tommaney. *The New York Times* (December 7, 1935), p 1; (December 10, 1935), p 22.

37. *The New York Times* (February 11, 1936), p 7; (February 18, 1936), p 46; (February 20, 1936), p 1.

38. *The New York Times* (February 20, 1936), p 1; (March 14, 1936), p 1; (March 17, 1936), p 1; (April 10, 1936), p 33; (May 19, 1936), p 1.

39. *The New York Times* (May 24, 1936), p 1, 2; and IV, p 10.

40. *The New York Times* (June 10, 1936), p 1; (June 11, 1936), p 1; (June 12, 1936), p 2; (June 13, 1936), p 1; (June 16, 1936), p 1; (June 19, 1936), p 1; (June 28, 1936), p 1; (July 1, 1936), p 1.

41. *People v. Silverman,* 297 N.Y.S. 449, p 457–467.

42. *The New York Times* (September 4, 1936), p 1; (September 5, 1936), p 1; (September 9, 1936), p 1; (September 18, 1936), p 1. Before ending his presentation, Todd gave his final version of the bribery conspiracy based on a letter from Commissioner Valentine to Geoghan on September 18, 1935. Valentine wrote: "Acting Detective Sergeant Charles Hemendinger . . . was the go-between for members of the Police Department in the collection of money paid to the police in the Drukman case." Valentine added that "all arrangements in connection with the bribe and fixing . . . were made at meetings in Sam Herman's restaurant." Finally, Valentine noted that Joe Adonis and Joseph Solvoei "are believed to have distributed the Drukman money; that Erickson, one of the biggest bookmakers in New York . . . may have helped the

Luckmans." Following the governor's announcement, members of the grand jury sent off a lengthy telegram to Lehman stating their shock and dismay at the "failure to remove the District Attorney: and at the "tone and content" of Lehman's opinion. They stated: "We looked to you for leadership. We looked in vain." Two days later, Lehman replied to what he called their "abusive and misleading letter." Lehman said it was both "monstrous" and "perverse" for the jurors to "assert that a man must be guilty just because a grand jury has brought charges against him. The governor added a swipe at the actions of Todd, noting his attempts "to damn by innuendo and to destroy by unsupported accusations." *Public Papers of Herbert H. Lehman,* p 735–743.

43. *The New York Times* (May 18, 1938), p 2; (October 14, 1938), p 1; (August 11, 1936) p 1; (August 12, 1936), p 1; also, Citizens Committee on the Control of Crime in New York, Inc., *Crime in New York City in 1939,* p 1.

44. Citizens Committee, op. cit., p 18–19.

45. J. H. Amen, *Report of the Kings County Investigation, 1938–1942,* (New York, 1942), p 8–9.

46. Ibid., p 9–10. Amen, who was Grover Cleveland's son-in-law, had been serving as a special assistant to the attorney general of the United States for the past ten years. He had recently been "in charge of the rackets for prosecutions under the so-called Federal antiracketeering act. Among the cases handled by Amen were the "fish racket" where he convicted Joseph "socks" Lanza and Louis Palermo, and the "artichoke racket." *The New York Times* (October 18, 1938), p 1.

47. Amen, op. cit., p 48–53.

48. Ibid., p 84–87.

49. *The New York Times,* (October 22, 1938), p 1; (October 23, 1938), p 39; (October 25, 1938), p 1; (October 26, 1938), p 2.

50. Amen, op. cit., p 56–57.

51. Ibid., p 58.

52. Ibid., p 60–65.

53. Ibid., p 60–65.

54. Ibid., p 73–74; *The New York Times,* (May 5, 1939), p 1.

55. Amen, op. cit., p 123–125, 178–181. "The lending policy of the shylock racket was done on a 6-for-5 basis. That is for every $5 loaned a $6 repayment was required. The time of repayment was generally six weeks. Due to the method of repaying the principal, the rate of interest was 342 percent."

56. Amen also worked on a number of individual indictments that stemmed from evidence uncovered in his regular investigations. The most interesting of these cases was the indictment of Joe Adonis and Sam Gasberg for kidnapping and extortion. Amen, p 177–178. Also see New York State Attorney General's Office, *A Report on the Administration by the Department of Corrections of the City of New York* (1943); Supreme Court State of New York—County of Kings, *A Presentment Concerning the Enforcement by the Police Department of the City of New York of the Laws Against Gambling* (1942) and *A Presentment on the Execution of Bail Bonds* (1941).

57. *The New York Times,* (May 11, 1939), p 1; (June 5, 1939), p 36; (August 26, 1939), p 32; (November 3, 1937), p 1.

58. See S. Seabury, In the Matter of the Investigation of the Departments of the Government of the City of New York, . . . *Intermediate Report* (January 25, 1932); Seabury, *Second Intermediate Report* (December 19, 1932); and New York State Supreme Court, Appellate Division—First Judicial Department, *Final Report of Samuel Seabury, Referee* (March 28, 1932).

59. See The District Attorney of Kings County and the December 1949 Grand Jury, *Report of Special Investigation, December 1949 to April 1954* (1955).

60. A very strong case against both the work of Nadjari and of special prosecuting in general is M. Nessen, "No More Nadjari, No More Special Prosecuting," *Empire State Report* (1977).

The Myth
of Crime
Control

9

In this chapter, we want to shift our focus on the issue of control from the arena of municipal politics, corruption, supersession, and special prosecuting to federal law creation and organized crime. Since Senator Estes Kefauver's congressional hearings in the early 1950s, federal politicians have recognized that criminal conspiracies are often national in scope and that attacking the Mob, Mafia, and Cosa Nostra generates considerable favorable publicity. For federal politicians, organized crime as it is commonly understood presents a happy pairing of duty and potential high visibility. As far as federal law is concerned, the single most ambitious, broad, sweeping, encompassing example of law creation dealing with organized crime came in 1970 when the Organized Crime Control Act was enacted by Congress shortly before the November, 1970 elections. It is not our purpose in discussing this Act to use it as a primer to display the conflicts and contradictions raging in the 1960s and the role of law within the dialectical process. Although all this is implicit, what we will concentrate on is revealing, through an analysis of the creation of the Act and its application, a linking logic underlying organized crime legislation and political repression. The key is to understand several levels of conspiracy and their interaction with law creation.

Organized Crime–What Is It?

The Organized Crime Control Act began its legislative life 22 months before its passage as Senate Bill 30, introduced by Senator John L.

McClellan and strongly backed by Senators Sam J. Ervin and Roman Hruska. By 1970, it had been eagerly adopted, if not embraced, by President Nixon and key members of his Administration, especially Attorney General John N. Mitchell. It is important to note that much of the substantive material incorporated into the Act was the product of President Lyndon Johnson's Commission on Law Enforcement and the Administration of Justice, created in 1965. This commission's final report, which appeared in February 1967, contained over 20 recommendations for federal action against organized crime. And, as originally proposed in 1969, S. 30 had eight provisions, or "titles," the first six of which were drawn from the commission's recommendations. When the Organized Crime Control Act emerged from the Senate early in 1970, it contained ten substantive titles; when signed by President Nixon it had 12, although the last two had little to do with organized crime.

In addition to the substantive recommendations made by the Johnson Commission, it also framed public discourse on organized crime by promoting a highly selective, indeed pernicious, characterization of organized crime. According to the commission:

> Organized crime is a society that seeks to operate outside the control of the American people and their government. It involves thousands of criminals, working within structures as complex as those of any large corporation, subject to laws more rigidly enforced than those of legitimate governments. Its actions are not impulsive but rather the result of intricate conspiracies, carried on over many years and aimed at gaining control over whole fields of activity in order to amass huge profits.[1]

The Commission was talking about a particular organization—variously called "Mafia" or "La Cosa Nostra." And it is clear that, during the period of Congressional debate over S. 30, organized crime was taken as a synonym for either group. Consider the following items taken primarily from the Congressional Record:

1. On September 3, 1969, Senator McClellan introduced a series of stories dealing with a narcotics ring allegedly run by "members of the Mafia family headed by Vito Genovese."
2. On December 18, 1969, Senator McClellan answered criticisms of S. 30 by noting that "Six of the 26 identified families of La Cosa Nostra operate in New York State; five in New York City alone." In the same remarks McClellan also discussed the case of Frankie Carbo," a member of the Lucchese family of La Cosa Nostra."
3. On June 3, 1970, well after Senate passage of S. 30, Senator

McClellan referred approximately ten times to the Mafia as organized crime.

4. On March 5, 1970, in the House of Representatives, Congressman Richard H. Poff from Virginia placed a newspaper story in the Record that discussed, among others, "Stefana Magadin, head of a Mafia family in Buffalo."

5. The final example of this Mafia/Cosa Nostra fixation comes from the hearings held before the Committee of the Judiciary of the House of Representatives in the spring of 1970. Called before Subcommittee No. 5 was Attorney General John N. Mitchell, whose unqualified support for S. 30 was prefaced by a long statement—replete with tales of the history of Mafia and stories of La Cosa Nostra.[2]

Over the last four decades, a criminal minority has put together in the United States an organization which is both an illicit cartel and a nationwide confederation, operating with comparative immunity from our criminal laws, and in derogation of our traditional concepts of free enterprise. This confederation, formerly known as the Mafia, but more recently identified as La Cosa Nostra, owns or controls many illicit businesses in the United States, and is rapidly increasing its substantial interests in legitimate commerce and industry. La Cosa Nostra emerged as a criminal fraternity in the United States in the early 1930's, after a series of gangland wars in New York and New Jersey left Charles (Lucky) Luciano undisputed boss of the American underworld.[3]

There are two primary points to be made about this exclusive characterization of organized crime: First, as Dwight Smith and others have ably pointed out, this particular definition and description serves to "isolate a small group of men of Italian descent and to accuse them, as members of a particular organization, of having perfected organized crime."[4] Under the titles of either Mafia or La Cosa Nostra, these individuals have become the embodiment of the alien conspiracy—a typical device, as noted many times before, of locating the causes of social problems outside the mainstream of American life, preferably in the secret expansionist designs of wicked foreigners.[5] In addition, the Commission's definition of organized crime has been attacked as a hindrance to knowledge, research, and legislation because "it is not applied to crimes that are really organized, such as anti-trust violations by large corporations."[6]

Although contemporary scholarship demolished the Commission's history and sociology of organized crime,[7] a more pertinent question is: Could and should Congress have known better in 1970? The answer is yes. For instance, in 1959, the Department of Justice issued "A Summary of Successful Federal Racket Prosecutions, 1953–1959." An analysis of the individuals named and their crimes indicates the predominantly local nature of organized crime, and more to the point it shows a decided lack of ethnic exclusiveness. Convicted for labor racketeering under the Hobbs Act and a portion of the Taft-Hartley Act were 134 individuals, 101 of whom were identified. Out of that total, at most 15% were of Italian or Sicilian background. Turning to "Convictions of Known Racketeers, Gamblers, etc., Under the Tax Laws," 73 individuals are mentioned. Slightly more than 16% of them were Italian or Sicilian.[8] Similarly, a careful reading of the Hearings of the Kefauver Committee—but not its summary—would have revealed the diversity in organized crime.[9]

We realize that such prosaic reports as the above "Summary of Successful Rackets Prosecutions" and the homework required to read the Kefauver Committee hearings could hardly compete with the sensational hoopla of then-Attorney General Robert Kennedy's drive against organized crime in the early 1960s, but it should have. In this brief inquiry into the meaning of organized crime as understood in 1970, Kennedy's role was crucial.[10] Whatever evidence there was to the contrary, Kennedy's attitude toward organized crime was characterized by a "zeal to break up the syndicates . . . reminiscent of a 16th-century Jesuit on the hunt for heresy."[11] Raised as a cold warrior, Kennedy framed his actions through a deep-seated belief in subversive conspirators.[12] This meant that a careful definition of the issue was not only unnecessary, but a waste of time. As Henry Peterson comments: "When you talked about organized crime people would ask you to define what you meant. Robert Kennedy came in and said, 'Don't define it, do something about it.'"[13] Questions of definitions were overwhelmed by the demand for action and the deep belief in deviant statuses, attitudes with a long history in the American experience. Without a proper definition, however, the Federal establishment was left with little more than an extensive enemies' list, compiled in the Kennedy years by Edward Silberling.

This retrospective look at the issue of meaning indicates a problem of more than antecedent interest. Not only does definitional turmoil go to the core of the Organized Crime Control Act, but it also reveals its significance in later evaluations of the Act's effectiveness. As we noted earlier, a recent review of the Federal effort against organized crime by the General Accounting Office (GAO) notes that there is no acceptable definition of organized crime. The GAO report states that in 1970 the U.S. attorney general defined organized crime as "all illegal activities engaged in by members of criminal syndicates operative throughout the United States, and all illegal activities engaged in by known associates and confederates of such members." But, as the GAO points out, this ambitious definition has been rejected by over half of the U.S. attorneys. In addition, the report holds that there is vast confusion among all the federal agency personnel participating in the so-called "war on organized crime." The confusion is well founded: "At one extreme the term was defined to include only members of La Cosa Nostra, while at the other extreme organized crime included any group of two or more persons formed to commit a criminal act."[14] In fact, the GAO strongly implies that the contemporary struggle is hopelessly adrift because of the lack of an agreed-upon definition. One other example from the GAO report concerns the Organized Crime and Racketeering Section that was established by the attorney general in 1954, and placed within the Criminal Division of the Justice Department. After two decades of work, "OCRS has not (1) clearly defined organized crime, (2) established quantitative or qualitative goals against which the effectiveness of strike force operations can be measured, or (3) developed a system to accumulate the data needed to assess strike force results . . . . The lack of specific definition of organized crime, . . . also makes it difficult to define the problem the strike forces were created to reduce."[15]

Even in a generally favorable analysis compiled by the Committee to Evaluate Department of Justice Policy with respect to Organized Crime Strike Forces (July 31, 1974), known as the Hoiles Report, this same problem is mentioned although distinctly underplayed. The Report states: "Some 'weakness' can also be found in the Strike Forces as a result of confusion as to the scope of their jurisdiction—that is, the definition of the term 'organized crime'— and occasionally this difficulty results in disagreements with U.S. Attorneys with respect to responsibility for certain prosecutions."[16] More to the point are some of the comments found in *Organized Crime Intelligence: Executive Summary* prepared by Management Programs and Budget Staff, Office of Management and Finance. The *Summary* notes that a "national strategy was proposed in 1972," composed of four parts:

1. the Organized Crime Strike Forces;
2. international efforts against organized crime;
3. recent legislation, i.e., the Omnibus Crime Control and Safe Streets Act of 1968 and the Organized Crime Control Act of 1970; and
4. the National Council on Organized Crime.[17]

The *Summary* goes on to point out that as of 1976, only the Strike Forces and the Federal legislation remain in existence. Significantly, "the National Council on Organized Crime held its last meeting in June 1971." Before adjourning, however, the National Council, in the person of Attorney General John Mitchell, stated in a 1970 memorandum that he intended to meet and eliminate the organized crime problem by 1976.[18]

> The National Council's target date of 1976 has arrived. The Strike Forces have been in operation for nearly a decade; yet, no one could seriously suggest that the problem of organized crime has been eliminated or brought under control. Even if the control or elimination of organized crime were viable strategic goals, it would be impossible at the present time to define or measure progress against such goals. To define control or elimination in this context implies an index against which these goals could be measured; however, at present there is no information base as to the totality of organized crime in the United States.[19]

Again, the crux of the problem is one of meaning. Without knowing what organized crime is, how can one know the effect of any strategy designed to combat it? At the least, it appears that the compilation of La Cosa Nostra charts and enemies' lists of known racketeers contributed little to resolving substantively the problem of defining organized crime.

To underscore the plight of intelligence about organized crime, which directly points to fundamental confusion in the meaning of organized crime, let us look at some of the answers found in one of the appendices to the Report on Organized Crime Intelligence, compiled by the Office of Management and Finance in 1976. Basically the document is a series of questions presented to the FBI concerning their knowledge of organized crime. We preface the following questions and answers by noting that "over 90 percent of the intelligence resident in OCRS comes from the FBI."

1. Is there a pattern of close family leadership among certain organized crime families? Are any families having disagreements with the "consortium"? What are the issues? What are the likely consequences?

   The FBI stated they could not answer from data available within the Bureau and estimated 2500 work hours would be required to respond.

2. What is the relationship of LCN interests to the "Dixie Mafia?" Are any sub-contractual or joint projects now in progress or expected? Are any "Dixie Mafia" or other non-LCN figures iden-

tifiable as the new leaders of traditionally LCN-dominated activities? Which activities in which cities? What is the present and expected (2 years) impact on organizational structure and illegal activity in the particular cities?

The FBI reported that they could not respond because the "Dixie Mafia" is not an organization as such and does not lend itself to a comparison with LCN.

3. What is the national pattern of interrelationships (by geographical and personnel connections) of stolen securities (theft and disposal), narcotics, and sports gambling? What are the gross revenue and net revenue gains to organized crime, and what is the impact on the general public in 1975?

The FBI reported they could not respond because "there is no way anyone inside or outside of organized crime could estimate the underworld's gross and net revenues, let alone their impact on the public."

4. What types of business are undergoing increased extortion problems in Strike Force cities? Do these efforts coincide with loan sharking, union, or hijacking problems in those cities? Do some businesses apear to be targets for a more concerted infiltration or takeover drive by organized crime?

The FBI reported that they could not respond ". . . because the underworld does not have a neatly packaged program of infiltrating only certain types of businesses. They (organized crime) generally operate on an *ad hoc* basis, penetrating when and where the opportunity presents itself.[20]

The answers to the other 11 questions are similar. The conclusion is that either the FBI is absolutely reluctant to divulge their secret information to other federal agencies, or more likely that their answers reflect the intelligence vacuum that corroborates the problem of meaning and certainly coherent definition.

We might also add that the impossibility of determining success or failure after enactment of the Organized Crime Control Act (1970) matches in many ways the acknowledged failure of the Federals earlier "muscular" activities against organized crime in the 1960s. We base this on the methodologically superior analysis of organized crime contained in the 1971 *Report of the New York State Legislative Committee on Crime, Its Causes, Control and Effect on Society.*[21] In 1970, the committee "in cooperation with the Policy Sciences Center, Inc. and funded by a grant from the National Institute of Law Enforcement and Criminal

Justice," studied the "dispositions of criminal cases against members of organized crime during the decade of 1960–1970." Their conclusions are

1. a decline in the arrests of organized crime figures during the decade
2. when arrested, organized crime figures displayed a strong immunity from prosecution and conviction
3. "there is an extraordinary attrition rate in the process from disposition to guilty conviction or plea to actual sentence."[22]

The final point we wish to make here about the particular definition of organized crime implicitly packaged in the Organized Crime Control Act concerns the utilization of the Mafia stereotype as the cover for repressive legislation—which can and did effectively harass and persecute political dissenters. Certainly it was recognized at the time of the House hearings that at least some of the provisions of S. 30 had a potentially larger target than the commonly understood or misunderstood organized criminal. This is borne out by the following exchange between Emmanuel Celler, Chairperson of Subcommittee No. 5 of the Committee of the Judiciary, and Attorney General Mitchell,

THE CHAIRMAN: Of course, S. 30 is called the "organized crime" bill. We had better not call it an organized crime bill. Maybe we should call it something else. I think it probably gives a misapprehension

ATTORNEY GENERAL MITCHELL: We have provisions from here that do not relate solely to organized crime. But, as has been said here this morning, the categories of "general crime" and "organized crime" frequently overlap. They are often difficult to distinguish. . . .[23]

Much more forcefully, this same conclusion was reached by Professor Herman Schwartz from the State University of New York at Buffalo School of Law who was invited to testify on S. 30. Schwartz stated:

It is interesting and perhaps instructive that although this bill is entitled the "Organized Crime Control Act," it is in no way limited to organized crime. Title VII, for example, extends to every conceivable kind of crime and proceeding, whether civil, criminal or administrative, no matter how petty or trivial. Partly this is because the supporters of this proposal want to catch every possible area in which organized crime operates; partly this is because these supporters have often declared that they really cannot describe organized crime adequately.[24]

Although defying anything remotely precise, the Cosa Nostra stereotype was nevertheless potent. It allowed—as some legislators demanded—the casting of as wide a legislative net as possible on the strange premise that the enemy, although known, was still somewhat amorphous and that any definitional limitations would inevitably allow some to wriggle through. How else can one explain the rejection of Senator Edward M. Kennedy's amendment to limit the special sentencing provisions of the Organized Crime Control Act only to persons convicted of specified organized criminal activity, and Representative Mario Biaggi's amendment to define Mafia and La Cosa Nostra as organized criminal groups; make membership in either a federal crime with set penalties; and provide that a false accusation of membership in either is libel?[25]

The Organized Crime Control Act

Even without a proper definition, the vast majority of Congress was willing to accept the provisions of the Organized Crime Control Act and to believe that they principally applied to something known as La Cosa Nostra. As mentioned earlier, the Act contained 12 titles when signed by President Nixon. However, the last two titles had little to do with organized crime. Title XI dealt with explosives, establishing a system of federal controls over the interstate and foreign commerce of explosives through licensing and permits, as well as prohibiting their distribution to certain categories of persons. There is something noticeably important about this particular title: It is the only one which explicitly bridged the gap between the Organized Crime Control Act and political dissension. It was not fictiously aimed at Mafia bombers, but rather, at increasingly militant antiwar groups. The last title was a typical piece of congressional self-righteousness, calling for the establishment of a commission to review the effect of the first ten titles of the Act. Using the descriptions from the *Congressional Quarterly*, the first ten provisions of the Act follow:

> Authorized special grand juries to sit in heavily populated areas or where designated by the Attorney General for periods up to 36 months, subject to the control of the Federal district courts, to return indictments, and to submit to the court reports concerning noncriminal misconduct by an appointed public official involving organized criminal activity, or organized crime conditions in the area (Title I).

> Repealed all previous witness-immunity laws and authorized Federal legislative, administrative and judicial bodies to grant witnesses immunity from prosection using their testimony, but not from all prosecution for any act mentioned in their testimony. This comprehensive new law provided "use-immunity," a narrower grant than the "transaction-immunity" authorized by most previous laws (Title II).

Authorized detention of recalcitrant witnesses until they complied with the order of the court, but for no longer than 18 months (Title III).

Authorized a conviction for perjury based on obviously contradictory statements made under oath—eliminating the rules that there must be direct proof that a statement was false and that there must be testimony from two witnesses (Title IV).

Authorized the Attorney General to protect and maintain Federal or state witnesses (and their families) in organized crime cases (Title V).

Authorized use of depositions in criminal cases subject to constitutional guarantees and certification by the Attorney General that the case involved organized crime (Title VI).

Limited to five years the period within which Government action to obtain evidence could be challenged as illegal; required court review of Government records to ascertain their possible relevance prior to their disclosure to a defendant who established that their origin was illegal (Title VII).

Declared it a Federal crime to plot to obstruct state law, particularly through corruption of government officials, in order to facilitate an "illegal gambling business," defined as one which violated a state or local statute, involved five or more persons, and operated for more than 30 days or had a gross income of $2,000 in one day (Title VIII).

Declared it a crime to use income from organized crime to acquire, establish, or operate a business engaged in interstate commerce, and prescribed use of forfeiture, antitrust devices, special investigative procedures and damage suits against such crimes (Title IX).

Authorized increased sentences (up to 25 years) for dangerous adult special offenders. Defendants found, during a special postconviction hearing, to fall into this category might include a person convicted of a third felony, a professional criminal convicted of a felony or an organized crime figure (Title X).

Constitutional Criticisms

Prior to the passage of the Act, some of the most articulate and detailed criticism came from the Committee on Federal Legislation of the Association of the Bar of the City of New York. Called before the House Committee on June 10, 1970, its analysis was presented by Sheldon H. Elsen, chairman of the Committee on Federal Legislation. The only title that they approved was Title V, which provided protection for Government witnesses. As for the rest, the committee urged a total revision especially because so much of it was unconstitutional and otherwise objectionable. for instance, Title III was in some important respects "contrary to the Federal Rules of Criminal Procedure," while Title VII eliminated "constitutional objections to the admission of the fruits of illegally seized evidence after five years." For this reason and others, the Committee judged Title VII obviously unconstitutional. The other titles were almost equally as suspect. The only part of the bill that they did not report on was Title II, which they were unable to adequately consider in time. Overall then, the Committee on Federal Legislation considered S. 30 a legislative disaster, containing "Kafka-esque" features and at least the seeds of official repression.[26]

Title VII also received detailed criticism from Professor Herman Schwartz, introduced earlier. His discussion of Title VII was divided into several sections and began with the claim that it "would in fact reduce whatever protection presently exists, since it would gravely weaken the exclusionary rule not only where electronic surveillance is concerned . . . but in the whole range of unlawful official activity." Schwartz held that Title VII could seriously weaken the findings and principles laid out in *Mapp v. Ohio*, 367 U.S. 643 (1961), *Miranda v. Arizona*, 384 U.S. 436 (1966), as well as other Supreme Court decisions that curbed police illegality by denying the use of unlawfully obtained evidence on the part of prosecutors. One of the prime issues in Title VII, then, was the government's attempt to legislatively overturn the then recent Supreme Court decision in *Alderman v. United States*, 394 U.S. 165 (1969), which held "that whether illegal electronic eavesdropping had tainted the prosecution's evidence must be determined in an adversary proceeding, and the defendant must be shown all the tapes so that he could effectively argue the issue." Moreover, Schwartz argued that Title VII went well beyond the question of electronic eavesdropping to cover, if not cover up, all illegal searches and seizures.[27]

The official and clearly disingenuous reply to the *Alderman* argument raised by Schwartz was simply that there is "no constitutional objection" to that part of Title VII that corrects "the *Alderman* decision, because that decision was merely an exercise of the Supreme Court's supervisory jurisdiction over the lower federal courts and not a constitutional interpretation.[28] However, the substantive issue raised by Schwartz and others, that sections of the Organized Crime Control Act sanctioned illegal law enforcement practices would not die down. It was also a feature, although a small one, of the discussion surrounding Title X.

During the House hearings, Chairperson Celler read the statement of the Association of the Bar of the City of New York in regard to certain procedures in Title X:

The trial court is directed to base its findings on a "preponderance of the information." Yet the sentencing decision may be far more critical than the initial determination of guilt or innocence which must be made on the basis of admissible evidence and beyond a reasonable doubt. Information of all kinds not only hearsay and rumor, but also presumably the fruits of unlawful searches or illegal wiretappings could be used and the defendant sentenced to 30 years without any of the real protections afforded by a jury trial.[29]

The reply to Chairperson Celler's reading was made by Will R. Wilson, Assistant Attorney General in charge of the Criminal Division of the Department of Justice, who accompanied Attorney General Mitchell to the hearings. Wilson stated that the Justice Department does not *now* use illegally obtained evidence. Wilson continued: "It is against the policy of the Department to do that. He is referring to old illegal wiretaps. Those are not used in the sentencing process." Undoubtedly struck by Wilson's simplistic and moralistic reply, Chairperson Celler asked him to read the specific language of the bill, and the following discussion ensued:

MR. WILSON: "Use of information for sentencing. No limitation should be placed on the information concerning the background, character and conduct of a person convicted of an offense which the court of the United States may receive and consider for the purpose of imposing an appropriate sentence."

THE CHAIRMAN: Is that consistent with what you just indicated?

MR. WILSON: That would permit any type of evidence permissible under present law. But, as regards information from illegal wiretaps, we certainly don't use that sort of thing as a matter of policy and haven't used it.[30]

The point of it all seemed to be this: the government, particularly the Justice Department, was to have free rein in its fight against organized crime, unhampered by too many cumbersome restraints in gathering evidence. But no one, apparently including mobsters, need worry about procedural safeguards, because the Justice Department was inherently fair as witnessed by their policy against using tainted evidence. Or at least, so argued Will Wilson and Attorney General Mitchell in the spring of 1970.

Political Repression: Application

For nearly three years, the pieties of Wilson and Mitchell retained some force and credibility in Congress. But in the late winter of 1973, Senator Edward M. Kennedy's testimony before the House Judiciary

Subcommittee No. 1 on federal grand jury abuse neatly countered them. Kennedy stated that Congress was partly to blame "for the present crisis," because of its failure to see the "sinister potential abuses" that were built into the Organized Crime Control Act. More importantly, the Department of Justice was to blame, Kennedy added, "for lulling Congress not only with excessive protestations of the need for this new Act as a law and order tool, but also with equally excessive and wholly unfulfilled promises of good behavior if only the Act would pass.[31] At the time Kennedy testified, the crisis of which he spoke was the attempted police-state exposed and partially unraveled by the process known as Watergate. And it is no overstatement to view the Organized Crime Control Act as one of the significant building blocks in the nightmare version of law and order conjured up by President Nixon and his associates. The seeds of official repression mentioned by the Association of the Bar of the City of New York had bloomed. And ironically enough, the most poisonous blossoms were contained in Titles I and II, which were for the most part ignored by the original critics of S. 30, especially the New York Bar.

What transpired between the passage of the Act and 1973 "was the campaign of grand jury harassment unleashed against Richard Nixon's political enemies," as Representative John Conyers put it. Speaking in the summer of 1976 before the Subcommittee on Immigration, Citizenship, and International Law of the House Committee of the Judiciary, Conyers indicated:

> It was the infamous case of the "Fort Worth Five" and other less publicized but no less outrageous horrors that made us realize that Nixon's Organized Crime Control Act of 1970, which introduced both subtle and sweeping changes in grand jury and immunity procedures was a prescription for grand jury "dirty tricks," not a panacea for gang-busting.[32]

With the passage of the Organized Crime Control Act, the Nixon Administration had constructed a mighty engine of repression driven by the use immunity provisions of Title II and the special grand juries of Title I. Immunity, which first appeared in the Federal Criminal Code during the Red Scare of 1954, had been transactional. Once a witness had been immunized, the witness could never be tried on the subject of his or her testimony. Title II changed this to a form under which witnesses in grand jury proceedings could be forced to testify on a grant of immunity and still be liable for prosecution for the events they described. All that was necessary was for the prosecution's evidence to be based upon neither the testimony itself, nor leads developed from that testimony. One can easily imagine how difficult a time a defendant would have proving evidence was tainted.

Once developed, this nefarious engine was turned over to what had been a moribund part of the Department of Justice—the Internal Security Division, another product of the 1954 hysteria over communism. The function of the renascent ISD was clearly the curbing of political dissent by demoralizing and intimidating radicals. To lead the ISD, Attorney General Mitchell chose Robert Mardian, who was once described as a "key member of the hard-line White House junta on civil rights.[33] Although Mardian directed the grand jury network, much of the field work was carried out by attorney Guy Goodwin, who headed the Special Litigation Section of the ISD. Although the purpose of the ISD was to curb dissent, it more specifically employed the traditional accusatory function of the grand jury as a cover for:

1. A secret White House-sponsored network for the systematic collection of political intelligence by illegal means and for purposes unrelated to law enforcement.
2. The laundering or legitimizing through grand jury interrogation of such tainted evidence.
3. The development of evidence through the grand jury process to support an indictment already handed up—a form of pretrial discovery not permitted in criminal cases.
4. The use of civil contempt, not to obtain testimony, but solely to punish uncooperative witnesses.[34]

This particular thesis has been most cogently developed by Frank J. Donner and Richard Lavine, who argued that the ISD's campaign was in reality the implementation of the infamous Huston plan, which was one of Nixon's instruments "in the relocation and centralization of the entire intelligence establishment in the White House."

The Huston plan was the result of a project personally initiated by President Nixon in the White House on June 15, 1970. The plan called for wiretapping of groups and individuals suspected of radical activity, the monitoring of their mail, and burglaries of their apartments, homes, and offices. In addition, the plan included intensified recruitment of spies on college campuses. As should be familiar, the Huston plan was supposedly forestalled by J. Edgar Hoover, who viewed it as a usurpation of his personal espionage fiefdom. But according to Donner and Lavine, "the operational aspects of the Huston plan, from wiretaps to break-ins, were implemented by a White House-sponsored agency which had two covers: it was located in the Department of Justice as a part of the Internal Security Division and it claimed to be nonoperational." The name of this agency was the Intelligence Evaluation Committee and its director was none other than the head of the ISD,

Robert Mardian. The point of the Donner and Lavine analysis appears to be that the IEC was the apex of a domestic intelligence triangle that included at one point the ISD grand juries and at the other the notorious plumbers—the White House gang of burglars and spies.

As proof of their thesis, Donner and Lavine discussed the web of illegalities and grand jury abuse surrounding such well documented affairs as the Daniel Ellsberg case, the so-called Weatherman grand juries convened in such cities as Tucson, Detroit, Cleveland, Madison, San Francisco, Seattle, and New York, the grand jury investigations of the Catholic Left in Harrisburg and Camden, as well as the machinations behind the grand jury probe aimed at members of the Vietnam Veterans Against the War, held in Tallahassee in the summer of 1972. In each case, witnesses were called upon to testify about events that were already known to the ISD through burglaries, illegal wiretaps, and mail interceptions. The above examples by no means exhaust the nasty work carried out by the Special Litigation Section of ISD. As Paul Cowan pointed out in *The New York Times Magazine* (April 29, 1973), Goodwin's group "presented evidence to more than 100 grand juries in 36 states and 84 cities," and subpoenaed somewhere between 1000 and 2000 witnesses. It was this vast display of vindictiveness that finally promoted Senator Kennedy to comment:

> And so it goes, as the Special Litigation Section of the Internal Security Division plies its trade, with its small army of grand inquisitors barnstorming back and forth across the country, hauling witnesses around behind them, armed with dragnets of subpoenas and immunity grants and contempt citations and prison terms. These tactics are sufficient to terrify even the bravest and most recalcitrant witness, whose only crime may be a deep reluctance to become a government informer on his closest friends or relatives, or an equally deep belief that the nose of the United States government has no business in the private life and views and political affiliations of its free citizens.[35]

A more systematic list of grand jury terror tactics carried out during the Nixon Administration was compiled by the Coalition to End Grand Jury Abuse and submitted to the House Judiciary Subcommittee, which was considering grand jury reform in the summer of 1976. With appropriate and compelling citations the Coalition's findings demonstrated that the government had, or had attempted: to gather domestic intelligence; to discredit nonmainstream groups; to frighten citizens from political activity; to disrupt legal dissent; to disrupt the news-gathering process; to cover up official wrongdoing; to break the attorney–client privilege; to punish citizens for their refusal to answer FBI questions; to punish witnesses for exercising their Fifth Amendment rights; to bring accused persons to trial on insufficient evidence; to entice the commission of perjury; to hide failures of law enforcement agencies; to chill the defendant's right to a public trial; to locate already indicted fugitives; to substitute for a search warrant; and, to disrupt personal lives by unwarranted geographical removal.[36]

The Disappointing Aftermath

And what of organized crime? Obviously, in one sense, it was used as a "strawman" to lay the groundwork for Nixon's desired quasi-police state. One might expect, therefore, that this strawman would have been laid to rest by the appalling Watergate revelations and the resignation of Nixon along with the jailing of Mitchell and others. But it has not happened. As was made clear in the previously mentioned 1976 Hearings, held before the Subcommittee on Immigration, Citizenship, and International Law of the House Committee of the Judiciary, the Department of Justice still clings tenaciously to the organized crime "shibboleth" and the necessity for almost all of the repressive paraphenalia of the Organized Crime Control Act of 1970, including most forcefully, use immunity. In fact, in a Justice Department "Memorandum Responding to Questions Concerning Grand Jury Practices and Proposed Changes" posed by Subcommittee chairman Joshua Eilberg, the utility of use immunity is vigorously defended by arguments totally concerned with organized crime.[37]

But even within the confines of traditional organized crime debate, this intransigent position has been seriously questioned. As the Coalition to End Grand Jury Abuse strongly informed the House Subcommittee, any form of compulsory immunity had been discounted by Attorney Peter Richards, one of the leading organized crime prosecutors in the country. Richards's background included service from 1964 to 1969 as a special attorney in the Organized Crime and Racketeering Section of the Justice Department. In the summer of 1976, he was a New Jersey deputy attorney general in charge of the Special Prosecutions Section of that state's criminal justice division. Richards, in an address before a summer seminar at the Cornell Institute on Organized Crime (funded by LEAA), "completely contradicted the Justice Department assertion that compulsory immunity is essential to the successful prosecution of organized crime." The Coalition also added this telling quote from Richards's talk to their testimony.

> Giving him (the organized crime witness) immunity in the grand jury, forcing him to testify by court order over his clear objections—we don't like to do it because we have found that it normally does not work. The

situation where a witness refuses to cooperate in the first place, then comes into the grand jury and changes his mind and cooperates and tells you the truth and gives you something valuable is extremely, very, very, very rare. I don't think I've ever seen it happen, as a matter of fact.[38]

What the above reflects, however, is not the maturing of organized crime prosecutors, but instead a kind of prosecutorial chaos in the organized crime field especially prevalent in the years following the Organized Crime Control Act. At the very least, this conclusion is the heart of the GAO report discussed earlier in the context of competing definitions of organized crime. The point of the Organized Crime Control Act, as far as organized crime was concerned, was to national-ize the effort to combat it. And it is precisely this effort that the GAO finds to have been a dismal failure. "In essence," the report states, "there is no coordinated Federal effort to fight organized crime." The Drug Enforcement Administration, Federal Bureau of Investigation, Internal Revenue Service, U.S. Customs Service, Securities and Ex-change Commission, Immigration and Naturalization Service, and the Organized Crime and Racketeering Section of the Justice Department all conduct their own private and basically uncoordinated campaigns.[39] Perhaps nothing better illustrates the essentially impossible and at least partially bogus nature of the endeavor than the absolutely derelict activity of the coordinating unit—the National Council on Organized Crime, which disappeared with such unseemly haste.

Law and Society

This is no brief for the GAO's notions about winning the war against organized crime. When all is said and done, the basic answer given by the comptroller general to the question why "organized crime still flourishes, despite ten years of work by federal strike forces to combat it," is simply the inefficient planning, organization, and direction of the Federal effort.[40] The GAO is, of course, being both overly harsh and simplistic. It knows full well that the Federal Strike Force program by itself has no more chance to eradicate organized crime than the strategic hamlet program had of stemming the tide of illegal war in Vietnam. It is but one of many instruments and policies developed over the years at every level of government in America in order to establish some semblance of control over organized crime, or to at least appease public sensibilities.

Indeed, as we have seen, one of the major problems with the so-called federal war against organized crime is the conception of organized crime itself rather than the performance of strike forces.

Organized crime is not some evil and monolithic presence standing apart from American society and planning its collapse; is it not some alien conspiracy whose aims are counter to the logic and tenets of competitive capitalism. Organized crime is the sum of innumerable conspiracies, most often local in scope, which are part of the social and political fabric of this nation. Furthermore, the fragmentation of federal effort, bemoaned by so many, is probably an accurate reflection of this social reality rather than merely a consequence of bureacratic bumbling.

It would, of course, be misleading to hold that all government organizations are insensitive to the embeddedness of organized crime, always placing it outside the political economy in some fundamental sense. But even when there is the glimmer of a deeper understanding, it is cast in a basically totalitarian mode. To make this clear, let us return to the National Advisory Committee on Criminal Justice Standards and Goals *Report of the Task Force on Organized Crime,* which claims, as discussed in the preceding chapter, that "the final explanation for the growth of organized crime and corruption concerns the structure of government in the United States—particularly at the state and local levels." The *Report* continues:

> The American pattern of fragmentation of governmental authority . . . tends to guarantee that attacks on crime syndicates or other corrupters will be fragmented, that results will be delayed, and that most reform movements can be outwaited.
>
> Although it might be argued that this fragmentation at least protects the public from a systematic tyranny by a corrupt leader, the same public must be prepared to pay the price of inefficient and protracted law enforcement efforts.[41]

The analysis above cavalierly dismisses the issue of systematic tyranny by a corrupt leader—one of the lessons of the Organized Crime Control Act—and is strongly reminiscent of so-called reform ideology promiment in the Progressive Era (1900–1916). At that time, the obsessive concern with organized crime and corruption and the decentralized political structure of American municipalities coalesced into a rhetoric of reform that masked strong antidemocratic impulses.[42] As Samuel P. Hays notes the basic issue in municipal reform was "how to reduce the influence in government of the majority of voters among middle- and lower-income groups."[43] This fundamental desire was hidden behind the rhetoric of "law and order" and constant rumblings about true democracy. Hays concludes:

> Municipal reform in the early 20th century involves a paradox: the ideology of an extension of political control and the practice of its concentra-

tion. While reformers maintained that their movement rested on a wave of popular demands, called their gatherings of business and professional leaders "mass meetings," described their reforms as "part of a world-wide trend toward popular government," and proclaimed an ideology of a popular upheaval against a selfish few, they were in practice shaping the structure of municipal government so that political power would no longer be broadly distributed, but would in fact be more centralized in the hands of a relatively small segment of the population.[44]

To repeat, then, this is no argument for centralization, effecient or otherwise.

There is one final issue to address in this critique. For all the confusion over meaning, the mendacity of application, the drive for centralization and its failure, little direct attention has been focused on the combative rhetoric framing the discussions of organized crime. Among the many examples already mentioned or alluded to, one more should suffice. In April, 1969, President Nixon, commented on S. 30 that "This administration is urgently aware of the need for extraordinary action and I have already taken several significant steps aimed at combating organized crime. I have pledged an unstinting commitment, with an unprecedented amount of money, manpower and other resources to back up my promise to attack organized crime."[45]

One of the major functions of "war" rhetoric is to clearly divide the enemy from the exemplary community. The descriptive vocabulary used in public pronouncements about organized crime is itself an engine that moves and converts an endemic social problem into the traditional mold of conspiracy and subversion. There is a rather long history of this conversion in American culture.[46] All we wish to say about it at this time, however, is that the conspiratorial tradition itself demands the Mafia/La Cosa Nostra mythology. Not empircism, but ideology is at the root of this demonology. Recognizing this may help make it clear why the Communist Control Act, the ISD, transactional immunity, and the OCRS were all created in 1954, and why so many cold warriors played such key roles in this social drama of almost 30-years duration.

Conclusion

Contradictions, we have argued, are the well springs from which legislation flows. This fact is often masked by the rhetoric that surrounds legislative innovations. As we have seen in this chapter, a variety of contradictions and conflicts may be attacked, quite conspicuously, by legal changes that are on the surface designed solely to cope with "the problem of organized crime." In this context of political realities and economic forces, it is quite clear that the creation of myths about the parameters of organized crime—its nature and its structure as well as its threat to national well-being—serves quite well to justify a vast array of otherwise questionable laws.

NOTES

1. GAO, *War on Organized Crime Faltering*, p 2. (Washington, DC: U.S. Government Printing Office, 1977).
2. The material is located in (1) 115 Congressional Record S10020; (2) 115 *Congressional Record* S 17089; (3) 116 *Congressional Record* S 28238; (4) 116 *Congressional Record* H 1564; (5) House of Representatives, Committee on the Judiciary, Subcommittee No. 5, *Hearings on S. 30 and Related Proposals* (Washington, DC: Govennment Printing Office, 1970), p 151–157.
3. House, *Hearings on S. 30*, op. cit., p 87.
4. D. C. Smith, Jr., op. cit., p 87.
5. R. O. Curry and T. M. Brown (eds.), *Conspiracy: The Fear of Subversion in American History.* (New York: Holt, Rinehart and Winston, 1972).
6. See again Haller's unpublished paper.
7. See the works already cited by Albini, Block, Chambliss, Haller, and Smith.
8. The prosecuted racketeers are

Joseph P. Ryan	Philip Masiello	J. W. Hall
Evan R. Dale	Frances L. Stickel	Albert Doyle
John J. Kristics	Nicholas A. Stirone	Emanuel Riggi
James Bateman	Paul H. Hulahan	Orville Rhodes
James Murphy	O. B. Soucie	William Poster
Henry Highfill	Carl Bianchi	R. M. Secor
Lawrence Callahan	L. A. Thompson	H. H. Hudson
B. Ricciardelli	Alfred Leanzo	Henry G. Varlack
James Lowe	Woodrow W. Cape	Peter Postma
David Roche	Samuel Havalauskas	Edwin H. Snyder
Joseph McConnon	Edward J. Pavlat	Morris Malinsky
Guy T. Long	Wadelmiro Arroyo	Joseph Meglino
Irving Green	Louis Rapkin	David Lustigman
Albert Pfeffer	Milton Tillinger	William Adrian
Isidore Schwarts	Samuel Vogel	Paul Baurhenn
William Anderson	William Bales	Oscar Ferrebee
Albert Doyle	Virgil Floyd	Theodore Gibbs
Jack Flaum	Dominick Franzee	Harry Hagan
Jack Geilhausen	Jack Green	Stanley Jochim
Guy Harmon	Peter Higgins	Thomas May
David Karpf	Clayton Lowry	Claude Palmiatti
Harry Meisenhelter	Raymond Nedley	John Sweeney
Bruno Patalito	Henry Schmidt	Thomas McKeever
Mario Valdario	Ralph Wright	Michael Nemirka
Lawrence Morrison	George Barrett	Gerald Connelly
Carmela Tormas	Sidney Brennan	Edward Gallagher
John Coleman	Alejandron Garcia	C. A. Lowry
H. H. Hudson	Jack Jorgeson	Dante Martire
R. S. Median	J. Moore	Thomas Pecora
Isaac Nathan	James Parran	Peter Weibert
R. M. Rodriquez	Frank Ventimiglia	Seymour Eichengrund

Eugene Williams	Robert Beshlian	Fred W. Bierig
Abraham Siegel	Herbert Korholtz	Daniel Smith
Cyril Lopp	Cecil E. Brown	Arthur H. Samish
Frank Erickson	L. B. Binyon	George W. Lewis
Harry Gross	Frank Costello	Louis Berra
Alex Birns	Sam Beard	William Giglio
Emmett R. Warring	John Doyle	Louis Smith
Frank Livorski	Howard M. Lawn	Charles Friedman
Umberto Anastasio	Michael Bowers	James D. Irving
John Ward	Frank Nathan	Sidney Brodson
Lionel Dominguez	Elmer Remmer	Paul DeLucia
Peter Licavoli	John O. 'Neil	Glenn Smith
Edward Curd	Dave Beck	Lorenzo Alagia
High Culbreath	Mateo Azcona	Rozier Bayley
Earl Artis	Thomas Callahan	William Cohen
Leon Chester	Isadore Eisenstein	Jang Kay Fong
Edward Copeland	Fred M. Ford	Joseph Frank
Young Ah Fook	Marin Highes	Frank Iaconi
John J. Gannon	John Kampeyer	Herbert Kaufman
Harold Jackson	Joseph Koza	Leo Link
Daniel J. Keating	Samuel Marosso	John L. McEwen
Alfred Marshall	Sanders Scott	Fred Shaheen
James Robinson	Edward Sandelar	Charles P. Spencer
Elain Simpson	John A. Stewart	Fred Talbot
Joe R. Steele	Charles Toye	Harvey Veino
Justin Tappero	Carrol Yates	
Leroy B. Williams	Edward Koonse	

Source: U.S. Department of Justice, A Summary of Successful Federal Racket Prosecutions, 1953–1959.

9. W. H. Moore, *The Kefauver Committee and the Politics of Crime, 1950–1952.* (Columbia, Missouri: University of Missouri Press, 1974).

10. V. S. Navasky, *Kennedy Justice.* (New York: Atheneum, 1971). See especially Chapter 2, Organized Crime: The Bureacracy and the General.

11. Ibid., p 46.

12. Ibid., p 46.

13. Ibid., p 46.

14. GAO, op. cit., p 8.

15. Ibid., p 17.

16. U.S. Department of Justice, Report of the Committee to Evaluate Department of Justice Policy with Respect to Organized Crime Strike Forces, *The Hoiles Report* (July 31, 1974), p 21.

17. U.S. Department of Justice, *Organized Crime Intelligence: Executive Summary* (March, 1976), p 5–6.

18. Ibid., p 6.

19. Ibid., p 6.

20. U.S. Department of Justice, *Organized Crime Intelligence: Appendices* (March, 1976), p 1–12.

21. New York State Joint Legislative Committee on Crime, Its Causes, Control & Effect on Society, *Report* (1971) Legislative Document No. 26; p 81–89.

22. The Committee also notes that "If one uses the data in this investigation to predict the probability of a member of organized crime being sent to jail or prison, one would find the following for each crime:

Arrested for	Probability of going to jail or prison
larceny	1 in 5
gambling	1 in 50
extortion	1 in 3
narcotics	1 in 4
assault	1 in 7

23. House, *Hearings on S. 30*, op. cit., p 185.

24. Ibid., p 381.

25. See "Crime and the Law, *Congressional Quarterly Almanac* (1970), especially p 554–554.

26. The Association of the Bar of the City of New York. Committee on Federal Legislation, The Proposed Organized Crime Control Act of 1969 (S. 30), in House, *Hearings on S. 30*, op. cit., p 291–341.

27. *Hearings on S. 30*, op. cit., p 377–382.

28. Ibid., p 319.

29. Ibid., p 187.

30. Ibid., p 187–188.

31. Kennedy's testimony, which was given to the House Judiciary Subcommittee No. 1 during *Hearings on the Fort Worth Five and Grand Jury Abuse*, (1973) and was added to House of Representatives. Committee on the Judiciary, Subcommittee on Immigration, Citizenship, and International Law, *Hearings on H.J. Res. 46, H.R. 1277 and Related Bills: Federal Grand Jury* p 498–513. (Washington, DC: Government Printing Office, 1976). The quote is from p 511.

32. House, *Hearings: Federal Grand Jury*, op. cit., p 345.

33. F.J. Donner and E. Cerruti, The Grand Jury Network, *The Nation* (January 3, 1972), p 5.

34. F. J. Donner and R.I. Lavine, Kangaroo Grand Juries, *The Nation* (November 19, 1973), p 519.

35. House, *Hearings: Federal Grand Jury*, op. cit., p 509–510.

36. Ibid., p 415–417.

37. Ibid., p 113–147; see especially p 119.

38. Ibid., p 406–408.

39. GAO, op. cit., p 5–7.

40. Ibid., passim.

41. National Advisory Committee on Criminal Justice Standards and Goals, op. cit. p 29.

42. S.P. Hays, The Politics of Reform in Municipal Government in the Progressive Era, in A.B. Callow Jr. (ed.) *American Urban History: An Interpretative Render with Commentaries.* (New York: Oxford University Press, 1969).

43. Ibid., p 431.

44. Ibid., p 435.

45. The President's remarks can be found in H.R. Doc. No. 91–105, 91st Congress, 1st Session (1969). We have taken them from two sources: W.S. Lynch and J.W. Phillips, Organized Crime—Violence and Corruption, *Journal of Public Law* (1971), p 70; and W. Wilson, The Threat of Organized Crime: Highlighting the Challenging New Frontiers in Criminal Law, *Notre Dame Lawyer* (1970), p 45.

46. The best work on this topic is D.B. Davis, *The Slave Power Conspiracy and the Paranoid Style*. (Baton Rouge, LA: Louisiana University Press, 1969). D.B. Davis, Some themes of Countersubversion: An Analysis of Anti-Masonic, Anti-Catholic, and Anti-Mormon Literature, *The Mississippi Valley Historical Review* (September, 1960) XLVII. B. Bailyn, *The Ideological Origins of the American Revolution*. (Cambridge, Massachusetts: Harvard University Press, 1967).

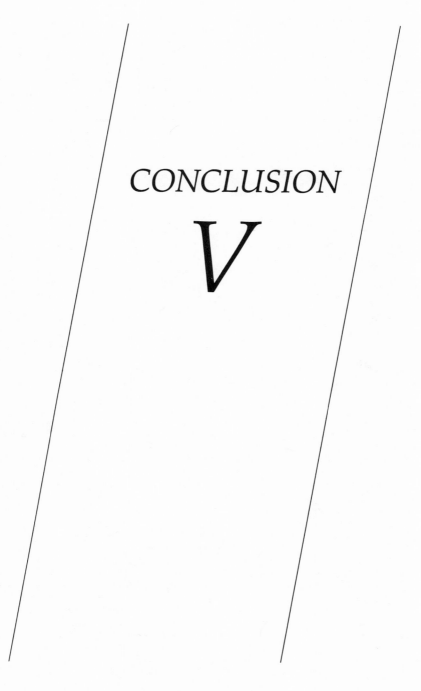

CONCLUSION
V

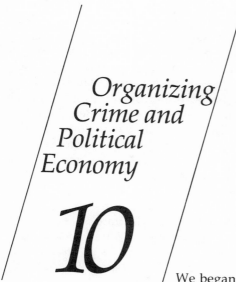

Organizing Crime and Political Economy

10

We began this inquiry by noting that:

> Traditional theories of deviance are essentially non-structural and ahistorical in their mode of analysis. By restricting investigation to factors which are manipulable within existing structural arrangements these theories embrace a "correctional perspective" and divert attention from the impact of the political economy as a whole. From this point of view deviance is *in* but not *of* our contemporary social order. Theories that locate the source of deviance in factors as diverse as personality structure, family systems, cultural transmission, social disorganization and differential opportunity share a common flaw—they attempt to understand deviance apart from historically specific forms of political and economic organization. Because traditional theories proceed without any sense of historical development, deviance is normally viewed as an episodic and transitory phenomenon rather than an outgrowth of long-term structural change.[1]

For the analysis of organized crime, this critique is telling: Unless and until organized crime is understood within historically specific forms of political and economic organization, then theorizing will continue to miss the mark.[2]

This is implicit in the examples presented and discussed. Explicitly then, by presenting work indicating the extraordinary range of and changes in organized criminality associated with nation-state development and the social history of capitalism, this book is an argument for a mode of analysis. The mode of analysis for organized criminality is that developed by Marx in his revision of Hegel's *Philosophy of Law* and quoted earlier, in which he states that "legal relations . . . could be neither understood by themselves nor explained by the so-called general progress of the human mind, but that they are rooted in the material conditions of life, which . . . are to be sought in political economy."[3]

We are, of course, not alone in this effort, and it may well be appropriate in closing to mention some of the more promising recent efforts to engage in this kind of analysis and research as it is applied to the study of crime. There can be no doubt but that an increasing methodological sophistication among historians concerned to do what E. P. Thompson calls "Plebian history" is radicalizing both our ideas about crime and criminality as surely as it reflects a renascent Marxism, or at least an ecclectic radicalism indebted to Marxist modes of analysis.[4] The point is that methodological sophistication, in revealing previously hidden aspects of the social lives of the mass of past humanity, has moved some historians toward a much more critical, indeed radical posture. At the same time, radical historians are developing the necessary techniques to penetrate the social lives of the most obscure. As these twin developments take place, the issues of crime—both organized and disorganized—have become *contextualized*, increasingly embedded in studies of political economy.[5]

The importance of this can hardly be overly emphasized as the following passage from E. P. Thompson's study of law creation and organized rural criminality in the eighteenth century indicates:

> Errington was a bailiff and Towers was a 'Minter'; that is, he was one of the debtors who had taken refuge in the supposed 'liberty' of the 'New Mint' (or 'Seven Cities of Refuge'). The Minters kept up an extreme loyalty—indeed, a whole ritual of solidarity—in defending each other from the bailiffs. They based their claim to 'sanctuary' upon the supposed privileges of ancient consecrated sites within and around the city. Several such 'sanctuaries' had been closed down at the turn of the century, and in 1720 only that at Southwark and the memory of one at Wapping survived. In the afermath of the Bubble, their inmates multiplied. We have in the case of the 'Mint' some kind of metropolitan parallel to the forest matrix of Blacking, with debtors as forestors and bailiffs as keepers. But the debtors were better-organized, the bailiffs more brutal. The bailiffs lived in an immediately symbiotic relationship to London's criminal society: under cover of their function they had the reputation for engaging in armed robbery and blackmail; a 'bum bailiff' and authority to hold debtors for a short time as prisoners in his 'spunging house'—and once held there a man, whether a genuine debtor or not, might be terrorized and bled of whatever money he or his friends had. The debtors organized to resist the bailiffs. Their 'society' was enrolled in a book; oaths of mutual support were made; and from the 'sanctuary' at Southwark they sent their emissaries, who were called "Spirits', out of the Mint in search of their antagonists.[6]

By grounding studies in notions of political economy, the symbiotic relationships at the center of criminality, law creation, and law enforcement within particular historical epochs are illuminated. This approach then removes the study of organized crime from the fruitless process of constant reification, one of the major consequences of ahistorical social science. By way of conclusion, let us take a brief look at selected examples of analyses that promise to contribute to this trend. Our intention is to suggest leads that others may pursue by noting some current examples worthy of further inquiry.

Aristocratic Organized Crime: Legitimation

Consider the fit between civil society, whose structure is revealed in studies of political economy, and certain patterns of organized criminality discussed by Barbara A. Hanawalt in an analysis of 14th-century England.[7] She reports primarily on extensive and vicious extortion rackets carried out by both the high and low nobility. The crimes, *and they were known as crimes,* carried out by members of England's nobility and their retainers or gangs were "an outgrowth of their real professions as administrators and warriors."[8] Hanawalt's report reminds one of Marc Bloch's finding in *Feudal Society* that "Violence was deep-rooted in the social structure and mentality of the age."[9] This endemic and often epidemic violence, Bloch adds, played an important role in the feudal economy. Organized violence was a knightly task:

> At a time when trade was scarce and difficult, what surer means of becoming rich than plunder and oppression? A whole class of masters and warriors lived mainly by such means, and one monk could calmly make a petty lord say in a charter: I give this land "free of all dues, of all exactions or tallage, of all compulsory services . . . and of all things which by violence knights are wont to extort from the poor."[10]

These patterns of organized criminality reflect the sociology of power in medieval societies. In these cases, there is a clear congruence between the structure of civil society and organized criminality. The successes and failures of noble organized crime were, of course, rather acutely tuned to the ebb and flow of royal power. And it is surely instructive to note that one of the methodologies by which royal and therefore state power ultimately increased was through the legitimation of much noble-organized crime. As part of the *quid pro quo* between the rural aristocracy and royal administration (throughout

Europe), justice in baronial domains was largely left in the hands of the barons and their henchmen. This meant that violence, extortion, and corruption would continue primarily in the interests of the rural aristocracy, which pledged in return allegiance and cooperation with the centralizing state.

The growth of state power through relationships with the rural nobilities in Europe is exceptionally complex. There are vast differences in the timing and, indeed, the extent of the struggle between the often-competing power centers. But in general, something of the quality of resolution and, therefore, of the process of legitimation, can be seen in the following studies.

As W. H. Bruford noted about Germany, "No German king was able to establish a system of common law. The maintenance of peace and justice had to be left to the territorial princes from the beginning of the thirteenth century."[11] Later, in discussing differences between the German high and low nobility in the 18th century, Bruford comments:

> Those of the country nobility who still managed their own estates had on these grounds a good claim to a privileged position, ... Even if not directly useful in a military or administrative way they were, as landlords, an essential factor in the economic system and had important functions to perform. In the management of their estates, the encouragement of good husbandry, the maintenance of order and dispensing of justice in the squire's court, they could if they liked be princes in small, with a vast power for good—and of course for evil—over the peasants of their land.[12]

In considering Germany east of the Elbe, Bruford adds that the Junker "administered the law and tried the peasants on these estates not only in civil but in criminal cases." The Junker was a "kind of sheriff, magistrate and police-chief in one."[13]

In the same vein, Frederick B. Artz in his history of Europe during the two decades following the Napoleonic wars remarks that in England "The lesser aristocracy policed and ruled the countryside."[14] Turning to East Prussia, Russia, and other areas in central and eastern Europe, Artz states that the aristocracy "lived like great feudal lords, administering law and preserving a prestige which the monarchy had never dared attack."[15] And finally, Joel Samaha, in analyzing the Justices of the Peace in Elizabethan Essex, notes that they formed "a true community of magistrates." They were composed of "magnates no less than minor gentry," and "combined in their office were the roles of policemen, detective, public prosecutor, and judge."[16]

The process of legitimation that decriminalized much of the organized criminality practiced by Europe's rural aristocracies was principally carried out during the course of the 16th and 17th centuries: the time that in England roughly corresponds to the transformation from a preindustrial to a modern or modernizing society. The momentous effects of such changes were not limited to the organized criminality of the aristocracy, as Samaha found in the above study. Samaha writes:

> In England during the late sixteenth century, the pressures of a rising population forced a readjustment in the exploitation of resources, mainly in the direction of increasing the country's food supply. The readjustment was not completely successful, even though it spurred on the commercialization of agriculture and increased the country's wealth generally. In part this was because the distribution of wealth was so uneven . . . . But at the bottom of the scale the situation differed markedly. Wage earners suffered terribly due to two factors—and here is the heart of the crime problem in Essex. The rising population contributed to a labor surplus, driving wages down while the crisis in the food supply, especially with the heavy added drain caused by the proximity of London and Colchester, sent food prices skyrocketing.[17]

Samaha is not discussing organized criminality per se, but it is evident that many of the crimes analyzed were organized. The complex shifts in the political economy of the burgeoning nation-states and modernizing societies in rural areas decreased the extent of aristocrat-organized criminality, primarily through a process of legitimation and hence decriminalization, while increasing it for the vastly greater number of landless laborers.

Rural Organized Criminality: Banditry

Demographic pressures brought about by profound economic transformations in the developing world economy markedly changed the contours of criminality, both organized and disorganized, in rural areas. In this regard, consider banditry a neat heading for much rural organized crime. Fernand Braudel, in his classic study of the Mediterranean region during the 16th century, notes:

> No region of the Mediterranean was free from the scourge. Catalonia, Calabria and Albania, all notorious regions in this respect, by no means had a monopoly of brigandage. It cropped up everywhere in various guises, political, social, economic, terrorist; at the gates of Alexandria in Egypt or of Damascus and Aleppo; in the countryside around Naples, where watch towers were built to warn of brigands and in the Roman Campagna, where brush fires were sometimes ordered to smoke out bands of robbers who found abundant cover there; even in a state so

apparently well-policed as Venice. When the Sultan's army marched along the Stambul road to Adrianople, Nis, Belgrade and on into Hungary, it left behind along the roadside scores of hanged brigands whom it had disturbed in their lairs. There were brigands and brigands of course. Their presence on the main highway of the Turkish Empire, famed for its security, is sober evidence of the quality of public safety in the sixteenth century.[18]

No contemporary historian has more lucidly discussed rural organized crime than Eric Hobsbawm. In his celebrated monograph, *Bandits,* Hobsbawm outlines his particular interests, holding that "For the law, anyone belonging to a group of men who attack and rob with violence is a bandit."[19] But the criminal law in and of itself is an insufficient guide for historians and sociologists. Reflecting this opinion, Hobsbawm concentrates on those bandits "not regarded as simple criminals by public opinion."[20] The subject that animates him is social banditry, different from other types of rural organized criminality such as the "activities of gangs drawn from the professional 'underworld,'" as well as bandit communities such as the Bedouin "for whom raiding is part of the normal way of life."[21]

The crucial difference for Hobsbawm in his typology of rural organized criminality lies in the relationships between bandits and peasant communities themselves:

> Underworld robbers and raiders regard the peasants as their prey and know them to be hostile; the robbed in turn regard the attackers as criminals in their sense of the term and not merely by official law. It would be unthinkable for a social bandit to snatch the peasants' (though not the lord's) harvest in his own territory, or perhaps even elsewhere. Those who do therefore lack the peculiar relationship which makes banditry 'social.'[22]

Social banditry occupies Hobsbawm's center stage because it is an expression of profound historical change—epochal cracks in political economy. Social banditry reflects the "disruption of an entire society, the rise of new classes and social structures, the resistance of entire communities or peoples against the destruction of its way of life."[23] In Europe, the last great age of social banditry, according to Hobsbawm, was the 16th to the 18th centuries which marks the change from a precapitalist to a capitalist economy.

This change, of course, affected more than European rural communities and rural organized criminality in Europe. The connections between the emergency of European capitalism and modern slavery is extraordinarily well documented.[24] And within the developing system of plantation slavery in the Americas, a variant of rural organized criminality is to be found: maroon societies, which were rural communities founded and managed by escaped rebel slaves.

> For more than four centuries, the communities formed by such runaways dotted the fringes of plantation America, from Brazil to the southeastern United States, from Peru to the American southwest. Known variously as *palenques, Quilombos, mocambos, cumbes, ladeiras,* or *mambises,* these new societies ranged from tiny bands that survived less than a year to powerful states encompassing thousands of members and surviving for generations or even centuries.[25]

Richard Price notes that maroon communities hold "a special significance" for the analysis of slave societies. Price is quite right, of course, but we would add that these outlaw communities, which were a reaction to colonial plantation slavery, itself one of the consequences of developing capitalism, must be seen also from the perspective of historical criminology.

Maroon societies did not exist in a vacuum; they were not simply refuges carved out of some intractable wilderness. Many of them were complex societies that forged crucial links with various elements of plantation society. Maroons were suppliers of certain kinds of goods and services and had a fairly steady commercial intercouse with both whites and plantation slaves. In return, maroons were supplied with arms, tools, and information. Examples include the Spanish middlemen who sold fish and game in the "town of Saint-Dominque for the maroons of Le Maniel, obtaining for them, guns, powder and tools"; and white settlers in the vicinity of Palmares engaged in an "extensive and complex illegal trade with the quilombos, exchanging guns for silver and gold taken by the Palmaristas on their raids closer to the coast.[26]

Trade links with plantation societies were one of the ways of integrating maroon societies with a wider world. There were other "alliances of convenience: such as that between "maroons in the Spanish territories and the pirates who represented Spain's enemies."[27] For over three centuries, maroons and pirates cooperated and participated in "widespread, illicit international trade."[28]

Piracy

The fact that maroon communities (part of the broad picture of rural organized criminality by definition) acted in concert with pirates begs consideration of the question of piracy itself. There can be no doubting that piracy and privateering were forms of organized crime.[29] Both were, naturally, in one sense timeless and ubiquitous. But more importantly, they were as acutely tuned to large-scale economic changes as were aristocratic and rural organized criminality. Piracy expressed in its location, intensity, structure, personnel, and commercialization the vagaries of nascent capitalism—the changes attendant on the development of the capitalist world-economy.

Piracy and privateering were vast illegal enterprises running an enormous gamut from petty "scavengers" prowling and "roaming the Aegean islands or along the coasts of western Greece" waiting to "capture a fisherman perhaps or rob a granary, kidnap a few harvesters, steal some salt from the Turkish or Ragusan salt-pans at the mouth of the Narenta,"[30] to activities "instigated by a city acting on its own authority or at any rate only marginally attached to a large state."[31] In the latter cases piracy and privateering were a "secondary form of war" substituting "for declared war." Such cases explain the action of Louis XIV who when he "could no longer maintain a regular battle fleet against England, . . . encouraged or allowed war by piracy; Saint Malo and Dunkirk became belligerents in place of France."[32]

In the 16th century, urban-based or -nourished piracy and privateering in the Mediterranean were centered around "strategic cities: In Christendom, Valetta, Leghorn, and Pisa, Naples, Messina, Palermo and Trapani, Malta, Palma de Majorca, Almeria, Valencia, Segna and Fiume; on the Moslem side, Valona, Durazzo, Tripoli in Barbary, Tunis-La Goletta, Bizerta, Algiers, Tetouan, Larach, Sale."[33] Out of the above list three "new towns stand out: Valetta, founded by the Knights of Malta in 1566; Leghorn re-founded in a sense by Cosimo de'Medici; finally and above all, the astonishing city of Algiers, the apotheosis of them all."[34] The point of this geographical excursion is to note the range of urban-based piracy during the 16th century and to appreciate the manner which piracy and privateering as illegal enterprises formed the foundation of certain municipal economies. Algiers is the most notorious example with its intense and total commercialization of crime.

In the same fashion as other large-scale illegal enterprises, piracy and privateering encouraged, indeed demanded, subsidiary enterprises whose function was part of the market structure of commercialized crime. The most important and infamous of these concerned the ransoming of thousands of captured prisoners. This growing "traffic in ransoms and the exchange of men and goods led to the establishment of new commercial circuits."[35] The major ransoming institutions in the Christian world were the Order of the Most Holy Trinity for the Ransom of Captives and the Order of Our Lady of Mercy.[36] Their work, however, was fraught with difficulties—not the least being competition between the orders fueled by charges and countercharges of discrimination and double-dealing. Other involved in the ransom business were merchants—Christian, Jewish, and so-called renegades—who had business interests spanning both the Moslem and Christian Mediterranean communities. As seems inevitable in such enterprises, the intermediaries themselves found ways to raise their profits in the ransom business by hiking interest rates, and virtually pocketing ransom monies. Stephen Clissold writes:

> The Christian merchants, in fact, found themselves in an ambiguous position. Some made fortunes by shipping stolen cargoes to Europe and re-selling them at enormous profit. However upright and compassionate they might be as individuals . . . it was to their advantage to keep the system of plunder and enslavement operating smoothly.[37]

The scale of piracy and privateering was a function of the scale of trade in general. When trade prospered so did piracy: "in short, privateering was a means of forcible exchange."[38] Furthermore, Braudel states that without question there is a "positive correlation between piracy and the economic health of the Mediterranean . . . . They rise and fall together."[39]

Urban Underworlds

The connections between organized crime and political economy manifest in rural areas and on the seas is also evident, as already hinted in urban areas. Even without considering Algiers and other piratical strongholds in which the entire municipal economy rested on the bedrock of organized criminality, other urban localities supported organized criminality. The root cause of urban criminality in the mid-16th century was the increasing morass of poverty, expressed by the burgeoning number of vagrants and vagabonds cluttering the roads and swelling the towns. So plentiful did they become at this time in the Mediterranean world that for Braudel and other historians they raise the question of the existence of urban underworlds. Their answer is that all the cities had their criminal quarters: Seville, Madrid, Paris, Palermo, Naples, Rome, and Venice—to mention only the largest. Urban governments responded to this situation by enacting a continuous spectacle, an ineffectual game of capture and expulsion of hordes of miscreants endlessly replenished. This double problem of poverty and criminality was a "structure of the times which progressed beyond the narrow confines of the unsympathetic towns, reaching nation-wide and European dimensions."[40] As we remarked in Chapter 6, it is crucial to recognize the transformations of these urban areas throughout the era of capitalist development: It is the quantitative and qualitative differences in urban economies and the ways in which they function in the capitalist world system that account in large measure for different patterns of organized criminality in the 19th and 20th centuries.

Conclusion

Some time ago, Barrington Moore stressed two criteria for creative work in social science: the historical approach and a critical stance.[41] It is evident that the merging of social science methods with the historical approach has been both radical and liberating according to Moore's criteria. This is the approach we have employed throughout this book.

We have often repeated the observation that both extant data and our own inquiries into what is usually called "organized crime" are incompatible with the alien conspiracy, Mafia, or Cosa Nostra view often espoused (unfortunately even today) in the news media and social science textbooks. This point, though worth making again because of the tenacity of the myth, is nonetheless not one of the major points to be made in this work. We have striven rather to provide empirical descriptions based on the conscious choice of a particular methodology (or methodologies) as well as a theoretical paradigm designed to explain and organize our empirical findings.

This foray into the history of organized crime, crimes, and criminality in various locales highlights certain deficiencies in the ways organized crime is commonly conceptualized and suggests a more fruitful mode of analysis.

We suggest not only adopting the historical methodology that we have employed in this work (including contemporary history), but also carefully and relentlessly emphasizing the lives of people in the context of a political economy viewed "from the bottom up" as a necessary palliative to conventional viewpoints. Further, we suggest that dialectical theory—with its conceptualization of contradictions, conflicts, and resolutions as necessary formulations to comprehend how people go about making their histories in the face of constraints inherited from their past—provides us with the best framework for understanding criminality, generally, and the processes by which crime gets organized, specifically.

NOTES

1. S. Spitzer, "Toward a Marxian Theory of Deviance," *Social Problems* (1975) 22: 638–639.

2. This admonition also holds true for historians of crime whose leitmotif is a type of historical impressionism. The most notorious example of this style is the remarkably interesting work of R. Cobb, *Paris and Its Provinces*. (London: Oxford University Press, 1975). On this point see R. Darnton, The History of Mentalites: Recent Writings on Revolution, Criminality, and Dearth in France, in R. H. Brown and S. M. Lyman (eds.), *Structure, Consciousness, and History*. (Cambridge: Cambridge University Press, 1978).

3. L.S. Feuer (ed.), *Basic Writings on Politics and Philosophy: Karl Marx and Freidrich Engels*. (Garden City, New York: Doubleday, 1959).

4. Thompson's work, especially his epic *The Making of the English Working Class* (New York: Vintage Books, 1963), has been criticized as an example of "culturalist Marxism" that is antagonistic to Althussierian notions of "structural Marxism." In an enlightening discussion of these issues, Richard Johnson, in the journal *History Workshop* (1978) 6, details certain theoretical and epistemological problems inherent in Thompson's work. Johnson writes: "This very cursory 'reading' requires much elaboration and development. But if it is anything like accurate, it may suggest a range of ways in which Marx's legacy can be (and has been) mis-appropriated. The mechanism here is the failure to recognize the range and levels of discourse in *Capital* and, often, to mistake the properties and pertinences of one level for those of another. The actual structure of the text aids selective appropriations . . . . In the same way, a *pathological* divorce develops between those who analyse particular situations (historians, journalists, or politicians) and those concerned to develop 'theory.' 'Culturalism' as an epistemological position represents one side of this divorce in a particularly extreme manner. Despite the emphasis on critique, it represents a form of intellectual work that, rather systematically, distances itself from what is most distinctive in the method of the mature Marx," (p 89). Johnson goes on to comment that in Thompson's work, "The economic as a set of objectively present relations only appears in an attenuated form, *through* the cultural, *through* the 'inwardness of experience' (p 91). Thompson answers such criticisms in his brilliant *The Poverty of Theory; And Other Essays*. (London: Merlin Press, 1978).

5. What is meant by political economy can be seen in the following statements by G. Lichtheim in *Marxism: An Historical and Critical Study*. (New York: Praeger Press, 1961). Lichtheim writes:

> What Ricardo meant by political economy—and it is this meaning which Marx took over from him, and which the Marxian school has conserved—is indicated in the very first sentence of the preface to his great work: "The produce of the earth—all that is derived from its surface by the united application of labour, machinery and capital—is divided among three classes of the community; namely the proprietor of the land, the owner of the stock or capital necessary for its cultivation, and the labourers by whose industry it is cultivated." After noting that "in different stages of society, the proportions of the whole produce of the earth which will be allotted to each of these classes, under the names of rent, profit, wages, will be . . . different . . ." he goes on to declare that "to determine the laws which regulate this distribution, is the principal problem in Political Economy." [p 170–171]

Lichtheim goes on to note:

> Ultimately, what concerned classical economists was "the wealth of nations," and the social conditions under which human effort went into the production of riches. To this Ricardo added the division of the total product among the major classes of society, and thus laid the basis for the Marxian synthesis of sociology and political economy. Marx's formulation of the so-called materialist conception of history ("In the social production of their life, men enter into definite relations that are indispensable and independent of their will, relations of production which correspond to a definite stage of development of their mate-

rial productive forces.'') implicitly defines the subject of his economic doctrine, inasmuch as it was his aim to lay bare the "law of bourgeois society by analyzing its economic mechanism. This meant welding into a whole sociology and economics, both conceived historically. [p 175.]

6. E.P. Thompson, *Whigs and Hunters: The Origins of the Black Act*. (New York: Pantheon Books, 1975).

7. B.A. Hanawalt, Fur-Collar Crime: The Pattern of Crime Among the Fourteenth-Century English Nobility, *Journal of Social History* (1975) 8.

8. Ibid., p 13.

9. M. Bloch, *Feudal Society*, translated by L.A. Manyon. (Chicago: University of Chicago Press, 1964).

10. Ibid.

11. W.H. Bruford, *Germany in the Eighteenth Century: the Social Background of the Literary Revival*. (Cambridge: Cambridge University Press, 1965).

12. Ibid., p 62–63.

13. Ibid., p 109.

14. F.B. Artz, *Reaction and Revolution, 1814–1832*. (New York: Harper & Row, 1934).

15. Ibid., p 9.

16. J. Samaha, *Law and Order in Historical Perspective: The Case of Elizabethan Essex*. (New York: Academic Press, 1974).

17. Ibid., p 112. (Italics ours.)

18. F. Braudel, *The Mediterranean and the Mediterranean World in the Age of Philip II*, translated by S. Reynolds. (New York: Harper and Row, 1973), Vol. 2.

19. Eric Hobsbawm, *Bandits*. (New York: Dell Publishing, 1969).

20. Ibid.

21. Ibid., p 14.

22. Ibid.

23. Ibid.

24. E.D. Genovese, *The World the Slaveholders Made*. (New York: Pantheon Books, 1969). Laura Foner and E.D. Genovese, (eds.), *Slavery in the New World: A Reader in Comparative History*. (Englewood Cliffs: Prentice-Hall, 1969).

25. R. Price (ed.), *Maroon Societies: Rebel Slave Communities in the Americas*. (Garden City, New York: Doubleday, 1973).

26. Ibid., p 13.

27. Ibid., p 14.

28. Ibid.

29. It is important to discuss the manner in which the terms piracy and privateering are to be understood. Our guide is Braudel, op. cit., p 866:

> Piracy in the Mediterranean is as old as history. There are pirates in Boccaccio and Cervantes just as there are in Homer. Such antiquity may even have given it a more natural (dare one say a more human?) character than elsewhere. The equally troubled Atlantic was frequented in the sixteenth century by pirates certainly more cruel than those of the Mediterranean. Indeed in the Mediterranean, the words *piracy* and *pirates* were hardly in current usage before the beginning of the seventeenth century: *privateering* and *privateers* or *corsairs* were the expressions commonly used and the distinction, which is perfectly clear in the legal sense, while it does not fundamentally change the elements of the

problem, has its importance. Privateering is legitimate war, authorized either by a formal declaration of war or by letters of marque, passports, commissions or instructions. . . . In the sense that the entire Mediterranean was an arena of constant conflict between two adjacent and warring civilizations, privateering was a permanent reality, excusing and justifying piracy; to justify it was to assimilate it to the neighbouring and in its way respectable category of privateering.

30. Ibid., p 871.

31. Ibid., p 869.

32. Ibid.

33. Ibid., p 870.

34. Ibid.

35. Ibid., p 888.

36. S. Clissold, *The Barbary Slaves*. (Totowa, New Jersey: Towman and Littlefield, 1977).

37. Ibid., p 105.

38. Braudel, op. cit., p 884.

39. Ibid., p 887.

40. Ibid., p 743.

41. B. Moore, *Political Power and Social Theory*. (New York: Harper & Row, 1965).

Index